W9-AUX-475

PENGUIN BOOKS

VITA'S OTHER WORLD

Vita's Other World was written after Jane Brown's book about the partnership between Sir Edwin Lutyens and Gertrude Jekyll, *Gardens of a Golden Afternoon* (Penguin 1985). She has since brought her gardeners up to date with a biography of Lanning Roper (1987) which was written at the request of his friends.

VITA'S OTHER WORLD

A GARDENING BIOGRAPHY OF
V. SACKVILLE-WEST

How fair the flowers unaware
That do not know what beauty is!
Fair, without knowing they are fair,
With poets and gazelles they share
Another world than this.

JANE BROWN

PENGUIN BOOKS

Penguin Books Ltd, Harmondsworth, Middlesex, England
Viking Penguin Inc., 40 West 23rd Street, New York, New York 10010, U.S.A.
Penguin Books Australia Ltd, Ringwood, Victoria, Australia
Penguin Books Canada Ltd, 2801 John Street, Markham, Ontario, Canada L3R 1B4
Penguin Books (N.Z.) Ltd, 182–190 Wairau Road, Auckland 10, New Zealand

First published by Viking 1985
Published in Penguin Books 1987

Copyright © Jane Brown, 1985

Designed by Yvonne Dedman

All rights reserved.

Made and printed in Great Britain by
William Clowes Limited, Beccles and London
Typeset in CCC Old Style

Except in the United States of America, this book is sold
subject to the condition that it shall not, by way of trade or otherwise,
be lent, re-sold, hired out, or otherwise circulated without the publisher's
prior consent in any form of binding or cover other than that in which it is
published and without a similar condition including this condition
being imposed on the subsequent purchaser

Frontispiece:
Vita, writer and gardener 'at home' – taken by an American photographer.

Contents

LIST OF COLOUR PLATES

The page numbers given are those opposite the colour plates,
or, in the case of a double page spread, those either side of the plate.

 LIST OF ILLUSTRATIONS

❧ ILLUSTRATION ❧ ACKNOWLEDGEMENTS

COLOUR
John Brookes: 1, 2, 3
John Medhurst: 4
The author: 5, 6, 7, 8, 9, 10, 14, 15, 20, 21
Iris Hardwick Library: 11
The Marchioness of Salisbury: 12
Harry Smith: 13, 17, 19, 23, 26
Nigel Nicolson: 16, 29
Edwin Smith: 22
Peter B. Brown: 24, 25, 27, 28

BLACK AND WHITE
Nigel Nicolson: frontispiece, 1, 3, 5, 6, 10, 12, 13,
   14, 15, 16, 21, 22, 24, 25, 26, 27, 28, 29, 30, 31,
32, 33, 35, 38, 40, 41, 42, 43, 44, 45, 50, 51, 52,
53, 54, 55, 56, 57, 59, 60, 61, 62, 63, 64, 65, 67,
68, 69, 70, 71, 72, 73, 74, 82, 88, 94, 97
Keith Harding: 2, 46, 47, 48, 49
Country Life: 4, 7, 11, 17, 18, 19, 20, 23, 58, 75,
   76, 77, 78, 79, 80, 81, 83, 84, 85, 86
British Architectural Library/R.I.B.A. Drawings
   Collection: 8
Aerofilms Ltd: 9, 66
The author: 34, 36, 37, 39
Christine and Stuart Page: 89
Kerry Dundas: 95
Leonard and Marjorie Gayton: 87, 91, 92
Edwin Smith: 90, 93, 98
Philip Turner of Carlton: 96

For Colin

 ACKNOWLEDGEMENTS

My thanks go to many people whose patience and encouragement have helped me with this book. My special thanks go first of all to Margaret Richardson, for suggesting that I write it, and then to Michael Dover, Caradoc King, Eleo Gordon, Annie Lee and Yvonne Dedman, for making it a reality.

For help with my research I am grateful to the staff at Kent County Archives Office, Mr John McKee of the Wallace Collection, the staff of the London Library, Mr and Mrs Robert Stephenson-Clarke, Dr and Mrs John Beale, Mr James Russell, Mr James Platt and Mr Jack Vass. For help with illustrations I am grateful to Keith Harding for his photographs of Vita's Kent, to Lisa Markwell of *Country Life*, to Christopher Allen of Aerofilms Ltd, to Christine and Stuart Page for their clever plan of Sissinghurst (which would have delighted Harold Nicolson) and to John Brookes for his photographs of Persia. And of course my thanks go to many people who work for the National Trust and have the care of Knole and Sissinghurst, and especially to Miss Pamela Schwerdt and Miss Sibylle Kreutzberger, Sissinghurst's head gardeners, and Mrs Pamela Kilbane, Sissinghurst's administrator.

But most of all I am in debt to Nigel Nicolson, for his kindness, his firm criticism when necessary, and his generosity with his time, his home and in his role as his mother's literary executor. When I read the letters between Vita Sackville-West and Harold Nicolson they were at Sissinghurst, though they are now safely in the care of the Lilly Library in Bloomington, Indiana; he arranged for me to see them at almost the last moment before they left England and arranged for me to use what I found, he has allowed me free access to the material on the garden that remains at Sissinghurst and to his mother's photograph albums for my illustrations, and as a finale to this box of delights he offered me the use of the painting he had commissioned from John Piper, *The White Garden at Sissinghurst, 1984*, for my cover. Such generosity is characteristic of him; for me it has been both a challenge and an inspiration.

# INTRODUCTION

This little space which scented box encloses
Is blue with lupins and is sweet with thyme
My garden all is overblown with roses,
My spirit all is overblown with rhyme,
As like a drunken honeybee I waver
From house to garden and again to house,
And, undetermined which delight to favour,
On verse and rose alternately carouse.
V. Sackville-West, 'Sonnet'[1]

VITA SACKVILLE-WEST'S carefree candour about her twin passions for poetry and flowers is the keystone of this book. The writing of poetry was the rightful and wholly natural occupation of her tribe and kind. Poetry was the muse of her constant companions Marvell, Milton, Donne, Keats, Shelley and Gray, and of her deity, William Shakespeare. When she was young poetry was still the respectable, admirable, even divine, public expression of passion, albeit an expression in which secrets could be hidden. Vita loved writing poetry. She longed to write good poetry and most of all she desired to be remembered as an important poet. Her early poems were highly praised, Edward Marsh chose her work for Volume 5 of his *Georgian Poetry* in 1922, she became a respected critic of modern poetry, and *The Land* won her the Hawthornden Prize in 1927. But as she grew older she grew doubtful and worried about being out of touch. She acknowledged the influence of T. S. Eliot and the Spender/Auden school, with whom she could not 'get into gear at all'.[2] She said she wanted to deal with more permanent things than politics, and she struggled to do so in her second epic poem *The Garden*, first published in 1946. But *The Garden* was not then really appreciated; only now, as we are becoming aware of the twentieth century's mutilation of the dream of England and a common and overwhelming desire to take refuge in our gardens, are *The Land* and *The Garden* able to be recognized as the guides, prophecies and comforters that they are.

And what of Vita's passion for flowers and growing them, which grew into a passion for gardening and the making of a garden? This had always been a peculiarly private passion of the Sackvilles, and it hardly had the same status as the writing of poetry. Her contemporary kind never really understood her passion for flowers and gardening; it was only completely shared by her husband Harold Nicolson. Other friends and lovers may have thought that they helped with Long Barn or Sissinghurst, but they never passed that last barrier into Harold and Vita's secret world. A member of that kind, Peter Quennell (who found them amusing targets in life), had the grace to admit this after their deaths: 'How much the garden owed to the Nicolsons, and how well it symbolized their long devotion, the alliance of a slightly feminine man and a predominantly masculine woman, I understood when I visited it after their deaths, and it was crowded, over-crowded indeed, with enthusiastic sightseers.' He is describing Sissinghurst Castle, of course – 'a place of individual beauty', the 'living product of two sympathetic human minds'.[3]

Vita and Harold were themselves slow, perhaps unwilling, to recognize that anyone but themselves should be interested in their garden. In the late forties and early fifties when Sissinghurst was becoming well known, they were constantly amused that 'Experts' should find it interesting, and touched and pleased that their visitors who paid a shilling should find it a joy. With Sissinghurst Harold and Vita had set out to create 'a thing of beauty where none was before' – at first for themselves and only later, by popular demand, for other people. It never ceased to amaze them that their 'own dear garden should be taking its place among the better gardens of England'.[4] As the visitors brought home the message to Peter Quennell, so of course they have brought it home to me. Now over 100,000 people visit the garden each summer. Some are just passing and curious, but most are regulars and return time and time again. Most of them have been observed by the National Trust's devoted administrator for the last fourteen years, Pamela Kilbane, to emerge 'thrilled by it all'. If you listen to them talking, as I have done, it is clear that they do not come just to see the flowers, to discover how the best new varieties have been fitted into the familiar schemes (as Harold especially wished) by the brilliant head gardeners Pamela Schwerdt and Sibylle Kreutzberger, but they come because Sissinghurst is acknowledged by so many to be an enchanted place. The creation of the enchanted place has been described in *Sissinghurst: The Making of a Garden* by Anne Scott-James.[5]

Many of today's visitors remember and love Vita for her regular gardening column in the *Observer*. Her pieces were published in four *In Your Garden* volumes,[6] and were subsequently edited by Philippa Nicolson into *V. Sackville-West's Garden Book*,[7] which is still a best-seller. But what would Vita have thought of this? To her gardening was a private passion, only displayed in public to earn money to spend on her garden. 'I am filled with loathing for my *Observer* articles,' she wrote when she was editing the last volume of pieces.[8] She found writing them a terrible bore, and it was a bind having to devote her Sunday mornings to the task. When she was awarded the R.H.S. Veitch Memorial Medal she was 'rather pleased but even more astonished' to realize it was all due to those 'beastly' articles![9] What endeared her to the unknown thousands was her manner of easy conversation on a wide range of subjects of interest to broad-minded gardeners. Was it not also endearing that she kept her appointment faithfully for fourteen years, and that her impatience bred an irresistible wit?

It was partly her essentially private nature, and perhaps partly her pride in her more serious reputation, that led Vita to this despair about being popular. She got very depressed about it. 'I don't think,' Harold had to write to comfort her, 'you will go down to posterity as a writer on gardening subjects – and if I did so, I should clamour aloud in the halls of fame.'[10] He thought she would be especially remembered for *The Edwardians, Knole and the Sackvilles* and *Pepita*. In addition to these and her long epic poems, she wrote eleven full-length novels, two superb travel books on Persia, a number of biographies, numerous substantial essays and short stories, and several volumes of short poems. But are these what she has been remembered for? There was Michael Stevens's solid and respectable critical biography, a thesis published in 1973 of which *The Times* said, '. . . it will have to be a truly outstanding biographer who can improve on this beautifully constructed, concise and stimulating work'.[11] Ten years later Victoria Glendinning proved that point and won the Whitbread Prize for her biography *Vita*.[12] Harold Acton, an old friend of both Vita and Harold, reviewed *Vita* in *Books and Bookmen* (September 1983) and celebrated the mixing of a huge and strong cocktail which lingered 'with a bitter-sweet poignancy'. And many remembered, or had hardly forgotten, that the publishing landmark of 1973 had been Nigel Nicolson's *Portrait of a Marriage*.[13] Much has been written in these two dazzling and important books, *Vita* and *Portrait*, about her passions, and something about her poetry, but very little about her gardening. Am I to redress the balance?

So I sit down to write with trepidation. I can hear Harold Nicolson, the respected biographer of George V and Lord Curzon, warning of 'impure' biography – composing the chosen life 'as an illustration of some extraneous theory or conception'.[14] Clearly my book could not have been written without those that have gone before. But Sissinghurst and its hundreds of thousands of visitors, *The Land* and *The Garden*, and, above all, Vita's deep sense of place – are these extraneous conceptions?

THE KEY to Vita's life is the fact that she was brought up in a secure and privileged world, the world of the great Sackville home, Knole, in Kent, where she was the centre of attention and attraction, and led to believe that this world would always be hers. My first chapter traces the meaning of Knole and the Sackville inheritance in her life. For much of my understanding of this I am in debt to another of Vita's biographers, Virginia Woolf and her *Orlando*, first published in 1928. *Orlando* may be a work of fantasy but it was written from the best of motives – with love and laughter shared – and in her wildest exaggerations Virginia Woolf strikes to the heart of Vita's deepest motivations.

It was no doubt at some sensitive adolescent moment that Vita discovered that, merely because of a quirk of history, the foundation of her lifestyle, Knole, could never be hers. Nothing is more traumatic than when the rules of the game are changed just when one is learning them. For Vita there were alternatives. The obvious solution would have been to marry an equivalent lifestyle. But it was not Knole's pomp and position that meant most to her. It is significant that she refused both Lord Lascelles, who offered Harewood House, its Barry terraces, Brown landscape and endless Yorkshire acres, *and* Lord Granby, proffering manorial Haddon Hall and the creamy yellow turrets of Belvoir Castle with further endless acres of the Shires. Vita's profoundest quality was her honesty. She chose to marry for love and take on a lifelong struggle to re-create her lost world (of necessity in miniature) to her inward satisfaction. In my chapters on her travels and her first home at Long Barn, she is gathering up the materials for this, as one collects coloured wools and glittering threads before sitting down to embroider.

The work of art that she had the energy, tenacity, means and time to create was the garden at Sissinghurst. But this garden could not have been made without the classical taste of her husband Harold Nicolson. And a work of art does not spring up overnight. Sissinghurst's garden is the result of both their educations and experiences (and those of a good many other people as well), and I have tried to gather up all the relevant strands that made the minds that made Sissinghurst – and so gave it the mark of its greatness, its generosity of soul. This is what gardening at its best is all about – the ability to endow a place with all the beauty, delight and peace that comforts the travail of the human heart. To make such an enchanted place is a painful and laborious process, but it is perhaps also a propitiation.

Almost as soon as they had made their garden Harold and Vita were faced with the threat of losing it with the beginning of the Second World War. These threats and tensions of war brought out Vita's best prose and poetry in defence, not only of her garden, but of her wider landscape and the life within it. She often expressed her belief that she was 'at heart nothing but an old Tory squire'.[15] This belief is the key to her closeness with the agricultural countryside of the Weald and her remarkable ability to express her sense of belonging. The Tory squires, and Whig ones, are gone and unapproachable, and yet they made the English countryside that we love and are having such difficulty understanding now that the vast majority of us are divorced from it. Somehow Vita appears as a friendly and accessible apostle of that past, and her ability to identify with her surroundings, her sense of place and her success in creating somewhere of her personal belonging, are the endless dimensions of her gardening that just may be the most important. Vita recaptured her roots with the kind of panache that sets a good example. She possessed her deep sense of place *and* she could express it vividly – does she not therefore more obviously belong in that much-loved company of Richard Jefferies, Edward Thomas and others who have taught us to understand where we are? In my last chapter I have explored this question.

All the people, long dead or then alive, who came into Vita's 'gardening' life and come into my book are armed with their own particular fusion with some aspect of her complex personality. In return for her gentleness and generosity she earned dazzling gifts from all of them, which she has in turn bequeathed to us in her writing and her garden. This then is a pursuit – a following of Ariadne's golden thread that leads out of a maze of faces, places and words and, I hope, ends in an enchanted garden.

Odiham, Hampshire, 1984

 PROLOGUE

We are born with the dead:
See, they return and bring us with them.
The moment of the rose and the moment of the yew-tree
Are of equal duration. A people without history
Is not redeemed from time, for history is a pattern
Of timeless moments. So, while the light fails
On a winter's afternoon, in a secluded chapel
History is now and England.
T. S. Eliot, *Little Gidding*[1]

THE PLACE is a small green hill in Sussex. The hill overlooks the brown green dips and other tree-covered hills of a treasured countryside. On this hill stands the church of St Michael and All Angels, Withyham. The church is as old as Domesday, but was struck by lightning in 1663 and all but reduced to a heap of stones. Within ten years it was rebuilt as it stands now, solid and grey, with a squat square tower looking across the trees to the delicate broach spire of St Mary's, Hartfield.

Inside it is dark and shaded. The grey light of a wet October afternoon is kind to the dust of ages. The gloom is warmed with one shaft of electric light across the front of the altar, which highlights the only living things here, a bowl of white lilies on a pedestal. The light passes the lilies and plays on the stone curls of Frances Cranfield, wife of the 5th Earl of Dorset, who kneels somewhat uncertainly (even though she has been doing so for 300 years) at the tomb of her thirteen-year-old son. Around her in the lofty square chapel with the faded blue starry roof are more Sackvilles. The textures of their real lives – velvet sashes, golden coronets, flowers, lace and smiles, are all turned to stone, gathering dust. Over them all are the flakes of coloured light from the enormous armorial Bonaventure window, decorated with leopards and brave words proving the Sackville descent through 700 years. They may not quite have come 'out of the northern mists wearing coronets on their heads'[2] but they are directly descended from one of William the Conqueror's companions, which is enough in England.

Beneath all this weight of the past, in a corner beyond the Bonaventure window, is Reynolds Stone's simple slate plaque in Vita's memory. Her ashes have been placed with the other Sackvilles in the crypt beneath. There is, strangely you may think, no mention that her name was legally Nicolson for most of her life, but there is mention of Sissinghurst and the word 'poet', which says it all. Vita has been returned by those who loved her to where she belongs.

St Michael's is the ancient heart of Sackville country. When Vita wrote, '... if I allowed myself full licence I might ramble out over Kent and down into Sussex ... out into the fruit country and the hop country, across the Weald, over Saxonbury and to Lewes among the Downs, and still should not feel guilty of irrelevance',[3] she was describing Sackville country. When Orlando took to the high place in Knole's park, 'so high indeed that nineteen English counties could be seen beneath: and on clear days thirty, or perhaps forty, if the weather was very fine',[4] Virginia Woolf had pierced to the quick the Sackville pride in their endless acres. When Orlando recognized from his viewpoint the pinnacles and chimneys of the houses and castles the family owned, and 'that the heath was theirs and the forest, the pheasant and the deer, the fox, the badger and the butterfly',[5] the Sackville right to the life of their inalienable land was fixed for all time. For centuries they owned over half of what is now East Sussex – from Lancing to the Pevensey Levels there stretched a line that was the base of a triangle, on the tip of which stood Knole. In time and in lordly wanderings it seemed an endless country, once upon a time. Once the rent roll had contained two dozen manors and all their meadows, orchards, lanes and shaws. No wonder Vita felt at home, and it seems of little importance now to recognize that long since these places have gone their own ways, leaving a sprinkling of Sackville Roads and Dorset Closes. The languishing sentinels of Sackville country are rather notable architecturally – the elegant Jacobean stone façade of the 2nd Earl's Sackville College in East Grinstead, and one of England's more conscious tributes to the Modern Movement, the de la Warr Pavilion in Bexhill-on-Sea by the brilliant refugee architects of the thirties, Erich Mendelsohn and Serge Chermayeff.

For exactly 500 years the Sackvilles lived at Withyham, in their castles of Buckhurst, Bolebroke and Stoneland. Bolebroke will appear later in this story; Buckhurst and Stoneland have been united, have crumbled and have been rebuilt. Old Buckhurst is now the home of the de la Warr branch of the family. They were all in their heyday in Tudor times, and then, because Queen Elizabeth I wanted her favourite, her Lord High Treasurer, her 'fine poetic genius', Thomas Sackville, nearer to her, she gave him Knole. The historians say that she granted him Knole in the late 1560s, but he did not actually get possession of it until after her death in 1603. Then it took him two years to move in – which is hardly surprising, since his not inconsiderable worldly belongings had to be carted through narrow tracks across the sticky clays and countless streams of the headwaters of the Medway. Something like twenty miles may well have seemed like twenty counties then, but in due course it was accomplished, and the Sackvilles had come to their most celebrated home.

1. Vita, aged five, with her dolls 'Boysy', 'Dorothy' and 'Mary of New York'.

KNOLE: THE MIGHTY SHADOW IN THE GARDEN'S DIP

Beneath an oriel window facing south
Through which the unniggard sun poured morning streams,
I daily stood and laughing drank the beams,
And, catching fistfuls, pressed them in my mouth.
V. Sackville-West, 'To Knole Oct. 1 1913'[1]

VICTORIA MARY SACKVILLE-WEST was born at Knole on 9 March 1892. Her mother and father were first cousins. Her father, Lionel Sackville-West, was the heir to the Sackville barony through his uncle, another Lionel, the 2nd Lord Sackville. Her mother, after whom the baby was named Victoria, was one of the five surviving children of that same Lord Sackville's romantic liaison with a Spanish gypsy dancer.[2] Victoria Josepha had been deposited in the obscurity of a Paris convent until she was whisked off to Washington to be her father's hostess at the British Legation in the 1880s. Though her father had come home in embarrassing circumstances,[3] Victoria Josepha had triumphed in Washington and come home in triumph to Knole in 1888. There she had met and fallen passionately in love with her cousin, and they were married in the chapel of Knole on 17 June 1890.

Victoria Mary was to be an only child. She will be called Vita from now on to distinguish her from her mother, as she was in life.[4] One of her mother's reasons for marrying her cousin was to keep 'the largest house in England still in private hands' as her home. Victoria quickly learned to manage Knole with great style and efficiency; she had electricity, central heating and bathrooms put in without upsetting the ancient splendours. She managed the family finances, speculated successfully on the Stock Exchange, opened a fashionable and profitable shop selling lampshades in Mayfair and it was she who 'was in constant consultation with the lawyers on the intricacies of the two great lawsuits, she who won both, she who saved Knole'.[5] Victoria was strong-willed, beautiful and capricious. And with all these things to do, as well as her entertaining and travelling, her attitude towards her daughter ricocheted between lavish affection and impatience and neglect. Vita grew up with this powerful star ruling her world, and though she respected and loved her father, she saw little of him. With her silent, goblin-like grandfather, who would fill his plate with fruit after dinner and leave it for her in a desk drawer, for whom she would grow mustard and cress and her first vegetables, she developed a solemn but fond companionship. They would play draughts together every evening after tea, but though Lord Sackville was the most constant chaperone of her childhood, she never understood what he was thinking.

For the years of Vita's babyhood Victoria and Lionel were passionately in love; by the late 1890s they had drifted apart, and from then on they led separate lives – for which there was plenty of room at Knole. With absentee or otherwise occupied parents, her silent grandfather, a series of nurses and governesses (who were chiefly for escaping from) and the sixty or so indoor and outdoor servants of Knole, Vita's childhood was crowded but often very lonely. Victoria had met the first of her string of rich companions, Sir John Murray Scott, in 1897, and he was often there; Lionel too imported his comforts. The presence of a lively, much too observant and untactful tomboy was so often not required.

The great house itself became the chief companion of Vita's childhood – it was, all four acres of it, the most adventurous of playgrounds. She was a healthy and sturdy child. Ever since her first escapade at the age of eighteen months when she had set out across the great Green Court alone but with a worried footman in hot pursuit, Vita learned to use the house as her friend and ally in mischief among the servants whose charge she was. She delighted in leading governesses a dance – into gloomy parts of the great house they had never known existed, doubtless abandoning her poor chaperones to wander the endless corridors and secret stairways alone. In such circumstances it seems hardly surprising that this lively, lonely child, who probably knew the house better than anyone, should find this mischief more entertaining than sitting primly in her mother's room, being made to play politely with inadequate and unimaginative visitors. It is also hardly surprising that there passed a fairly constant stream of nannies and governesses, these unfortunates falling foul of either Vita's waywardness or her mother's temper.

But there were other playmates – the other occupants of Knole – for the house was (and is) filled with the faces of those who once walked in its galleries, the portraits that Vita 'knew so well they almost spoke'.[6] The bewildered, brave, compassionate and challenging faces that people the state rooms of Knole – these were her allies in her wargames with wooden swords, her secret army so aptly dressed for gallantries and deeds of derring-do, when less stalwart mortals had to go in for their tea or retreated in tears. They, after all, were only a little less alive than her silent grandfather, and certainly only a little less dazzling than her beautiful mother dressed for entertaining the Marlborough House set to dinner. Moreover their presence was constant, they could be relied upon to hear tales of woe or triumph and not be too busy or wanted elsewhere. What is more, they belonged to her, and she to them. Her name had taken its place alone on that last rung of the Sackville ladder of descent, so one day they, and Knole, would be hers. It had belonged to her great-great-aunts, Mary and Elizabeth – there was no nonsense about females not counting when they were Sackvilles, or at least no one mentioned otherwise to this strong and wilful child who merged herself so naturally into the past and present (and why not the future?) of her home.[7]

2. Knole: 'the effect is less that of a palace than of a jumbled village upon a hillside . . . it is *of* England . . . these irregular roofs, this easy straying up the contours of the hill, these cool coloured walls, these calm gables, and dark windows mirroring the sun' (V. Sackville-West, *Knole and the Sackvilles*, pp. 18/19).

3. Vita with her father Lord Sackville at Knole, *c.* 1900.

In those turn-of-the-century summers when Vita was eight or nine, Knole must have been a dazzling companion. From the quiet, almost secret entrance between the houses opposite Sevenoaks church, one was swept down the hill and up again, as on a switchback, through groves of chestnut and beech in the hilly park. From the top of Echo Mount, beneath the undaunted gaze of hundreds of dainty deer, Knole's gables, roofs and chimneys came into view. It looked more like a small village than a house [2], and its immediate domain stretched over 1,000 acres of commons and woods, with names like Squire's Shaw, Lord's Spring Wood, Duchess Walk and Anquetil Crown Point.[8]

The solemn gabled west front was quiet, but in the Green Court young gardeners were sizing up the dawdling housemaids, until a stern voice from an open window reminded them of their duties! The 'village' was full of life and the sounds of work. Imagine those great rooms and galleries, the blinds half down to protect the tapestries from the sun, but the windows open and the brocaded curtains lifting in the breeze. The breeze brings the house to life, the sun makes the coloured glass in the windows pattern the polished floors, birdsong comes into the house, everywhere is full of light and colour. There is a smell of fresh polish and clean washed frilled cushions, books and wraps are left around, a small dog sleeps on a window seat, the gun dogs sprawl in the doorways. And as well as the real animals there were the animals of Vita's imagination, the carved armorial leopards who guard Knole [4]:

> Often on the painted stair,
> As I passed abstractedly,
> Velvet footsteps two and three,
> Padded gravely after me.
> There was nothing there, nothing there,
> Nothing there to see.[9]

Vita's life was concentrated on the garden side of the house. She loved the Colonnade Room [5] with its light grey walls of grisaille with swags and urns and masks, and glittering silver light sconces. The colonnade opened on to the garden. At one end of it were the cosy Georgian sitting rooms, and at the other was the dark panelled dining room, where Dryden, Congreve, Pope, Swift, Addison and Dr Johnson gazed down on family meals. Between the colonnade and the dining room was the stair which led to Vita's room, and then on up to the retainers' galleries, the attics at the top of the house, where she could run and play on wet afternoons, where they had found the trunks which Cromwell's men had forced open. Vita was perfectly free to roam, even in the 'show' rooms. Imagine her skating along those crazy floorboards in the Cartoon Gallery, snaking to the pattern of that wonderful ceiling. She loved

4. Knole: the Painted Stair, as it was in Vita's childhood, when extensive restoration work had just been carried out. The decoration dates from the same period as that of the ballroom, i.e. 1603–8, and the Sackville leopards on the newel posts are repeated in *trompe l'oeil* on the outer walls of the stair. The painter's tricks, the elaborate patterns and strange mythological beasts and figures which adorn the stair, all painted in shades of greens and grey, could not but have played tricks on a child's mind.

5. *(above)* Knole: the Colonnade Room as it was in Vita's childhood, when it was the focus of the family's life, especially in summer when the doors (on the right, out of the picture) on to the garden were opened. This was one of the rooms where Lady Sackville had electric light installed, using silver sconces from the King's Bedroom to great effect against the grisaille walls. The door at the far end leads to the lobby, with stairs up to Vita's room and the door into the dining room or Poet's Parlour.

6. *(opposite)* Knole: the ballroom as it was in Vita's childhood. The decorative plasterwork and panelling date from between 1603 and 1608 and were done for the 1st Earl of Dorset, most probably by the King's craftsmen William Portinton and Richard Dungan. The former was almost certainly responsible for the frieze of pairs of mermaids and chimaeras (monsters with lion's head, goat's body and serpent's tail) which so fascinated Vita. The portrait by Hoppner of the children of the 3rd Duke of Dorset, George, Mary and Elizabeth (who all became successive owners of Knole; see page 35), was clearly moved from its usual place in a private sitting room for the photograph. It became one of Vita's most treasured memories of the house – the young attendants at her wedding were dressed as 'the Hoppner children'. The painting is no longer at Knole.

this room too, and always remembered coming into it in the evenings with the sunset flaming through the west window and taking her breath away. And she crept for quiet into that dear little dark green closet ante-room to the King's Bedroom.

Knole, in those days, was a house full of flowers. There were bowls of roses and lilies everywhere, and elegant tubs of tropical rhododendrons, gardenias and jasmine beside fireplaces and tables. There were flowers on painted furniture, flowered brocades and velvets, flowers on the Chinese screen in the dining room, even the brass light switches were engraved with tiny flowers, and there were silver flowers in the King's Bedroom. The ballroom [6], where Vita so delighted in the frieze of mermaids standing on their tails, is full of flowers exquisitely carved in wood and

stone. Imagine her then, escaping from her mother's temper or some cloying visiting playmate, running up the colonnade stairs to the Organ Room, where a small door by the fireplace led down into the tapestry-hung chapel, where she could hide in the pulpit and never be found. Imagine her, recovered, sauntering down again, waving to the sad lost little white face of Henry, Prince of Wales (d. 1612), who seems to be longing for just such a lively companion. Imagine her, called in from play, looking grubby and sullen, wearing her treasured khaki, retrieved from some important battle or cricket match to show a group of visitors around.

When Vita was a child Knole was officially open to visitors for the last three days of every week. But sometimes there were extra invited parties, and rarely, it seems from the visitors' books, was anyone turned away. Knole was a popular attraction. It may not seem much to us now, but on 9 August 1901 there were twenty-seven visitors to what was essentially a family house, not organized in any special way for them, and thus there were sometimes disruptions. Hence the grubby guide. Even at eight she was very knowledgeable about the house. If family memory failed there was Brady's guide book, printed for Lady Plymouth in 1839 and still going strong (and Vita's father was occupied in writing another). She admitted she learned her history from Knole, and that it was a biased history which she later felt made her ignorant of realities. For her the centuries 'meant Thomas, Richard or Edward Sackville, Holbein, Van Dyck or Reynolds, farthingale chairs or love seats'.[10] But the visitors were enchanted. On 13 April 1902 the poet and diplomat Cecil Spring-Rice came with a party. He later wrote that he had fallen in love with the ten-year-old Vita (as he had done once with her mother) on that day. For this occasion, and for other important visitors, she would have been dressed as her mother liked her to be, in a silk dress with a sash, her brown hair softly curled – this Vita looking hardly less lovely than the 3rd Duke's children in the famous painting by John Hoppner which was then one of Knole's greatest treasures.[11]

Visitors came to Knole all summer, and in the depths of winter, when the house smelt of apple-wood logs and Lady Betty Germaine's pot pourri. Strangers and friends came from all over the world – Sackvilles from New York, the Reverend Maule from Knole Road in Bournemouth, Mr and Mrs Clarke from Mexico, Caroline and Minnie Cadby from Golders Green, Mr Horncastle and his friends from Hythe. They came in their barouches and Delauney Bellevilles – the Stanhopes and their guests from Chevening, Lady Verulam, Lady Mary Lygon and Lord Beauchamp, packages of Elphinstones, Drummonds and Grosvenors, the Marlborough House set – the Crown Prince and Princess of Romania, the Duke and Duchess of Abercorn, Mr and Mrs Willie James, Lord and Lady Wolverton and George Cornwallis-West. The Knole visitors' books are full of their names and different styles of life and writing – from the flamboyance of Stopford Sackville, a descendant of the last Duke of Dorset, to the scholarly neatness of one Arthur Higgs of Balliol.[12]

George Cornwallis-West, who stayed at Knole a lot when Vita was very young in the years before his marriage to Jennie Churchill, found that the house stood out in his memory more than all the other houses he knew. His visits created in him, he

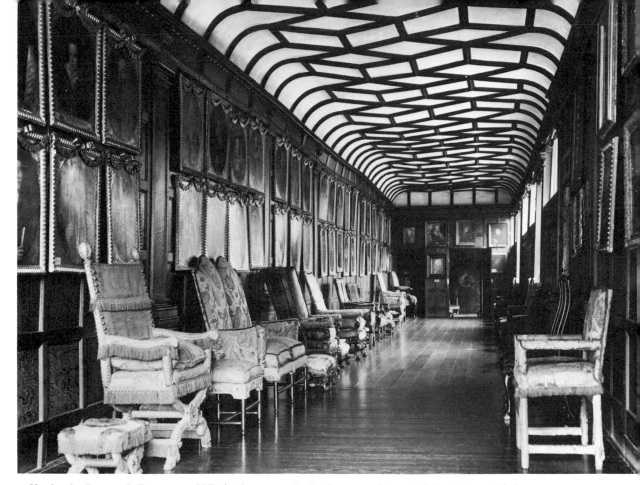

7. Knole: the Brown Gallery, one of Vita's playrooms. In the foreground is one of the chairs, with its footstool, that came from Whitehall Palace, and the wall covering of portraits in gilt beribboned frames is a gallery of famous faces, including Drake, Raleigh, More, Philip Sidney, Mary Queen of Scots, Cranmer and Elizabeth herself, mostly attributed to Jan van Belkamp.

wrote, 'the love of beautiful things. How potent it was to come face to face with the portrait of James I as a rather bewildered old man by Mytens and see beneath the picture the actual chair the King was sitting in ...'[13] How much more potent then was Knole for the little girl whose rocking horse had belonged to the 4th Duke of Dorset, who was allowed to play with the jewels that Gainsborough had painted, who was touched with Orlando's disease, a literary weakness that substituted a phantom for reality, and who flaunted her family and its possessions to the rich, sophisticated and admiring visitors. There is something especially powerful about a home which is partly on 'show' and often peopled with strangers. One joins in the charade, but in the shadows of the evening when the visitors are gone it is possible to creep back and enter – like stepping on to the stage of an empty theatre – into full possession of the grandeur. I have no doubt at all that Vita donned a velvet cape that swept the floor and paraded down the Brown Gallery [7], saluting Blake and Thomas More and the dashing Philip Sidney, laughing at Jan van Belkamp's gang of solemn-faced portraits and Harry Howard in his quaint black velvet cap. I have no doubt at all that she sat in one of those fabled Whitehall Palace chairs with the dolphins at her feet and held court until the shadows disappeared. This was how Knole seeped into her soul. It became a part of her as surely as the food she ate.

A ND THEN there was the garden. In spring and summer the doors of the colonnade were opened on to the gravel walks where the peacocks strutted among flurries of white pigeons; '. . . you have to look twice before you are sure whether they are pigeons or magnolias', wrote the grown-up Vita in *Knole and the Sackvilles*. She goes on to describe the garden of her childhood – turf of brilliant green, the sound of bees in the limes, the heat 'quivering like watered gauze above the ridges of the lawn'.[14] She describes an enclosed garden, with herbaceous borders beside long green walks, little square orchards with apple trees 'under which grow iris, snapdragon, larkspur, pansies and such like humble flowers'.[15] There are interior walls with rounded arches 'through which one catches glimpses of the house, so that though the garden is divided it also has complete harmony – half is formal and roughly half is wilderness – wilderness of beech and chestnut threaded by mossy paths which in spring are thick with bluebells and daffodils'.[16]

The wonder of it is that she might have been describing the garden Johannes Kip drew for *Britannia Illustrata* between 1711 and 1715, a copy of which has always hung in the lobby of the Brown Gallery [8]. This, along with the view from the upstairs windows, would have supplied Vita's first overall image of Knole's garden. Substitute beds of herbs and vegetables for the herbaceous borders, and Vita could still have been looking at the garden that Lady Anne Clifford had known here in the early seventeenth century when she was married to the 3rd Earl of Dorset. Just as the quality of unchangingness applies to the house, it is even more deeply experienced in the garden – or it could have been in the garden of Vita's childhood. If, with the fancy of hindsight, the purpose of Knole's garden was to perpetuate the images and sensations of an Elizabethan garden through the centuries, until a Sackville came along who would harness the experience to make a great twentieth-century garden (if Knole's garden fatefully sought oblivion in the cause of Sissinghurst's fame), how did this come about?

K NOLE'S GARDEN belonged to Knole even before the Sackvilles came. The twenty-six acres were enclosed by a great Kentish ragstone wall by the Lennards of Chevening, who were tenants of the house in the years before Thomas Sackville took possession in 1603. Lord High Treasurer Sackville was the originator of the Sackville sumptuousness and he spent a fortune on his house in what were to be the last years of his life. He died, in a Privy Council meeting, in April 1608. (He was married to the daughter of Sir John Baker of Sissinghurst Castle.) It seems safe to surmise that his lordly generosity in keeping a household of 200 to be fed meant that the garden was mainly functional and fruitful – twenty-six acres of the old, basically medieval *hortus conclusus* – with squared walled enclosures, some filled with flowers, miniature trees and arbours, but most producing herbs, salads and vegetables with orchards for fruit. Knole's garden was large – much larger than contemporaries at Ham House or Montacute, and it must have been a country garden of great delights – with damask, musk and sweetbriar roses, violets, wallflowers, pinks, sweet williams and honeysuckles, rosemary, mints and thymes. The orchards, or tree gardens, would have been filled with limes and junipers as well as medlars, quince, cherries, apples and pears, and ornamented with seats and treillage. All to bring peace and fruitfulness to the aura of the house.

During the seventeenth century Knole's garden missed greatness by some of the finest of whiskers, when one considers what was happening to gardening in England. Thomas Sackville was succeeded, for one year only, by Robert, the 2nd Earl, and then by Richard, the 3rd Earl, who kept Knole splendid but squandered the rest of his fortune so presumably spent none of it on new fashions in gardening. This was a blessing, for his wife, for fourteen unhappy quarrelsome years before his death in 1624, was Lady Anne Clifford. Lady Anne must have had ideas about gardens, and when she left Knole to marry Philip Herbert, 4th Earl of Pembroke, it was for these two that Isaac de Caus made Wilton into one of the most celebrated gardens of Europe in the 1630s. Wilton was given great scroll parterres, a highly organized wilderness presided over by Flora and Bacchus, coronets rising and falling in fabulous fountains and a grotto in a grove of cherry trees. It was, Roy Strong writes, the 'supreme expression of English Renaissance garden design and a vivid reflection of the ideals of the court of Charles I'.[17] Even though Edward, 4th Earl of Dorset, was also at the court of King Charles, none of these Renaissance fancies reached Knole. The garden was never touched by visions of the Venetian villas of the Brenta, nor by the taste for Inigo-Jones-inspired museum gardens filled with classical figures. Though his house was raided by Cromwell's soldiers and the 4th Earl suffered for his loyalty to his King, at least there were no emblematic representations of Divine Rights to be swept away and Knole's garden was left in peace.

The seventeenth century was also the century of John Evelyn, whose influence would not have been missed at Knole. His advocation of 'salletts', herbs and flowers, his introduction of yew and holly for hedges, as well as his advice on the planting of trees, would surely have been taken. But perhaps, most importantly, Evelyn made it socially prestigious for gentlemen to take an interest in their gardens, and with the Restoration, where the royal gardens led the rest would surely follow?

In 1677 Charles, the 6th Earl, succeeded to Knole, with the benefit of the wealth that his mother Frances Cranfield, daughter of the Earl of Middlesex, had brought. Charles was another splendid Sackville – a courtier, poet and patron of poets, writer of popular songs, lover of Nell Gwyn, friend of Dryden, Pope and most other Restoration scribblers as well as William Penn, and a genial man of the world. Painted in his dressing robe by Godfrey Kneller, Charles looks like an an indoor man, plump and pallid, given to dinner parties and endless conversations on politics and art. Not a gardener. He was a close friend of King William and Queen Mary, and he probably added the very presentable wrought-iron gates to Knole's garden soon after 1688 (when Jean Tijou was working at Hampton Court for King William, though Knole's are modest and by an unknown craftsman). Charles retired from his busy public life in 1698 and was spirited away into captivity at Bath by his third wife, Anne Roche, and he died there in 1706. And so the seventeenth century had passed Knole's garden by – no great axial thrusts inserted as at Longleat and Ragley, no Italian Mannerist fancies like Wilton nor fanning *pattes d'oie* as at Hampton Court; even though the Dorsets had walked with kings and queens and with those lords with the most fashionable gardens, they had not transported those fashions home to Knole. It remained a large version of a gentleman's country garden.[18]

1706 is the year from which the earliest records of Knole's garden survive.[19] Perhaps it was the first year it was thought worthy of making such paper contracts for garden matters, for it was the year that the 6th Earl's eighteen-year-old son Lionel (who was to be created 1st Duke of Dorset in 1720) came into his own.

At first it seems that the young Earl had difficulty finding a satisfactory gardener. In March 1706 Richard Baker was 'to take charge and look after garden at Knowle' and 'reserve the fruit for his Lordship' for £30 a year and a room in the house. His perquisites included the cabbages and kitchen herbs over and above what were needed for the house. He took over a long list of tools – the hoes, turfing irons, glass frames, iron 'rowlers' and wheelbarrows, but only one pair of shears. Baker did not last long, for by 27 December 1706 Robert Kaidyer or Keydy is signing for the tools; by August 1711 Phillip Davies is in charge, but by then there had been major works put in hand.

It seems acceptable that the young Earl might have wanted to introduce some new ideas and improvements. Vita says that this Lionel was 'amiable rather than brilliant'[20] but he was much at Court and frequently at other fashionable houses. One imagines him inquiring lightly over dinner about a likely man to improve, but not change, Knole – perhaps inquiring of his father's old friend of the Kit Kat Club, Sir John Vanbrugh of the Board of Works. At the Board there was a draughtsman with ambition in garden design, Thomas Akres, who lived in Duke Street, St James's. It was this Thomas Akres who arrived at Knole with a contract dated 15 January 1710 to carry out various works for the young Earl of Dorset. The contract refers to a plan, which has not been found, so it is not clear whether Akres was the designer of the improvements or if it was some more exciting person. The improvements are, however, matters of detail, and though they are important in the unchanging life of Knole's garden, they are not significant in terms of historical design. The contract is reproduced in full for the charm of its language and spelling and its insight into early eighteenth-century gardening. Thomas Akres

> 'is to lay out in form the little partar before the cloyster as is expressed by the letter A in a platform or scheme thereof given by the said Thomas Akres and signed by him and to lay the said partar with Ruf and gravell and plant the same with handsome evergreens of about 4 foot high

'to lay out the Bowling Green called the Mount in the said draught or scheme for a bowling green and to plant a little wood at each end with flowering shrubs and a hedge round either of elm lyme hornbeam or yew and to take away the wall which supports the Tarris and make it into a slope and to lay all the slopes and bowling green with turf and to new make the slopes between the partar and the bowling green and plant with pyramid yews of about 4 feet high to cultivate the Kitchen Garden by the stew ponds trench it with dung and lay it out for a kitchen garden

'to cultivate and dung all the dwarf trees and borders under the wall in the plantations of dwarfs set out under letter [?] and carefully prune all the dwarf trees and hedges of apples and filberds

'to lay out the little kitchen garden in beds and quarters proper for a kitchen garden to cultivate earth and dung that slip of ground between the walls and the woods within the two hedges and plant two hedges one of fruit the other of yew

'to lay out the low ground by the wood and to digge a canal forty foot wide and about 4 foot deep to make the pond at the end something regular and handsome and to find all workmanship and materials to digg all gravel turf earth and sand to find all plants at his own expense to mow rowle beat and edge all within grass walks'[21]

Akres was paid a total of £396 – £100 on starting and the rest in instalments as the work progressed. He signed for the last payment on 22 November 1711, so the work was done within two summers. When Phillip Davies accepted care of the garden tools in the summer of 1711 the list included the boots 'proper for the Horse when he rolls the grass', large baskets for carting grass, three salad baskets, forks for hand weeding, edging irons and Dutch and other hoes.

Kip's engraving of Knole and its garden [8] was published by David Mortier in 1715. Much of the work that Akres carried out fits with Kip's image, and it seems likely that the artist visited Knole and recorded it immediately after these important alterations were carried out. Kip's accuracy can be trusted with foregrounds (if not with distances) and the new trees *look* about four feet high and certainly look newly planted. In *Britannia Illustrata*, among its companions, Knole stands out as a country garden, very different from the swirling parterres Kip drew at Longleat and the great rectangular canals of Wrest Park.

Thomas Akres signed a second contract, for the maintenance of the garden, and he seems to have been retained on a kind of consultancy basis to supervise at a fee of £180 a year. In the parterre and bowling green the gravel paths and sand alleys were to be weeded and rolled, the grass was to be well cut and rolled and the borders kept free from weeds. The kitchen garden was to be well manured and regularly trenched to produce herbs, roots, salads, melons and cucumbers. In the wilderness the grass walks were to be cut, swept and rolled, and all the fruit and nut trees were to be pruned and trained, and all the evergreens clipped 'in their proper shapes'.

The Akres contracts are the richest and most rewarding in the Knole archives relating to the garden. Succeeding papers and record books are full of detail, but are only concerned with the day-to-day running of the garden. What it is most amazing to realize of all is that the essential details of Akres' gardening, as Kip recorded them, can still be traced in a modern aerial photograph [9]. The two images show

the outline of the house to be virtually unchanged in the intervening 260-odd years. The enclosure on the west front remained throughout most of the nineteenth century – it has now gone, though the oaks are still there.

The modern photograph shows the garden to have been stripped of all its decorative borders and dwarf trees around the house, but the central path to the colonnade room is there in both. Both also show the importance (though merely a nod at axial formality) of the gravel walk across the south front, once ornamented with clipped evergreens, then pedestal pots of geraniums in Victorian times, and now bare. This is where the peacocks strutted when Vita was a child; in earlier days there were other birds with exotic plumage and perhaps even chained bears, 'the surliness of whose manners Orlando was certain concealed trusty hearts'.[22]

When comparing Kip's engraving with the modern photograph, allowances have to be made for some distortion of the perspective. Kip did not, after all, have a neat aeroplane from which to view his objective, but had to work painstakingly from survey and measurement to give himself wings. The garden wall seems to have been originally higher, for the gate in the south-west corner of the house was once arched over. This is still the main entrance from the park into the garden, but other breaks in the wall have been made, notably the large break which attempts to provide a vista for the colonnade front, which is a modern innovation.

8. (above) 'Knowle in the Parish of Sevenoaks in Kent being the Mansion House of Charles Sackvile, Baron Buckhurst, Viscount Cranfeild, Earle of Dorsett and Middlx', by Johannes Kip and Leonard Knyff, published in *Britannia Illustrata* in 1715. (There is an error in that Charles Sackville had died in 1706 – possibly when the drawing was started – and the garden so closely fits with the work contracted and done in 1710/11 that the drawing must have been completed or adjusted after that date, by which time Knole belonged to Lionel, the 7th Earl.) Reference to the contract for 15 January 1710 for work to be done seems to show that, in this illustration, the work has been completed. On the south (garden) front of the house 'the little partar [parterre] before the cloyster' (the colonnade) had been made of turf with gravel paths and planted with evergreens. The mount and bowling greens with adjacent hedges and shrubs can be seen, and between the mount garden and the parterre, running almost the whole length of the gravel walk along the south front of the house, it appears that a bank of turf has replaced the terrace ('tarris') wall, and the pyramid yews 'about 4 ft high' are all planted. The kitchen gardens, which Akres thoroughly restored to order, are to the north-east of the house, probably extending to sheltered gardens behind the stables (where remnants survive today) along the north side of the house. The 'canal', 'something regular and handsome', is also in the north-east corner, the site of the stew ponds, and eventually, in Vita's childhood, of the Mirror Pond and sunken garden [see pl. 12].

9. (below) Aerial photograph of Knole from the south-west, c. 1960. This, when compared to Kip's illustration [pl. 8], allows the following comparisons and similarities over a period of 250 years:
• The central path from the colonnade front is there in both, but all the beds and borders that were within the arms of the house have gone. (Close inspection of the photograph reveals circular shadows in the grass on each side of the central path which could be the positions of the raised flower beds, with basket surrounds, that were there in the latter half of the nineteenth century.)
• The gravel walk across the south front is there in both.
• The walk inside the west garden wall has been retained.
• The proportion of the space in the south-west corner seems the same in both, with the central avenue of trees identifiable in the photograph.
• The change of level running south from the south-east corner of the house is there in both.

In general the validity of the comparison between the Kip engraving and the aerial photograph is amazing. The walk inside the west wall has been retained; the proportion of the space in the south-west corner seems the same, even the central avenue of trees is still there; the modern tennis court fits the equivalent enclosure of old; the change of level running south from the south-east corner of the house, marked by steps in Kip's engraving, is still there, still retained by a wall in part, part of which has the loggia against it; fragments of the next wall in an eastwards direction still exist and the piers which stand in the centre of the east lawn are survivors of the gate shown by Kip. Many of the trees in the wilderness are mature specimens, old enough to have been planted by Thomas Akres.

Lionel, the 1st Duke of Dorset, reigned at Knole until 1765, through a sizeable portion of the eighteenth century that was so momentous for English gardening. Perhaps, and quite justly, Akres' work had pleased him and he did not wish to make alterations. Perhaps Vita was being a little kind when she called him amiable rather than brilliant, and he did not see eye to eye with the wits of that very witty age. It could be said that the tasks and honours that befitted his station, and his bewigged and beautiful appearance in the Kneller portrait in the ballroom at Knole, were not those that demanded the subtlest diplomacy or most agile nerve. He carried the Act of Settlement to Hanover and escorted German George on his journey to England, he was Lord Warden of the Cinque Ports, Lord Lieutenant of Ireland, Constable of Dover Castle, a Knight of the Garter, Gentleman of the Bedchamber – am I less than kind? Duke Lionel certainly was a *busy* man.

His successor was his son Charles, 'somewhat feebleminded and dissipated and thoroughly unsatisfactory' according to Vita.[23] He was little threat, for he died in 1769. He was followed by the 3rd Duke, John Frederick, who protected Knole for the next thirty years. And how did he protect it? Remember, Capability Brown was rampaging England and would have happily swept away walls, walks and wilderness to set Knole floating in a sea of its very becoming parkland. The devoted Mr Brady supplies the answer when he says of the 3rd Duke: '... he was much attached to the place and expended considerable sums in its repair but would not suffer the primitive form and character of its exterior to be altered.'[24] So it was the Sackville weakness, a prevailing melancholy, that demanded that Knole be kept as they had always known it, an unchanging refuge in a changing world.

I love that John Frederick for his melancholia and his protection of Knole through a dangerous period; he was also rather a lovable person – patron of the delightful Gianetta Bacelli, who reclines in chilly grace beneath the Great Stair, he was the bringer of music to the galleries, the music of Boccherini, Haydn and Corelli, the planter of some of the finest woods in Knole's park and a legendary figure in the history of cricket. But the melancholia claimed him – because of Gianetta he waited till he was forty-five to marry, and he died seven years later, leaving Knole to his five-year-old son but actually in the capable hands of his widow, Arabella Cope.

From Duchess Arabella's time there are more records of the garden in the Knole archive. From 1798 there is a series of beautifully scripted garden books giving details of the daily life of the garden.[25] The first begins on 6 January 1798 when seven gardeners were employed and paid 9 shillings each for a six-day week. In the summer the rate rose to 10 shillings. Duchess Arabella must have instigated new régimes, for by the time she got her head, in 1802, the number had risen to seventeen gardeners doing a six-day week for 12 shillings each. She seems to have been fond of gooseberries, for there are numerous mentions of gloves for the gooseberries and overtime for picking them. Overtime was worked in summer for mowing and in the early autumn for fruit-picking; loads of dung were brought from the White Hart in Sevenoaks, flower roots bought from Vineyard Nursery in Hammersmith, and the garden expenses for 1803 totalled £357 11s. 1d. On Trafalgar Day 1805 the gardeners Tarrant, Langridge man and boy, Parkhurst, Budgeon, Baldwin, Dudwell and boys T. and W. Wells were placidly planting, weeding and mowing, cleaning out the bird houses and charging extra for destroying wasp nests. Beer was served for a celebration in the ice house, as it was regularly for a celebration at the end of February or in early March. There were parcels to be collected and delivered to Her Grace at Bognor, boxes of fruit to be sent to Penshurst, the weekly Sunday morning attendance for orders at the house and the flower pots on the terrace to be constantly refilled.

Young George, the 4th Duke, was full of promise at Harrow and Christ Church, but just after he came of age he was killed in a hunting accident at Powerscourt in Ireland. Knole passed jointly in turn to his sisters Mary and Elizabeth. It was for Mary, Countess of Plymouth, that Mr Brady wrote his guidebook. His mellifluous and pompous praising of the views from the park stung Virginia Woolf into her sardonic laudations of distant armadas and waves and even 'the craggy top and serrated edges of Snowdon herself'.[26] But Brady also tells us about the exotic birds, the shell-backed seats, flower baskets and rustic summerhouses similar to those Repton had designed for the Royal Pavilion at Brighton. Lady Plymouth's days at Knole lasted until 1864 – with her visitors and her guidebook, her fashionable Victorian gardening (undoubtedly she introduced the herbaceous borders) and her musical afternoons, she brought the garden into an elegant old age. Mowers enabled larger areas to be lawn, the dividing walls which had crumbled were removed, and the whole garden was opened out. The regularity of the tree planting had long since given way to time, old hulks were cleared and the healthy oaks, beeches, limes, yews, mulberries and hollies were left to continue on till today. Fewer paths and avenues were kept, but still the form and experience of the garden were retained by old practice and old desire.

When the Countess died in 1864 Knole remained the property of her sister Elizabeth de la Warr, then passed to the 1st Lord Sackville, Elizabeth's son.[27] It came to his brother Lionel, Vita's grandfather, in 1888. And so we have slipped into her time.

As a child Vita had her own garden 'because of the tradition that every child must automatically love and cherish a garden of its own',[28] but she was honest enough to admit later that it bored her – 'weeds grow too fast and flowers too slowly'.[29] She let it get untidy and the gardeners would descend and tidy it up, so she felt it wasn't really her garden at all. A little tyrant and a bully she may have been (so was Gertrude Jekyll as a child), but *not* in the garden, which was ruled by a more terrifying tyrant. It was just the unreachableness of the enchanted garden, forever in the guardianship of the Gardener, that made her long to have command of such enchantment. At least, that is one way that gardeners are made:

> The head-gardener was the terror of my life. He was an immensely dignified man, with a hooked nose, keen eyes, and a great black beard, giving him the appearance of a major prophet. From time to time he used to descend on me with accusations of having robbed his peach trees or destroyed his borders by picking flowers, accusations which were sometimes well founded and sometimes not. In those days I regarded him as an ogre and a spoil-sport, but looking back on him now I see that he was merely a typical head-gardener of the grander sort, justly exasperated by the depredations of an irresponsible child. Absolute lord in his own domain, he must have counted me among the worst of his garden pests.[30]

Vita also offers another reason for Knole's unchangingness: she allows the prophet affection and respect and many virtues, but

> His faults, I regret to say, were also many. They proceeded from no vice inherent in his nature (for he was an upright man) but from sheer obstinacy and a dislike of changing anything to which he had grown accustomed. He thus disliked cutting vegetables while they were still fit to use and preferred to let them run to seed rather than allow them to be delivered young and succulent to the kitchen. This, I have since found, is a failing common to nearly all professional gardeners. Then, of course, when it came to the flower garden, he had no taste at all. He grew, and grew very skilfully, the most hideous and ill-assorted plants with no regard whatsoever for colour, suitability or elegance. Such a thing as a colour-scheme had never entered his mind; nor, so long as he could keep his health and his job, would it be allowed to enter it. Every now and then my father, spurred on by some gardening friend, would make a protest; but although the black-bearded prophet would listen respectfully and politely, it never made any difference to the garden. Things went on in exactly the same way as before.[31]

So Vita's idea of a garden was firmly fixed in childhood, long before the complications of growing up absorbed her mind. Sensations – the smell of clipped box, the scent of wet gravel under yews and of honeysuckle sweetness drifting from a high trellis – once fixed in early childhood are never lost. Nor was her idea of a garden as a set of spaces through which one wandered or ran – where she could dodge and surprise through archways, where the reddest strawberry or waviest asparagus fern was always just out of reach and one would surely be caught astride the box edging leaving a footmark on the sacred soil. Oft repeated glimpses and the scents of paradise, and the occasional taste of its fruits, no matter what the risks – of such things are gardeners made. If she was an arrogant and pampered child, the sense of place that Knole gave her made her humble; she loved its 'soul, benign and grave and mild, towards me, a morsel of mortality'.[32] If hers was a childhood crowded with over-attentive servants and the emotional warrings of her parents,

Vita, as a basket of westiria.

10. Vita as her mother liked her to be, dressed for a party, with her hair waved and on her best behaviour. Here she is dressed 'as a basket of westiria' (Lady Sackville's spelling).

she was able to escape into the garden [12] where 'the past mingled with the present in constant reminder out in the summer house after luncheon, with the bees blundering over the pond'.[33] In this setting she escaped into writing her endless historical romances of Edward Sackville, Jean-Baptiste Poquelin and Richelieu. With Edward Sackville she conjured up the 4th Earl of Dorset as 'the embodiment of Cavalier romance' – conjured up with all her undoubted talent and the added piquancy of her understanding of the Sackville disease, the touch of melancholia that had kept Knole unchanging and would touch her too; and her undoubted ability to lose reality in fantasy. Perhaps, in her case, it was rather to create a fantastic reality.

Vita's dependence upon Knole, its contents, its garden and its lost estate, were fixed immovably by the time she was sixteen, in 1908. Violet Keppel confirms it at the time: 'Vita belonged to Knole, to the courtyards, gables, galleries; to the prancing sculptured leopards, to the traditions, rites and splendours. It was a considerable burden for one so young.'[34]

Old Lord Sackville died in 1908. Vita became 'the Kidlet' of the headlines as her parents fought and won their right to Knole. But the family's triumphant, circus-like return home, pulled by estate workers in a carriage from the station, was, in terms of Vita's future, a tragi-comic charade. All that she had depended upon, had belonged to, would not now be hers. Suddenly the rules had changed and Knole was entailed away to her Uncle Charles and her cousin, ten years her junior, Edward Sackville-West. Fortunately, or of necessity, for the moment she had other things to do, other places to go.

11. *(opposite above)* Knole: the east front, with two pairs of vases brought by Lady Sackville from La Bagatelle flanking the steps.

12. *(opposite below)* Knole: the Mirror Pond and sunken garden as it was in Vita's childhood. She wrote in this summerhouse, it was her hideaway in summer: 'the past mingled with the present in constant reminder out in the summerhouse after luncheon, with the bees blundering over the pond'.

13. Lady Sackville and Vita. This 'miniature' was made from a group photograph (the waistcoats of the men standing behind can be seen) by the Sevenoaks photographer and artist C. Essenhigh Corke, who took all the Sackville family photographs, and painted watercolours of the interiors and exteriors of Knole (printed in Lord Sackville's guide book to Knole published 1906) between 1890 and *c.* 1920. This miniature was produced on a gilt-edged card and sold in packets of sweets.

2

THE GRAND TOURISTS

Lone and unshackled, let us to the road
Which holds enchantment round each hidden bend,
Our course uncompassed and our whim its end,
Our feet once more, beloved, to the road!
V. Sackville-West, 'Song: Let us go back'[1]

VITA's early life was filled with grand touring escapades, which equipped her, as the Grand Tour had equipped her eighteenth-century cousins, with her tastes for life outside of Knole. Her need for exciting and beautiful places, her need to experience other lifestyles and other landscapes against which to pitch her own, was one of the strongest motivations of her personality. When she met and married Harold Nicolson, their mutual respect for each other's moments of mad adventure, a shared taste for the same places, and a basic need for home as a foil to faraway places were the deepest bonds of their relationship. This compatibility remained the unassailed rock of their love and understanding, from a first rapture for the alpine meadows above Interlaken in the summer of their engagement (1913) until they became the most ennui-ridden pleasure cruisers in the last winters before Vita's death.

Vita's grand tours were more than matched by Harold's early life, as the child of a diplomatic family for ever on the move. During March 1919, in a crisis in their marriage when she was trapped at home with two small sons, Vita chided Harold: 'I met such a thrilling man yesterday who seemed to have lived everywhere that I most want to go.' She had heard of a castle for sale at the foot of Mount Olympus, she said, and continued: '... how much I like people who live in unexpected parts of the world – it always appeals to me irresistibly – when Mar[2] meets people who have just arrived from [the] Caucasus or Tahiti or China she gets pink with excitement and she just can't help it.'[3] She was being most unfair, for it was just Harold's experience of some fairly exotic places (Teheran, Tangier, St Petersburg) and his awareness of the exciting world 'out there' which had fascinated her in the first place – that and his golden curls. But Harold has to wait a little yet.

Before sitting down to write this book I pondered for hours on how much or how little need be said about the string of lovers who have become such a well-publicized part of Vita's life. I have concluded that the majority of them are incidental to the

·

14. Vita dressed as Portia, probably aged about seventeen and at the height of her passionate discovery of Italy.

pursuit of her deeper feelings about places. She held her feelings for most people in the topmost levels of her mind, and apart from Harold Nicolson, there were probably only three outstanding people who pierced the depths of emotional friendship – Virginia Woolf, Geoffrey Scott (who did make her read his *Architecture of Humanism* and discuss such things) and Dorothy Wellesley.[4] None of the others matter too much here – we are 'beyond the barriers beyond which not even lovers could pass'[5] – except, that is, for one. For longer hours, long after the others had been easily dismissed, I wondered about Violet Keppel. And then I found the quotation that told me that she did count. On 13 October 1948 Vita (then aged fifty-six) wrote one of her then rare letters to Violet after a visit to her flat in the Rue Casimir Perier in Paris and to the castle she had found for herself outside the city at Provins:

> I loved Casimir Perier and Saint Loup. Above all, I loved Saint Loup: seldom has a place suddenly taken me as Saint Loup did. It was a queer feeling – almost as though I belonged there – I can't enlarge on this even to you – it is too private a feeling. It did, however, make me realize that curious bond between us, our intense sense of the character of places. We both have it so strongly that it becomes a pain. I don't even know if you will understand what I mean as I write all this – but I expect you will.[6]

At the end of my first chapter I showed Violet's understanding of Knole's meaning for Vita. Violet also wrote:

> It is not an exaggeration to say that places have played at least as important a part in my life as people. Indeed, it is almost as though the places have generated the people; equipped and apposite, they have sprung spontaneously from the background which created them. It was necessary to see Vita at Knole to realize how inevitable she was.[7]

Violet was the braver of the two and she knew herself better. Vita, even aged fifty-six, was still afraid of this feeling, though it was the bond between her and all the people that really mattered to her. Sometimes it was a bond held briefly and brilliantly because of one place (as with Geoffrey Scott and Florence), with Virginia Woolf it was the unreachable desire for *Orlando*'s past and Knole, and with Dorothy Wellesley it was a very present joy shared in poetry and gardening through the twenties and early thirties, dissolved by Dorothy's eventual unhappiness and isolation.[8] With Violet and Harold, though, the bond seemed to hold through space and time – but Violet and Harold were very different places.

When Vita flew from Knole she flew with Violet. She had met Violet Keppel in 1904, when she was twelve and Violet was ten. Violet was the daughter of Mrs George Keppel, the King's favourite, and she had had an even more romantic childhood than Vita.[9] Their mothers deemed them suitable as friends, and they themselves admitted that they were equally unsociable, both consummate snobs and had shared heroes – D'Artagnan, the Chevalier de Bayard and Raleigh! Violet was not the sort of girl to let anyone keep any secrets, and all Vita's secrets of Knole were soon shared; in turn Vita's personality was magnified and glorified for Violet by Knole's splendours – and it was Violet's ability to fuse people with places that flattered and fascinated Vita. It was hardly surprising that they became madly romantic – wandering through the show rooms in the moonlight, reading Dumas, Scott and Baudelaire aloud to each other. Dressing up led to acting out plays of their own devising – and the scenery was always on hand and perfectly in place – the arras rustled, the candles guttered in their silver sconces, and the actors were so wrapped up in their own pasts they didn't notice how their audience yawned!

Violet enhanced Scotland for Vita. They stayed at the Keppels' summer retreat, Duntreath Castle, overlooking the Strathblane Hills just north of Glasgow. Violet loved Duntreath and it glowed in her mind – it was so old, touched with menace, and it smelt of cedarwood, tuberoses and gunpowder. Vita was captivated – she long remembered how Violet filled her room with tuberoses, how they dressed up and Violet chased her down the long dark passages with a dagger. Vita's alternative was Sluie, near Banchory, above the birch-covered banks of the River Dee. This was Sir John Murray Scott's summer house, and Vita went with her mother (and old Lord Sackville as chaperone) most summers between her eighth and sixteenth birthdays [15]. Sluie was a comfortable Victorian house in a soft countryside of

15. Sluie: an early house party with Vita aged nine or ten.
Front row: Vita's grandfather, Lord Sackville; Miss Murray Scott (who is equipped with her knitting); Lady Sackville, Vita's mother (who is holding some kind of knitted garment and seems duly puzzled).
Back row: Sir John Murray Scott is second from left and his other spinster sister may be the lady on the right. The other two are unknown to me.

bracken and heather-covered hills – she loved it because it released her from care about her appearance and tiresome routines – and it released her mother also, into a carefree and delightful persona that she could love unreservedly.[10]

She does not seem to recall the Murray Scott home in Gloucestershire,[11] but she did stay with her mother and Sir John at the palatial apartment at the corner of the Boulevard des Italiens and the Rue Lafitte that he had inherited, along with its fabulous contents, from Sir Richard and Lady Wallace. Vita, when left alone, scooted in Sir John's wheelchair past the gilded chiffoniers and bow-fronted chests laden with Meissen china. The presence of the Wallace treasure made Lady Sackville a very different person, and she insistently drummed Vita on the finer points of Directoire, Empire and Louis Quinze. Vita *did* learn and was always a good judge of such things, but interiors never really interested her – as long as things that came from her beloved Knole were in their place in her homes she took them for granted. Occasionally she enjoyed dusting and polishing them. Strangely, it was not anything from the Rue Lafitte that caught her affection,[12] it was the ornaments from the garden of La Bagatelle, Marie Antoinette's pavilion in the Bois de Boulogne (which the Wallaces had also left to Sir John), which she remembered for the rest of her life. She loved the sophisticated rurality – the playing-at-shepherdess atmosphere – of La Bagatelle, and in her lonely imagination the groves must have been peopled with aristocratic ghosts, the classical statues and the satyrs and caryatids, lions and rams that ornamented the ranks of magnificent bronze urns, accurate replicas (by kind permission of Emperor Napoleon III) of those that guarded the walks of Versailles.[13] Pairs of those same urns still ornament the garden at Sissinghurst.

It was also important that Vita first experienced Florence with Violet Keppel. She went there for the first time in the spring of 1909, with Violet and Rosamund Grosvenor as companions. Violet wrote: 'Vita's reaction to Italy was exactly what mine had been to France. She was bowled over, subjugated, inarticulate with love.'[14] In 1910 Vita returned 'shivering with excitement and joy at my beautiful beloved Florence'.[15] In 1911 she went back again with her mother, who wrote: 'she looks and acts as if the whole of Florence belonged to her'.[16] She went again in 1912, and Harold and she spent part of their honeymoon there in 1913.

It is easy to dismiss Vita's passion for Florence as typical of her time and kind, but that doesn't make its effect on her any the less powerful and creative. Guides to Florence are still quoting André Suares on one of the more precious joys of a lifetime – 'to enter Florence for the first time at the age of twenty and to say to oneself at every step with a leaping heart "I am in Florence."'[17] Vita would more likely have exulted 'I am Florence' and 'Florence is mine'! Florence elaborated and glorified everything she loved about Knole; for Knole's one lovely *trompe l'oeil* Great Stair there were whole rooms in the Museo Degli Argenti; for Knole's exquisite Renaissance overmantels by Cornelius Cuer, there was the whole of the stupendous Duomo and, more comprehensible, the little Battistero, where Dante was baptized; there were reverberations of Knole's solemn courts in all of Brunelleschi's cloisters. Here was not just one house with a history but a whole city of the massive and

44

arrogant buildings of the Medicis and a countryside full of villas, all with their own dazzling ancient pasts. In the old prints and paintings of these villas she found the kin of Elizabethan Knole, houses surrounded with orchards and productive fruitful gardens. She found the companions to all her tastes and desires, to all she wanted to be or wished she had been, in the living and the dead. All her 'thoughts of escape and disguise, of changed name, travestied sex, freedom in some foreign city'[18] had been given reality by Florentines. She found the richness of the velvets and brocades she loved to wear in Bennozo Gozzoli's pageantry of the Medici perpetuated into the courtly cavalcade of the *Three Magi* to Bethlehem; and there were all those deliciously ambiguous Florentine boys as well as the ultra-spiritual, paradise-promising faces of the Fra Angelica angels. There was also, to be seen daily, what Harold Acton has so nicely called 'the Tuscan type persisting'[19] – the lean young profile peering into a bookshop that could be Dante, 'the hatless young women along the Via Tornabuonino have all the poise of their forebears in Ghirlandaio's frescoes', and when they dress up for a ball 'many of the old marriage-chest panels seem to come to life as under a magician's wand'.[20] As it happens Vita and Violet had beaten him to it – Philippe Julian remembers driving through the crowded streets with them in 1951 – 'the two women indulged in a leisurely survey of the passers-by, their verdicts those of a pair of latter-day disciples of Oscar Wilde: "Ah, my dear, that profile, *pure* Donatello." "Look, Vita! the flower-seller! Divine! A Botticelli, and do look at that one, a little on the heavy side, but *very* attractive, a Michaelangelo, darling! Heavens, but these people *are* beautiful!"'[21]

To Vita Florence was a carnival after the everydayness of Knole. As a place where beauty blended with nature, creating a living proof of the possibility for happiness which exists even in a world that is unsure of itself, it reflected her hopes and dreams, and taught her many lessons that will rebound again and again in this book. She absorbed, whether she knew it or not, the feelings of the best Italian gardens of the Renaissance from the villas of Medici and Gamberaia; their geometry is the Romanesque panelling of the Badia at Fiesole or the Battistero laid upon the ground; from the misty vistas of the Boboli Gardens there is the constant panorama of civilized leisure – that ever-surprising view of the city resting in its vale – paradise on a horizontal plane ornamented and organized by Lombardy poplars, holm oaks, umbrella pines, box and rose laurels. Florence's past is polished and alive, not dusty and dead[22] – the landscape of the amazing *Adoration of the Shepherds* by Hugo van der Goes spread before the eyes.

Anyone who sees and loves Florence cannot but learn the lessons of its gardens. The not un-English intimacy of the Arno Valley landscape makes a peaceful sympathy with the scale of the villa gardens, the avenues and vistas link the two, and the walls of box and yew that create the secret rooms ornamented with statues and sparkling water make frames for pictures of the villas and the countryside. The garden becomes 'a salon flooded with unlimited light and air', belonging as much to the countryside as to the house, becoming the mutual ground on which the two meet and the character of man is balanced with the character of the countryside.[23]

Michelozzi's Villa Medici is seen as the supreme example of this ultra-civilized background to 'lives of luxurious culture', and it was the Villa Medici – 'always the most interesting owing to its remarkable position'[24] – that became embodied for Vita in the tall thin frame of the young architect Geoffrey Scott. She had first met him in 1909 when he was restoring Bernard Berenson's Villa I Tatti; he had published *The Architecture of Humanism* in 1914, and in 1917 had married Lady Sybil Cutting, the owner of Villa Medici [16], and restored the garden for her. It was

16. Villa Medici at Fiesole near Florence, the supreme example of an ultra-civilized background to lives of luxurious culture and the essence of Vita's passion for Florence. The photograph of the villa, the home of Lady Sybil Scott, and the garden restored by Geoffrey Scott was taken in 1923 by Vita.

a marriage doomed from the start, and by 1923 Scott was ready to fall in love with Vita. But his best influence, and probably his greatest attraction for Vita, was in his brilliant book, and Vita's copy has the passages marked wherein she found something of herself: 'Romanticism ... allows the poetic interest of distant civilization to supplant the aesthetic interest of form ... it is inspired by the distant and the past; but it is inspired also, by Nature.'[25] And something of which she might like to be? The possessor, not of the Sackville melancholy, but of 'the laughter of strength'? That laughter, Scott analyses, is present visually in one style only, the Italian baroque architecture of the seventeenth century, with its fusion of the fantasy, surprise and variety of nature disciplined by the laws and logic of scale and composition. The triumph of the baroque was that 'it intellectualized the Picturesque'.[26] Was it Scott that made romantic, picturesque Vita see that her life, and any expression of it, also needed that balancing discipline of classical laws?

After Florence, the influence of the rest of Italy and most of France could but be light-hearted. Venice did not score at all and left her blasé. She loved parts of the Alps and certain chunks of France, which she visited several times, light-heartedly, throughout her life. She thought the Dordogne 'a lovely lost corner of France with enough castles for even me'.[27] Like Gertrude Jekyll, she was captivated by the scents and flowers of the south of France – rosemary, cistus, peach, almond and apricot blossoms, honeysuckles, jasmines and magnolias. Not surprisingly, she loved the châteaux of the Loire, and Vézelay and Burgundy – 'a wide rolling country in gentle colours with little vineyards on the slopes and soft creamy oxen dragging timber'.[28] She made several walking tours in the Alps and learned a lot about the flowers – by the time she went to the Col de la Valois with the adoring Hilda Matheson as a peaceful companion in July 1929 she was becoming an expert – 'the flowers are marvellous,' she wrote home to Harold,

> I will tell you some that we have found – rock roses, alpenroses, gentians (*verna*, *balearica* and *acaulis*), soldanella, lychnis, anemone, geums, silene, thyme, camassia, violas, violets (little bright yellow ones), saxifrages and sedums in great variety, forget-me-nots, potentilla and our own little vanilla orchis . . . you remember those little natural gardens we used to find in the Dolomites with silene, gentians and dianthus growing together – well, here they are. I think I must bring you here one day, you will love it . . . the hut is 8,000 feet up, simple and clean, marvellous air, I am writing lying on the grass studded with bright flowers – great grey peaks all around. You cannot think how lovely the combination of mauve violets and blue gentians is on the grass . . . flowers really do intoxicate me.[29]

As for Spain – 'my own country, you know'[30] – at first her visits were pure histrionics – absorptions in her bohemian roots – gypsy dancing and bullfights. Later on she was able to see more clearly – 'real El Greco illumination over Toledo today, huge grey and white clouds shot with sun and puffs of little trees in blossom on the hills – the Alcazar garden even more lovely and romantic than I remember with Banksia roses out and oranges everywhere'.[31]

After all this, there was Russia. Vita first went with her mother and Sir John Murray Scott when she was eighteen to stay at the Château Antoniny on its estate 100 miles square between Kiev and Warsaw. An immense yellow Mercedes had taken them bumping fifty miles across atrocious country (Vita and her mother laughing so much they were nearly ill at the spectacle of the genial, twenty-five-stone Sir John, 'whose bumps were bigger than anyone else's'[32], and blaming

Napoleon for not stopping long enough to make better roads). The château was completely incongruous in the middle of the steppe, and filled with magnificent and alien grandeur. Armies of guests gabbled in a language Vita had never heard before (Polish), there were eighty saddle horses and a private pack of hounds, Cossacks sleeping across her doorway, hereditary dwarfs to hand out the cigarettes, and night-long mazurkas – these were her memories of Tsarist Russia just before the Revolution. But her real captor was Russia herself: 'How much I loved Russia! Those vast fields, that feudal life, that illimitable horizon – oh, how shall I ever be able to live in this restricted island? I want expanse!'[33] Having none, she returned to writing about her Renaissance heroes in escape, disguise and freedom. In the June of 1910, following her return from Russia, she met Harold Nicolson for the first time at a dinner party before a play.

VITA AND HAROLD were of course present at a party of a different kind. Those last four summers before August 1914 were their summers of house parties, balls and escapades of a kind of brinkmanship gaiety that was never to be seen again. They went to the Desboroughs' Taplow Court (an ugly, overgrown villa, furnished like an hotel) and mingled with the golden company that would one day not return. It rather depends who one reads about who loved whom in that dream time, but Violet flirted with Julian Grenfell (who was the reality of Vita's play-acting: tall and statuesque, torn between art and action, subject to fits of depression and gentleness – beside him Vita's was a wavering talent and melancholy), and both Patrick Shaw-Stewart and Edward Horner fell in love with Vita.

She went to Compton Beauchamp, a delicious old manor house at the foot of White Horse Hill in the Berkshire Downs. It was surrounded by a paved moat, built to keep the house dry and for the sheer beauty of a ribbon of clear water making an island of the old house. Here there was mystery – a haunted monk's walk through the beechwoods, and long vistas through high box hedges, terraced lawns, flower borders in profusion, old fruit trees in walled gardens – all overlaid with an ancient well-being. Vita learned a new dimension of houses and gardens. She found what she liked and what she didn't like.

Into the latter category came Crewe Hall, Barry's recreation of a Jacobean palace in Cheshire. The architect had used all the traditional devices – arcades, galleries, oriels, carved screens, mythical beasties (of a stiffening pride after the playful Sackville leopards), and Nesfield had added parterres of coloured gravels, impeccable carpet bedding and a sundial like a candy stick thrusting out into the unconcerned and unconnected lake. Vita hated it.

St Fagan's Castle, near Llandaff, was much more to her liking. Its tiered battlements were thick with flowers, fig trees and aromatic shrubs in those summers, there were pots of campanula and yucca everywhere, and a rosary which was 'a dream of loveliness'. Vita remembers Lady Plymouth roaming about the garden dressed in faded browns and pinks – *this* was the 'real genuine article in all its ancient glory', she wrote in 1913.[34] St Fagan's brought her a view of a new magic –

its rough stones and a series of bowers, pergolas and steps leading a dance down to the ponds, its old orchards strewn with crocus, narcissus and tulips, with a touch of Ruskin – 'you would think it a pleasant magic if you could flush your flowers into brighter bloom by a kind look upon them: nay, more if your look had the power not only to cheer but to guard!'[35]

I wish Vita had said more of another garden she visited – for her earliest visits to the Manor House at Sutton Courtenay in those years were to begin a lifelong admiration for Norah Lindsay, which was influential on Vita's gardening. In those days before the Great War Norah Lindsay was making her garden – she had married Lt Col Harry Lindsay in 1895 and he had received the Manor House as a wedding present from his cousin, Lady Wantage. Norah Lindsay was to become one of the most gifted gardeners of this century – her romantic approach, her ability to produce 'the perpetual refreshment to the spirit offered by the garden, which becomes a wonder and a blessing', her allegiance to the 'crumbling shrines of the ancient garden gods of Florence and Rome', were all that Vita most admired. Well before the war the Manor House was leading where Hidcote was to follow. The garden was in three main parts – the Long Garden, the Pleasaunce and the River Garden. The Long Garden [17, 18] was a large room with stone walls and high box hedges, smaller rosemary and lavender hedges around mixed borders, pergolas covered with flowering creepers and carefully kept lawns. Norah Lindsay's forte was luxuriance and she had a genius for *laissez-faire*. The Long Garden housed many plants with 'squatter's rights' – in just the right places – companies of 'lupins, anchusas, mulleins, all the easy English flowers, raise their tainted spires in spring and summer, and treading on their heels come mallows, thalictrums, hollyhocks, the tall bushy campanulas and the tropical rods of magnificent eremuri ... all comfortable and healthy growing in informal drifts ... one group follows another in rapid succession so there is never an inch of bare earth.'[36] The Pleasaunce was carpeted with daffodils, jonquils, narcissi and crocus in spring, and filled with roses, brooms and gorse beneath its shady old apple trees for the summer. The walk to the River Garden was paved with a long brick path, inlaid circles and rectangles holding tubs for water lilies and other water plants, and the lawn walk hedged with enormous old roses led to a lush meadow and the River Thames gleaming in the distance.

Not far from Sutton Courtenay, but a world away in style and atmosphere, Vita saw the Astors' Cliveden at its most magnificent. Forty gardeners grew flowers to garland the house for every party – she always remembered the wonderful indoor flowers at Cliveden, and much later she was very proud to earn Nancy Astor's praise for Sissinghurst, especially valued as she didn't really *like* gardens.[37] And there were two other places that were particularly hers – the Horners' Mells Manor and Hatfield House. Mells, tucked away in Somerset, once a rich and much-blessed abbey, supposedly the plum that little Jack Horner pulled for himself from a pie of monastic properties he was delivering up to Henry VIII, still sits serenely within its walls, beside its ancient church. Then, even before the Great War, Mells's taste had

consciously rejected Victorian bedding – vines, wisteria and roses clambered over
old walls and rafters, masses of rosemary and lavender burst out from under the
house windows on to paved terraces with tubs of agapanthus set out. There were
many oblong flower beds with just enough narrow grass paths 'to keep one dry shod
in wet weather' – 'there is no bedding out, no complete banishment of the useful.
Old fashioned border stuff lies below fruit trees . . . and the fruit trees . . . are not so
numerous as to exclude lilac bushes and rambler roses'. Roses garland the sundial –
this was planting in the spirit of generations of Horners gone by.[38]

And Tudor Hatfield was a fit companion for Knole, with its long galleries, maze,
vineyards and lime arcades that Pepys and Evelyn praised, the mulberries in the
corner of the Privy Garden planted by James I [19] – all that Francis Bacon said a

17. *(opposite above)* The Long Garden, Sutton Courtenay Manor House, looking towards the house.

18. *(opposite below)* The Long Garden, looking away from the house. This fantastic wonderland garden,
here photographed in its prime in 1930, well displays the extravagance of Norah Lindsay's taste in
gardening. The classical clipped evergreens are a foil to the spires of verbascums, delphiniums, lilies,
thalictrums and lupins, with roses flowing on arches and treillage. The Red Queen might pop up at
any moment and order on the croquet game; it is a garden that symbolizes exactly the moods of
ecstasy mingled with despair that surrounded Vita's youth and early married life, when she knew this
garden and its brilliant, but eccentric, maker. The garden no longer exists in this form.

19. *(below)* The Elizabethan spell of Hatfield: the Privy Garden with the mulberry trees planted by
James I. It was here, at a ball in January 1912, that Harold Nicolson told Vita that he loved her.

garden should be – 'square, encompassed on all four sides with a stately arched hedge: the arches to be upon pillars of carpenter's work' and massed with lilies and other delights.[39] Even some (very splendid) Victorian bedding could not spoil Hatfield's old Elizabethan spell; it was highly appropriate that it was here, at a ball in January 1912, that Harold told Vita that he loved her.

> Then in the sunlight stood a boy,
> Outstretching either hand,
> Palm upwards, cup-like, and between
> The fingers trickled sand.
>
> 'Oh, why so grave?' he cried to me,
> 'Laugh, stern lips, laugh at last!
> Let wisdom come when wisdom may.
> The sand is running fast . . .'[40]

EVENTUALLY Vita decided that she would laugh 'as he desired' and she married Harold Nicolson in the chapel at Knole on 1 October 1913. They began their honeymoon at Coker Court,[41] then they went to Florence and on to Constantinople, where Harold had been Third Secretary at the Embassy since September 1912.

To Harold Nicolson travelling was a way of life. He had been taken across Russia when he was eighteen months old (at the age when Vita was merely venturing across the Green Court!), he had spent his childhood in the wake of his ambassador father, and on his own account he had come to love the Swiss mountains and the Haute Savoie.[42] He had lived for spells in Italy, France and Germany to learn the languages. On his eightieth birthday his sons and his daughter-in-law gave him a special card carrying quotations from each of his decades. His tenth birthday (1896) was marked with the following passage from *The Desire to Please*:

> My father during all the years of my childhood and boyhood lived abroad. The pantechnicon vans would roll across the Caspian, the Mediterranean or the Aegean and there, in a house which looked now on the Andrassy Strasse, now upon the Golden Horn, now towards Trafalgar, or now across the Neva to the fortress of St Peter and St Paul, the Nicolson home would be reconstructed. Behind this exotic tapestry was a gap of which only today am I fully conscious. What I really wanted was to see the trees grow year by year in fields that had known me since I could not walk. I wanted to come back after long absence and to mourn the fall of a familiar elm or to rejoice to think that willow-cuttings had shuffled into willow coppices of their own. I longed instinctively to feel a little less un-English in my own country, a little less foreign when abroad. I wanted to feel autochthonous, the son of some hereditary soil . . .[43]

That last sentence explains much of his fascination with Vita, a fascination that grew into love. His biographer, James Lees-Milne, has concluded that it was 'Vita's deep atavistic love of Knole which Harold had to understand was the really serious rival he had to face'.[44] I feel that Harold's strength was that he was too wise to set up in rivalry to Knole, but tackled this problem in two ways – by finding a little atavism of his own, and then – when Vita had settled down – by becoming the substitute for Knole. He embodied all that Kent meant to her, and the fact that he would always listen and commiserate when it was Vita and Knole *contra mundum* was an abiding source of her gratitude and love.

Harold found his atavism with his uncle, the Marquess of Dufferin and Ava, and Ireland (and, to save his own self-respect, discounted it). His biography of his father, *Lord Carnock*, which he wrote in the late 1920s and published in 1930, shows every sign of filial respect and professional admiration, but little of affection. Harold's filial affections were directed towards his Uncle Dufferin, about whom he wrote *Helen's Tower* in 1937 [20]. Here he was on *his* home ground, which was similar to the Sackville heritage, and he levels with it thus:

> Lord Dufferin ... possessed a romantic nature. To me, the feuds of the Hamiltons and the Blackwoods are as unreal as those of Montagu and Capulet. My Hamilton forbears of the seventeenth century are no more to me than dim Ulster 'undertakers'; nor do the tales of their violence and rapacity stir a single fibre of atavism in my soul. To Lord Dufferin these unreliable legends were something more than mere border minstrelsy. To him the fancy that in his own person and by his own marriage he had healed these ancient rivalries afforded him the same satisfaction as he derived from the perusal of *Marmion*.[45]

My thesis is that a good garden can only be created from deep within memories and beliefs. It is with Lord Dufferin that we find Harold's deepest memories, rather than with his parents. In *Lord Carnock* he records his parents' marriage on 20 April 1882 in the chapel of the embassy at Pera, and that 'they drove out that spring afternoon to Therapia where they stayed for four days in the Summer Embassy and then returned to Constantinople. From that hour the private life of Arthur Nicolson was serene with happiness. There is no more which can, or should, be said.'[46] On the other hand, of memories of Lord Dufferin and his world there is much to be said; *Helen's Tower* is rich in anecdotes, even though some of them concerning his lordship's interest in his tiny nephew have to be stretched a bit! There is the oft-told story of Harold's hope that his uncle dropped viceregal business for a moment to receive the news that his sister-in-law, Katie, had had 'another dear little boy'.[47] The beginning of *Helen's Tower* is sprinkled with the flashpoint images of childhood: his first memory is of the smaller dining room at the Paris embassy on a May morning in 1892 when Harold first spied a powdered and bewigged footman and made brief acquaintance with his then ambassador uncle. He, his mother and his nurse, Miss Plimsoll, had come overnight from Buda Pest via Strasbourg (where they had stayed with another aunt, Clementina, who had married, not half so usefully as Lady Dufferin, Herr Ministerialrata Beemelmans, and lived in a dim, trim little house in the Herrenzimmer where the curtains were 'weighted with the smell of cigars'). Later comes the tale of the balloon, given to him by M. Chauchard of the 'Magazin de Louvre' – an enormous pink cockerel of a balloon. Harold's attention slipped momentarily, caught by yet another of the grandeurs of the embassy, and the balloon left his hand, sailed serenely to the heights of the magnificent ceiling and stayed there. Panic ensued – 'I stood there on the black and white marble pavement of the hall tortured with anxiety in regard to my balloon and my conduct.' It was eventually downed by a stiff paper dart armed with a pin, the ultimate resource of the agitated footman – 'My cries of rage and sorrow echoed throughout the Faubourg St Honoré.'[48]

Was it because of his feelings for his Uncle Dufferin and this longing to be associated with his grandeur that Clandeboye took such a hold on Harold's feelings too?[49] He remembers it with intense detail; for him the sense of touch brings back a dimly remembered incident or atmosphere 'with almost stereoscopic clarity, enhanced as it is by the attendant associations of sight, scent and sound'.[50]

> In such a manner I would be affected when, after years of absence, my fingers closed upon the handle of the entrance door to Clandeboye – a large round handle that needed two hands, the scrape of wood on stone, a puff of inside air, the smell of stone and plaster of the outer hall, the fainter smell of varnished deal and velvet cushions of the inner hall, and the other mingled smells of that large house – grapes and marsala in the dining room, French polish in the salon, calf bindings in the library, dried rose leaves and picture varnish in the great gallery, sandalwood which spread outwards from the pompein cupboards of my aunt's dressing room. The outer hall, filled with many lovable objects – curling stones with silver plaques, the stuffed and startled head of a rhino, a Russian bear, a Burmese bell, Greek inscriptions, a mummy case, a second bear . . .[51]

Attached to this romantic noble figure Harold discerns more admirable attributes . . . Lord Dufferin's love of Ireland, its very soil and the dilemma of destitution and misery of the Irish landscape, along with his own position as the heir to lands won by plunder and oppression. To assuage his feelings of guilt he spent vast sums on his estates, making his lakes and his two-and-a-half-mile long avenue in the cause of employment. He dreamed of escaping to Scotland, of castellated pinnacles above grey lochs and freedom from the pangs and pities of an Irish estate but 'always, at the last moment, the charm of Ireland would tug again at his heart'. 'Here I am,' wrote Lord Dufferin in 1853, 'home, home, home, *home*, – amid drenched fields, leafless bushes and a misty mockery of a park – which against my better reason I cannot help loving more than any other place in the world.'[52] Harold, despite his diplomatic polish and wit, perhaps knew that he had to come to that too.

There is also the unremitting rule that every gentleman of taste has to have dabbled with his soil. When he made his park, the young Lord Dufferin wasn't being entirely altruistic; his was the last great landscaped park made in Ireland. A modest river was enlarged into a series of lakes complete with islands, gulfs, channels,

20. Helen's Tower, Clandeboye, built by the 'romantic' Marquess of Dufferin, Harold's uncle, as a memorial to his mother in the nineteenth century. It was in the grandeur of his uncle and his love for his Irish estate that Harold found an atavism of his own, on which he focused the most potent memories of his childhood.

hidden reefs and peninsulas, and the road from Belfast was cut by the avenue 'which pursued its relentless and weed-covered way through fields and farms until it ended in the sudden tang of seaweed with the sound of waves upon the rocks of Helen's Bay'. Lord Dufferin added a bridge so that the trains could reach his private station and 'steam into his Sir Walter Scott dreams'.[53] He was also, true to type, interested in architecture. Harold's lifelong fascination with this art must have been born of early memories of the bound volumes of drawings in the library at Clandeboye, for alterations to the house which there was never enough money to carry out – 'they combined the simplicity of Balmoral with the elegance of Chambord'![54] Uncle Dufferin, undaunted (though not entirely successfully), became his own architect, and 'his first problem, as is the experience of most amateur architects, was the problem of levels'.[55] Writing this in 1937, the designer of Sissinghurst would have known.

Harold too had read *The Architecture of Humanism*, and he perfectly analyses his own (and Geoffrey Scott's) classical taste in relation to Lord Dufferin's (and Vita's) romanticism.

> It would seem indeed as if the misunderstanding that arises between the romantic and the classical temperament is due, not so much to any conflict between imagination and reason, as to the fact that whereas the classic finds pleasure in recognition, the romantic derives his own greatest stimulus from surprise. To the classic, as to Dr Johnson, 'the value of every story depends upon its being true'. A story is a picture either of an individual or of human nature in general. If it is false it is a picture of nothing. Yet it is not truth only which is essential if classical interest is to be durably aroused; that truth must be 'recognizable' in the sense that it must contain a sufficient proportion of thoughts, feelings and associations analogous to those of our own modern experience. The Middle Ages, the sixteenth and even seventeenth centuries do not provide those 'parallel circumstances and kindred images to which we readily conform our minds'. Their lack of actuality, and even of reality, deprives the classic of those pleasures of recognition which he most enjoys, and leads him to regard these dim events, either as misty fantasies, or else as so remote from his own experience as to possess an archaeological but not a human interest. To the romantic on the other hand, what is enjoyable is that very sense of expanding experience, occasioned by the unexpected, the unfamiliar or the different. So far from relishing only what he can, in terms of his own experience, assess and comprehend, he derives actual pleasure from the unrecognizable. And thus, when applying himself to persons, he is equally interested in remote and unfamiliar types as in individuals of the shape of whose mind and habit are akin to his own.[56]

This is how Harold explained Lord Dufferin to himself, and he loved his uncle and rejoiced in all his connections with him. It is perhaps also how he explained Vita's romantic passions away, and why most of them were of little concern to him since he had little regard, let alone envy, of such 'misty fantasies'. But love allows for at least a little vanity. If Harold's attachment to the Dufferin legacy was the quelling of his vanity over the atavism, over the often-voiced opinion that his family 'of impecunious high civil servants' was hardly a match for a Sackville, then

Vita carefully guarded his feelings about this for the rest of her life. And in return he guarded her feelings about Knole. One of the tendernesses of their love was this mutual respect for each other's weakness; there was no rivalry, merely mutual commiseration.

There was one more powerful Irish influence on Harold's youth – Lord Powerscourt's fabulous garden, made by Daniel Robertson from a plan of the Villa Butera in Sicily. Powerscourt's 300-yard long upper terrace of granite, open at the west end into the gardens ornamented with statues and vases, its second terrace of grass with a central flight of steps and an alcove in granite decorated with bronze vases and Tritons spouting water, the acres of dark conifers, the deer park with a deep glen containing the highest waterfall in the British Isles – this was Harold's lesson in the baroque, the fusion of romance and classicism. But it was also very, *very* grand, and he could not hope to aspire to such grandeur, nor did he, nor Vita, want it. They wanted the perfect balance all right, but in new and rather more elusive terms, and this taste united them completely.

And the fruit trees grew in profusion,
Quince and pomegranate and vine,
And the roses in rich confusion
With the lilac intertwine,
And the Banksian rose, the creeper,
Which is golden yellow like wine,
Is surely more gorgeous and deeper
In this garden of mine and thine.[57]

VITA AND HAROLD reached their first home in Constantinople, No. 22 Dhji-han-Ghir, just a month after their wedding, and they were to be very happy there until the following June [21, 22]. 'Our house,' wrote Vita, 'is the most attractive house you have ever seen. It is a wooden Turkish house, with a little garden and a pergola of grapes and a pomegranate tree covered with scarlet fruit, and such a view over the Golden Horn and the sea and Santa Sophia! And on the side of a hill, a perfect suntrap!'[58] The living quarters included an upstairs sitting room for each of them, a drawing room and a smoking room, with adjacent bedrooms and the dining room on the cooler ground floor. It was a place that suited them both.

All Vita's earlier experiences of places were eclipsed by her first sniff of the East. She was free from home, happy in Harold's uncomplicated love and in the companionship of an agreeable embassy staff, which included Gerry Wellesley and Reggie Cooper, and with time to explore the ancient city. Constantinople was the happiest possible beginning to her love affair with the paradoxes of the East; her first glimpse of a garden as a refuge from a hostile nature. She celebrated her garden in her poem 'Dhji-han-Ghir', some of which I have quoted above. She further described its broken walls, its neglected pools and fountains and its distant view to

21. *(left)* Vita in the garden of No. 22 Dhji-han-Ghir, their home in Constantinople, in early spring 1914.

22. *(right)* Vita and Harold in their garden – the house is in the background. Vita's own photographs of the interior show their rooms filled with furniture from Knole – tapestries, chairs, books, tables, pictures and mirrors went with them and were abandoned during the war, though they were reclaimed afterwards and safely returned to Long Barn.

the sea and the Bithynian shore. There is little evidence that they did very much to this first garden, they merely enjoyed it, which was most important of all.

It was Harold who captured Constantinople and all it meant to them in his novel *Sweet Waters*; he names his heroine Eirene, after Constantine I's church dedicated to heavenly peace, and portrays in her all the things he loved most in Vita. Eirene is introspective and serene, she has 'lost' her father and lives with her capricious mother whom she hates and loves in constant turns; much of her awkwardness and introspection comes from her half-knowledge that her mother is the plaything of a rich Greek. Eirene is tall, statuesque, with smooth pale cheeks under smooth dark hair – 'he had thought her like Demeter – she had looked like Demeter, serene and impervious'.[59] With Angus Field of the golden curls, the young man who awakens Eirene, there is much of his more light-hearted self; but more telling is the portrayal of Hugh Tenterden, the respected diplomat with aristocratic roots in Kent, who coolly rescues both the political situation and Eirene in the nick of time. Did Harold regret those golden curls which made him seem perpetually good for a lark but not to be taken too seriously? The golden curls always won Vita over – but he made Hugh Tenterden markedly balding – and Tenterden had that Kentish aristocracy behind him, he was 'a breaker of hearts' and was certain to be made an ambassador. Under the skin Harold wanted to be Hugh Tenterden, but he never was. But he did have his Eirene. *Sweet Waters* is perhaps the most disarming of all the books that either of them wrote – it captures that first brief happiness in Constantinople perfectly. It also portrays another life on the brink of extinction, for the south-eastern Mediterranean was just as doomed as Europe in that spring of 1914. The scents of crushed thyme, the Stamboul spring that brought the Judas trees into bloom and baskets of narcissus and tulips on to the streets, the gardens of grey ilex in the shimmering heat, magnolias, roses that burst from bud to tired petal in a single hot day as the summer advanced – the symbolism of the gardens of Pera and Therapia is woven through the book. At the end of *Sweet Waters* the brigand King Nicholas of Montenegro declares war on Turkey and the Balkan War has begun. In June 1914 Vita and Harold returned home to England because she was expecting their first child. They never went back.

23. Vita's first published article, which she clipped out of *Country Life*, 3 June 1916. Major-General Sir Charles Townshend (1861–1924) and his troops were besieged by the Turks in the garrison at Kut and finally surrendered after a heroic stand on 29 April 1916. Major-General Townshend was interned at Prinkipo Island, but was well-treated and released in order to plead for the Turkish cause at the Armistice conference. The Armistice was signed on 30 October 1918.

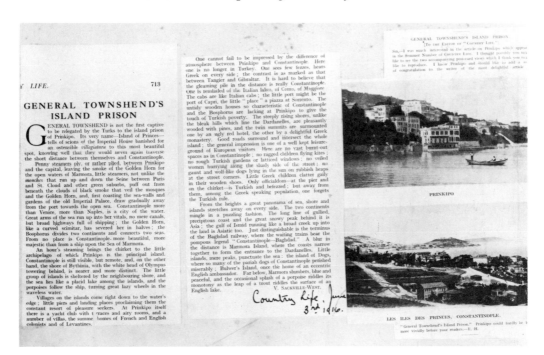

3

AN ELK-HOUND AND A ROSE BUSH: LONG BARN 1915-25

My Saxon weald! my cool and candid weald!
Dear God! the heart, the very heart of me
That plays and strays, a truant in strange lands,
Always returns and finds its inward peace,
Its swing of truth, its measure of restraint,
Here among meadows, orchards, lanes and shaws.[1]
V. Sackville-West, 'Night'

HAROLD NICOLSON was released from the frenzied diplomatic activity that accompanied the outbreak of war just in time to get to Knole for the birth of his son, Ben, on the morning of 6 August 1914. The following spring Harold and Vita bought Long Barn as their first country home.

When Vita followed the ferny path uphill through Knole's park it took her along the Broad Walk to where the track to St Julian's crossed the ridge. The view across her ancestral woods, if she turned a little to her right, included a small village. It was quite natural that the daughter of the house should migrate down the dipping lanes, past the squat square tower of St George's, Sevenoaks Weald, past the triangular green surrounded with estate cottages and a Victorian school, and farther down into a wooded hollow to find a home. It was, with less imagination than Vita possessed, a cottage on the estate. She could, and did many times in the years to come, walk from Knole to Long Barn, her dogs trundling at her heels, and, even if it could be fitted comfortably into one of Knole's smaller courtyards, it was a refuge, a rustic retreat and eventually a beloved home. Long Barn seemed unconcerned with time and had an ancient serenity, even if it did look rather like the home of the good gnome of the woods, wearing a heavy cap of a roof upon its head.

When the Nicolsons bought Long Barn for £2,500 in March 1915 it was a conglomeration of the fourteenth, fifteenth and sixteenth centuries with many alterations and additions [26]. It had been rescued from dereliction by Mrs Lilian Gilchrist Thompson, the wife of the Rector of Kippington (a village now part of Sevenoaks), and restored and put up for sale. It carried a legend of being the birthplace of William Caxton, it had yielded a golden rose noble of the time of Edward III, and it had seesawed in its fortunes from dower house to labourers'

24. Vita as she liked herself best, as a young mother with the new-born Ben in 1914.

25. Harold and Vita at a flower show at Knole – taken shortly after Ben's birth, probably in September 1914. Here she *is* Eirene, of Harold's novel *Sweet Waters*.

cottages over the centuries. In her letter of 23 February 1915 Mrs Thompson offered the Nicolsons the cottage complete with the alterations they had asked for – extra water and heating, a new brick terrace – and whatever furniture they wanted from what was there. Even though her mother had taken her on great antique-buying sprees during her engagement, Vita was not particularly interested in such things and she tended to take them for granted. She and Harold believed that 'flowers, chintz and Jacobean furniture were the happiest companions'[2] and this is what they acquired, probably from the well-stocked attics of Knole – refectory tables, high-backed chairs, carved and inlaid chests and Persian rugs. Vita never got excited over furniture the way she did over garden ornaments and statues.

In January 1916 they accepted a revised estimate from Bentleys the builders, of Tubs Hill, Sevenoaks, for re-erecting a barn moved from Brook Farm across the road (which Lady Sackville had bought for them) as an addition to the original house. The barn was put up in the spring of 1916, and the builders also paved a little formal garden outside Vita's sitting room window. It was a five-bay timber framed barn with a typical sixteenth-century crown post roof. It made Long Barn an L-shaped house, focused on the brick terrace [27]. From the terrace level the garden sloped down to meadows and a distant misty view over the Wealden trees. A breeze seemed to blow, even on the hottest days.

26. Long Barn: the 'cottage' as Harold and Vita found it and bought it for £2,500 in March 1915.

27. Long Barn: the 'barn' has been added and the terrace walls have been built in this photograph, taken about three years later, when Vita's first plantings are beginning to cover the retaining walls.

Though they always referred to it as 'the cottage', Long Barn was becoming quite a substantial house. There was a breakfast room overlooking the entrance front, with a long flagged passage – washed with light from the garden door – which passed Vita's sitting room on the right (with her bedroom above) and the dining room and Caxton's room on the left. Beyond Caxton's was the kitchen and the path to a cottage where the children were eventually housed with their nurse, and also the linking corridor to the barn. The barn became the Big Room, a fifty-foot-long sitting room with bedrooms for guests above and Harold's writing room at the far side, overlooking the rose garden. When it was finished Long Barn sported seven bedrooms and four bathrooms.

In April 1916 they bought 182 Ebury Street as their London home, where they spent weekdays, with long weekends at Knole in winter and Long Barn in summer. Their younger son, Nigel, was born at Ebury Street in January 1917. Gradually Long Barn claimed more and more of Vita's time – it was here that she slipped into the role of a young mother and domesticated herself, and she later felt that this was the time when she was most liked, or at least she most liked herself. 'I myself took to gardening quite late in life,' she wrote in 1938. 'I must have been at least twenty-two.'[3] She was just turned twenty-three by the time they acquired Long Barn, and for the next three and a half years she was happy and contented.

Vita did much of her garden planning in bed. She was keen on making lists and resolutions of what she would do – especially on days when pregnancy, post-pregnancy or the more regular *maladie* kept her body helpless but made the mind extra keen. Her early Long Barn notebooks have scattered entries – they often turned into scribbling pads for the boys, but it is only from these and her letters to Harold that a picture of her early gardening can be gathered. She began with ingenuous questions – when and how to plant lilacs? when to plant thyme, sedums, saxifrage? what are good climbing roses? She did all the usual things – she sent for catalogues, made a point of finding and looking round local nurseries, and noted things in other people's gardens. And being Vita, she turned to a source she knew well, she planted 'flowers that English poets sing'[4] – roses, daffodils, iris, wallflowers, love-in-a-mist, borage, lavender, stocks, columbine, poppies and hollyhocks. Her first desire was for flowers on the house – clematis and the hybrid perpetual rose 'Madame Delville', with enormous pink flowers, and 'American Pillar' and 'La Guirlande' were among the first purchases for Long Barn. She dreamed, she made more lists, she planned – hedges of hornbeam, beech and thorn (especially the mix of pink and white thorn she had noticed in Constantinople), Lombardy poplars, hedges of roses, water-loving plants and trees that would appreciate the damp and soggy lower part of Long Barn's garden and woodland. She acquired some perennials from Stubbs, the gardener at Knole (the successor to the black-bearded prophet?), who was therefore one of her first helpers.

On 25 August 1917 Vita and her mother went to visit Gertrude Jekyll in her magical haven Munstead Wood, the house Edwin Lutyens had built for her twenty years before in a wood near Godalming in Surrey. Lutyens was beginning his

28. *(above)* Harold on the terrace at Long Barn, July 1915.

29. *(below left)* Harold and Vita at the entrance to Long Barn, July 1915.

30. *(below right)* Vita and Ben, aged eleven months, at Long Barn, July 1915.

passionate friendship with Lady Sackville, and it rather went without saying that anyone who was to be important to him had to pay court to his imperious fairy godmother – 'Aunt Bumps', as he called her – and so pay court Vita and her mother did.[5] Vita wrote of Miss Jekyll: '. . . she is rather fat and rather grumbly . . . and the garden was not at its best but one can see it must be lovely.'[6] Lady Sackville recorded: '. . . she is seventy-four, very ugly in her features, but has fresh clear skin, and charming voice and *timbre de voix* and a very kind smile. She was charming to Vita and me . . . she admires Vita and so does McNed.'[7]

They would not only have admired Vita and conversed in French, they would have been conducted slowly around much of the house that McNed had built, with its cool white walls, plain and beautiful oak stairs and beams, and its Long Gallery overlooking the little north court with rippled stone paving and pots of ferns, hostas and hydrangeas. They would have slipped out of the door beneath the gallery overhang and crossed the little court to where the Nut Walk and other paths led out into the garden. They would have been told that the Nut Walk was resting (its time was spring, when the hazels were undercarpeted with yellow and white polyanthus primroses) and that the way to proceed was via the Michaelmas daisy borders, a riot of blue and mauve at the beginning of *their* display. Vita was never to be fond of Michaelmas daisies, so this was her first disappointment.

They would have come through the pergola of Jekyll-favourite climbers, her trusted 'Aimée Vibert' with rose-edged buds and warm-white flowers, and 'Madame Alfred Carrière' and 'La Guirlande' everywhere. Then the highlight of the Munstead garden in late summer – the 200-foot-long herbaceous border, drifting from cool beginnings with sentinel yuccas to the flaming company of scarlet and orange dahlias, kniphofias, gladioli, cannas and hemerocallis with orange African marigolds at their feet. Vita and her mother might not have been shown the walled Spring Garden, the green and secret Hidden Garden, nor even perhaps the June Garden of roses, lilies, lupins and columbines, for these were all resting (or was their disarray what Vita meant by the garden not looking its best?), but they would have wandered through the gate in the high wall to the flower garden and nursery ground. Here the lavender was being cut and the 'Pink Beauty' hollyhocks might have still been caught in their prime. One picture Miss Jekyll was proud of, and of which Vita took good note, was *Lilium auratum* against a yew hedge, with *Tropaeolum speciosum* scattered 'like bright jewels' on the ground beneath.[8]

Wandering back to the workroom door they passed the shrub banks with junipers, magnolias, damask, Provence and moss roses and *Cistus florentina* in flower. In the woodland the Fern Walk was looking its best – lush grand greenery with just a touch of yellow and more *Lilium auratum* as flowery incidents of light. Inside the workroom there were Miss Jekyll's exquisite shell pictures, her silver and wood carving, and perhaps on the bench the complicated planting plans for Barrington Court.[9] One doesn't really imagine Miss Jekyll signing copies of her books for hopeful embryo gardeners, but Vita acquired and used *Home and Garden*, *Colour Schemes for the Flower Garden* and *Annuals and Biennials*. She probably also acquired an insight into the riches of good gardening that could come to a lady of very similar artistic tastes to her own. She perhaps also accepted that no garden could be all things to all seasons, and in later years she must often have thought of Munstead Wood as she despaired of Sissinghurst in August.

Many of the things that I have described at Munstead Wood appear in Vita's gardening sooner or later, and she seems to have been immediately influenced by Miss Jekyll's taste in roses; perhaps she took her notebook or Miss Jekyll gave her a list – anyway, roses immediately flooded into Long Barn. The first priority was to cover the house with the creamy-flowered, glossy-leaved rambler 'Albéric Barbier', the fragrant yellow noisette climber 'W. A. Richardson', and the buff 'Gloire de Dijon'. For the beds outside Harold's writing-room window there were to be hybrid teas (mostly to be found in Harkness's current catalogue) – the salmon pink 'Madame Abel Chatenay', the coppery splashed yellow 'Betty' and apricot 'Lady Hillingdon'; 'Lady Ashtown', pale carmine pink, 'Killarney', pale pink, 'Mrs W. J. Grant', rosy pink; the favourite 'Caroline Testout', bright satin pink, the crimson madder 'Madame Isaac Perière'; and the cardinal red miniature 'Juliette', which Vita put into pots. All the beds were to be underplanted with *Nepeta mussinii*, because from her earliest gardening days Vita had hated bare rose beds. She also wanted to try rose hedges (which she had seen at Sutton Courtenay) – a hedge of 'Gloire de Dijon' with the crimson rose 'Grüss an Teplitz', two or three of the first then one of the second repeated – surely either Norah Lindsay's or Gertrude Jekyll's answer to a question? These roses, listed by Vita in her earliest gardening notebook, are exactly those that Miss Jekyll was using over and over again in her planting schemes at this time.[10]

Harold was working at the Foreign Office in London up until the end of 1918, and it was during week-ends and summer holidays of those last war years that Long Barn was given its English rustic version of an Italian villa garden. They had the south-facing slope and the distant view; two wide terrace lawns were cut and retained with stone walls, the first one being edged with twenty Irish yews, the second walled with box (and called the Pleasaunce); box-edged flower gardens were made outside their respective writing-room windows, and modest avenues of Lombardy poplars were planted to lead out into the wilder garden. Vita was fascinated chiefly with her flowers, and she set out to recapture all her best memories; Knole's orchards were represented by the Apple Garden, with spring flowers and then clumps of lilies and delphiniums under the old trees; the stone walls were home for saxifrages, violets, violas, gentians and geums as well as the more homely pinks and alyssums. She tried an orange border with lilies, 'Illumination' tulips, Iceland poppies, rudbeckias and 'Orange King' roses – and with her Renaissance taste she mixed orange with blue – centaurea, scabious, lithospermum and anchusas. To Long Barn's woodland she added medlars, hazel, dogwoods, pink and white thorn – things she had seen while walking in the Belgrade Forest – with old roses because she loved them. And she tried flowery incidents of martagon lilies, which were a great success.

31. *(above left)* Ben, aged nearly three, with a firm grip on the flower trug *and* on the *Lilium candidum*, summer 1917.

32. *(above right)* Vita, Ben and Harold stripping lavender on the terrace at Long Barn, summer of 1917.

33. *(below)* Vita, Ben and Nigel on the terrace steps at Long Barn, summer 1919.

Vita's mother was a great spur to her gardening in those early days. Lady Sackville took note of how gardening was a suitable occupation for a lady at home, how Lutyens adored Miss Jekyll, and she would not have wanted to be left out. Vita remembers how she and Lutyens arrived at Lady Sackville's house in Sussex Square, Brighton, one day in the summer of 1919 to find her triumphantly waving a watering can over borders ablaze with 'every probable and improbable flower'.[11] 'Aren't they lovely? they are all in pots!' – she had sent her maid out to buy everything in preparation for Vita's arrival, thereby solving the problem of the perpetually bright herbaceous border. After that Lady Sackville lost her enthusiasm, but it was converted into her generosity in buying lavishly for Vita's garden – it was she who first went to the Chelsea Flower Show and wildly ordered all sorts of things they wanted (and didn't want), she who paid for the building of the Dutch Garden at Long Barn which Ned Lutyens was to design for them, and, much earlier, she who started paying for a gardener. Vita chose him because of his name, William Cowper – which she was later disappointed to find was just Cooper, but all the same she found him splendid – 'I love the garden now that I don't have to struggle with the clay myself,' she wrote on 17 July 1919.

It was also at this time that the vital influence of Ned Lutyens was working on Harold. Harold's nostalgia for the role of gentleman grand designer, and his private feeling that – had he not been a diplomat – he would have wanted to be an architect, were the basis of his affection for Lutyens. In turn Lutyens was in need of good company at that time in his life – the war had finished off his country house practice, his great commission for New Delhi was all pressure and little progress, his family were living out of London, and he worked long hours alone. His belief that life and architecture were games 'to be played with gusto' had been severely shaken by the war, and his sensitive soul was deeply saddened by the pity of what he saw on his visits to the battlefields in his role as architect to the War Graves' Commission.

It was in 1917, when Lutyens was re-furbishing 34 Hill Street for Lady Sackville, that Harold got to know him, lunching with him and visiting his offices. Harold was 'thrilled with the orgy of his architectural drawings' displayed on tables and floor, and intoxicated by his Delhi plans, among the most lovely things he had seen; also his war graves and cemetery designs, 'little "pergly" walks of crab apples and irises, with chapels and solemn trees and his great altar'.[12] The Delhi drawings occupied an office in Apple Tree Yard behind St James's Piccadilly, and in 1917 Lutyens was designing the great Mogul garden for Viceroy's House. They would have been able to talk about Lady Hardinge's photographs and her praise of Srinagar in Kashmir and the Persian gardens that she thought were 'a dream of loveliness' and wanted to emulate for Delhi.[13] Especially on this imperial scale (the walk from Viceroy's House loggia to the end of the gardens is almost a quarter of a mile), Lutyens would have enthused over the ultimate test of his Jekyll-inspired and long-held garden design philosophy: 'a garden scheme should have a backbone – a central idea beautifully phrased – and every wall, path, stone and flower bed has . . . a relative value to the central idea.'[14]

The cemetery designs on the table at that time included Warlincourt Halte B.C., with its blocks of graves marked out with holly hedges and groups of fastigiate oaks, and Trouville, where the banks were clothed with *Clematis vitalba* and Virginia creeper which Miss Jekyll had noted were to 'intermingle where they meet'. Gezaincourt B.C. had some of Miss Jekyll's most evocative planting of the flowers of home – borders of jasmine, laurustinus and *Iris stylosa*, patches of *Iris pallida* and *I. florentina*, groups of roses and hedges of blackthorn, whitethorn, birch and hazel.[15]

I feel that Harold must also have seen Lutyens's layout for Folly Farm in Berkshire [34], which was just completed at that time. This is the most intimate of Lutyens's gardens in terms of the relationship between house and garden. Folly

34. Folly Farm, Sulhamstead, Berkshire: sketch plan of the layout. Of all the products of the Lutyens/ Jekyll partnership this is the one that most beautifully expresses the interdependence of house and garden. Lutyens had started work at Folly Farm in 1906, but the garden did not reach this, its final phase, until after the outbreak of war. Whether the Folly Farm plans were lying around in Lutyens's office when Harold visited him is problematic, though quite likely; however, it is Folly Farm that illustrates so perfectly what was to be Harold's gardening philosophy.

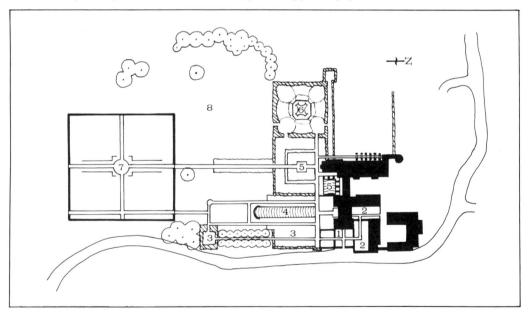

KEY

1. The enclosed entrance court.
2. The barn courts – small-scale, cottage-garden type courtyards between the original seventeenth-century farmhouse and an old barn.
3. The first important axis of the Folly Farm plan extends through the Barn and entrance courts via the Lime Walk to what was a pleached hornbeam arbour, but is now a small White Garden.
4. The canal, centred on Lutyens's Dutch extension built in 1906.

5. The flower parterre is a formal garden with its axis centred on the sweeping vernacular extension built in 1912. The two extensions were joined by a corridor where Lutyens used his supporting brick pillars to create the cloistered Tank Court – a formal pool reflecting the sublime geometry of his architecture.
6. The sunken rose garden – the ultimate in richly-carpeted garden rooms.
7. The kitchen garden.
8. The lawn.

35. *(above left)* Sir Edwin Lutyens ('McNed') at Long Barn in July 1925, when he was fifty-six. The year before, E. V. Lucas had written of him in *The Book of the Queen's Dolls' House*: 'He builds a New Delhi, eighty square miles of palaces and avenues, he builds a Queen's Dolls' House, an affair of inches but such as Japanese cherry stone carvers could not excel. His friends are legion; his mind electrically instant to respond to any sympathetic suggestion; he never broke his word, he never let you know if he was tired, and with it all he was out for fun.'

36. *(above right)* Folly Farm, the flower parterre, centred on the 1912 wing: 'There should be present to the mind of the visitor an awareness of the designer's intention . . .' (Harold Nicolson, 1953).

37. *(below)* Folly Farm, the sunken rose garden by Lutyens, *c.* 1916: 'There should be small enclosed gardens, often constructed around a central pool and containing some special species or variety of plant' (Harold Nicolson, 1953).

Farm [36, 37] has courts straight out of *Le Roman de la Rose* or Moorish Spain, it has
the discipline of strong vistas, which grow from the house, and garden rooms of
exquisite geometry and detail, filled with pools and flowers. Against Lutyens's
philosophy and his garden designs it is only necessary to put Harold's later and
more polished explanation:

> The essence of garden design, as of all forms of architectural planning, is the alternation
> of the element of expectation with the element of surprise. There should be present to the
> mind of the visitor an awareness of the designer's intention; that intention at the same
> time must be varied, and indeed, interrupted by the unexpected.[16] The main axis of a
> garden should be indicated and indeed emphasized, by rectilinear perspectives, by lines
> of clipped hedges ending in terminals in the form of statues or stone benches. Opening
> from the main axis there should be small enclosed gardens, often constructed round a
> central pool, and containing some special species or variety of plant. From time to time
> this variation should be broken and an unexpected feature . . . be introduced.[17]

The outcome of Harold's friendship with Lutyens was that he eventually came to
Long Barn. Vita proudly showed him round it all: '. . . he looked round very carefully
and I asked him "What would you do McNed?" – he replied "Sell it" – Mar was
crushed!'[18] But he helped them decorate the staircase with the blue fretted panels
they had brought from Constantinople, and Sackville leopards, and drew in Vita's
garden notebook to amuse the boys.[19] In 1925 Long Barn acquired its touch of
Lutyens's design. He and Lady Sackville went to stay for the week-end in May;
Nigel Nicolson writes:

> 'I can easily imagine what happened. On Sunday morning, after breakfast, the two
> men walked on to the brick terrace in front of the house, and my father said, 'I wish we
> could do something with that mess down there', and Lutyens would have said – 'Well,
> let's do it now!' Then they would have roughly paced out the area (it was just a bit of
> field), returned to the terrace, where there was always an oak outdoor table, from where
> they could see the site, and began playing about with pencils, rulers, squared paper and
> india rubbers. 'What about this?' 'Or that?', the other would reply. The result – L-shaped
> beds raised by low brick walls – has a more Lutyensy look than Nicolsonian, and I've
> little doubt that it was his basic design. He never returned to see it finished.[20]

So Lutyens designed Long Barn's Dutch Garden [38], and Lady Sackville paid
£600 for it to be built in the following July. Apart from this the garden grew more
by instinct than strict control, but it was a practice ground for both Vita and Harold.
It was essentially *cottagey* – the brick terrace was full of bumps and so were the
lawns, the steps were extremely rustic and the brick piers that Vita and the boys
enjoyed building were definitely D.I.Y. If Ned Lutyens had come back and seen the
brickwork of his Dutch Garden he would have disowned his design! But then, a
rustic refuge was what they both needed.

To put things into perspective – that summer of Vita's visit to Miss Jekyll (1917)
was the last summer of her 'happy honeymoon'. In September 1917 Violet came to
stay at Long Barn and her love affair with Vita flared into the drama of *Portrait of*

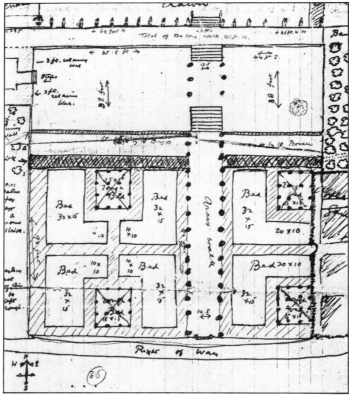

38. Harold's plan for the Dutch Garden at Long Barn, drawn up in conversation with Lutyens.

a Marriage. None of that need be repeated here, but it is necessary to realize that the traumas of the ensuing four-and-a-half years, the pains which both Vita and Harold inflicted upon each other and upon their children, the turbulence and viciousness of much that was said and done, all took place against the gentle, quiet background of Long Barn in its Kentish landscape setting, the house they called their 'little mud pie'. Harold went to work in Paris on the Peace Conference in January of 1919. In their correspondence Long Barn became a weapon. 'I wonder what else in the garden you will want to hear about, tyrant? I went out and walked round it to see – and have come back determined that another year we must have masses and masses of flowers,' wrote Vita in June.[21] And on 11 July: 'I dined out on the terrace. It is the stillest of evenings, not a breath of wind, and a great quiet moon rising above the trees' – the great pink roses of 'Madame Delville' were an exotic touch in a perfect Kentish rurality.[22] Harold, frantic with work, replied in a tired, almost unreadable scrawl that she was to get three more 'Madame Delville' and 'plaster the home with them'.[23] On 18 July, as the Peace Conference drags on, Vita counters: 'Colette goes on flowering but she's beginning to look reproachfully at me as much as to say "You did tell me that Mr Nicolson would be back soon"', and later again,

'Colette goes on flowering gallantly but she is very tired of waiting for Mr Nicolson ... Poor thing, she started flowering for his amusement in May.'[24]

Throughout that August Vita gardened, clipped box in the sun, and dreamed tantalizingly about all the places she would like to have a house – Seville, Cospoli, Caucasus, Greece, Tahiti and Florence – none of which were likely postings for Harold. Finally, when the last treaty had been signed and he returned home in October, Vita leaped off to France with Violet in revenge. From Monte Carlo on 29 October she wrote: '... my precious boy, whenever I see something lovely I think of

39. Sketch plan of Long Barn and its garden as it was in Vita's time. The site slopes fairly steeply from north to south, and there are retaining walls behind the buildings as well as the smaller walls, added in the Nicolsons' time, to support the garden terraces. The village of Sevenoaks Weald is to the north of the house, and the garden is surrounded by fields, with a distant southwards view across the Weald of Kent.

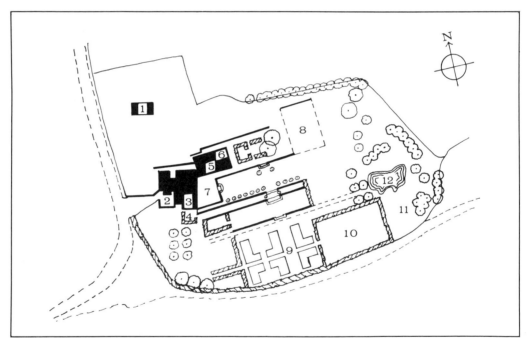

KEY
1. The cottage, used by the Nicolsons for additional accommodation.
2. The entrance court.
3. Vita's sitting room, overlooking –
4. Her small box-edged garden which gives way down the slope to a bank of azaleas and shrubs and then the Lombardy poplars.
5. The Big Room, occupying most of the ground floor of the barn addition.
6. Harold's writing room on the ground floor, overlooking more garden parterres, these filled with roses.
7. The brick paved terrace.
8. The tennis court.
9. The Dutch garden beds, designed by Harold with the help of Sir Edwin Lutyens.
10. The Apple Garden, an old orchard area to which Vita added more fruit trees with spring bulbs beneath them, and a border of flowers for summer.
11. The woodland, or 'Delphic grove', which was very damp in patches.
12. The pond, which began life as a very wet patch, and was later turned into a swimming pool with a concrete lining.

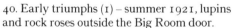

40. Early triumphs (1) – summer 1921, lupins and rock roses outside the Big Room door.

41. Early triumphs (2) – May 1922, *Iris susiana* and tulips.

you and wish you were there – you always say enjoy things a little for my sake but you have no idea to what extent I do that . . .'[25] Beauty was a powerful weapon, rarely wasted by either of them.

It would be useless for me to pretend that her garden was given a lot of Vita's time and attention during these years or that detailed reports filled her infrequent letters, because it was not so. But the thread, however tenuous, was still there – in her poetry, in her novel *Heritage* which was published in 1919; the garden was always there when she needed calming down, it was there for Harold to dream of and it provided the one subject on which they could converse when all others were forbidden. In the end, Long Barn and all it meant to them won. It was the mooring mast for their high-flying spirits and slowly, slowly, but relentlessly, it tugged them home. For the single truth remains with me, after reading all that has been written about them and most of what they wrote to each other, that without Long Barn there would have been no Sissinghurst, for they would have gone their separate ways.

In July 1920 Vita sat down to write herself out in her 'autobiography', the manuscript which forms the basis of *Portrait of a Marriage*:

> I lie on green bracken, amongst little yellow and magenta wild flowers whose names I don't know. I lie so close to the ground that my only view is of tall corn, so crisp that in the breeze it stirs with a noise like the rustle of silk. All day I have been in a black temper, but that is soothed away. There is no place, out here, for temper or personality. There is only one personality present: Demeter.[26]

... And later on ...

> Evening has nearly fallen: sunset light on the hill opposite has turned the yellow cornfields rose pink. I have dined out on the terrace, writing this all the while on my knee ... everything is so hushed and I feel so secluded and serene – not melancholy tonight. The country is too lovely for that. How lucky for me that I live in this fruitful and tender country: its serenity soaks into one. Moors and crags would kill me I think. The weald is an antidote...[27]

In the autumn of 1920 Harold came back to work in London. The following March Vita returned to him and Long Barn and the only serious crisis in their marriage was over. For her thirtieth birthday on 9 March 1922 Harold gave her a greenhouse and some encyclopedias. In *Orlando* the occasion is marked:

> Thus, at the age of thirty, or thereabouts, this young nobleman had not only had every experience that life has to offer, but had seen the worthlessness of them all. Love and ambition, women and poets, were all equally vain ... Two things alone remained to him in which he now put any trust: dogs and nature; an elk-hound and a rose bush. The world in all its variety, life in all its complexity had shrunk to that. Dogs and a bush were the whole of it.[28]

Knole and the Sackvilles and *The Heir*[29] were both published in 1922 as Vita's tributes to Knole, and these and her earlier novels and poetry entitled her to brushes with literary society, the P.E.N. Club, the Sitwells, Lady Ottoline Morrell, Hugh Walpole, even Arnold Bennett, and the Bloomsberries. Occasionally she went to grand parties, such as the one at Blenheim where she sat next to Winston Churchill and adored him – but she was settling to longer and longer periods at Long Barn. She enjoyed her greenhouse, the first of many garden gadgets which always were to amuse her, she contemplated bees and cider-making as subjects for poetry – and these were the beginnings of *The Land* – and she wrote her first gardening piece for the *Evening Standard*, 'Notes on a Late Spring'.[30] Harold went to the Lausanne Conference with Lord Curzon in the winter of 1922/3, then returned to work in London and plunge himself into the social whirl that he loved, at the same time writing books on Tennyson, Byron and, later, Lord Curzon. Geoffrey Scott, Pat Dansey (for whom Vita wrote *Grey Wethers*), Virginia Woolf, Dottie Wellesley and Raymond Mortimer were all part of their lives, but no one marred the contentment that the Nicolsons shared in their garden at Long Barn at the week-ends.

42. Vita with Canute and Pippin.

43. *(above left)* 1926 – Vita, on arrival in Teheran, in Harold's garden in the Legation compound.

44. *(above right)* Vita and Raymond Mortimer in Seyed's courtyard at Kum.

45. *(below)* 25 August 1926, the coronation of Reza Khan. The Shah's coach, in a procession of Baluchi, Turcoman, Bakhtiari, Kurd and Berber outriders, drives through a city festooned and draped with carpets – a city that Marco Polo would have recognized.

4

PARADISE:
PERSIA 1926 AND 1927

That day must come, when I shall leave my friends,
My loves, my garden, and the bush of balm
That grows beside my door, for the world's end:
A Persian valley where I might find calm.
V. Sackville-West, 'Nostalgia'[1]

ON 4 November 1925 Harold left on the long journey to take up his new post as counsellor at the British Legation in Teheran. His partings were painful; Vita sent letters on ahead to await him on his stops, she gave him a St Christopher medal, and Nigel, aged eight, wrote to his father: 'It must be funny to leave Long Barn for two years, you will forget what it looks like! But it will be lovely to come home to find the new garden blooming with lovely flowers and your room will be "fete de fleurs" arranged by Mummy who will have roses in her hair.'[2] Harold wrote from Cairo: 'Oh Vita, it is hot and dusty and the eucalyptus trees are all white with eight months dust, the bougainvillea is garish – I want my Weald, my Weald, I want to go tock, tock, tock on the terrace bricks . . .'[3]

But on 27 November he arrived in Teheran, and Persia fulfilled all her promises and reclaimed him: 'Oh Viti, the beauty of this country. It seizes me by the throat. Great plains flat as billiard tables, ending in mountains . . . one sees for 150 miles . . . one seems to crawl like some tiny insect across this vastness. And over it all is a pink light of sunset even in blazing noon.'[4]

Immediately, to form a link with home, he plans to make a garden for his Teheran house. Whether by instinct or by plan pre-arranged with Vita, he plays out the strongest linking cord he can. She had used the motif of a garden link with home in her first novel *Heritage*, a Hispano-Kentish tragedy soaked in the Wealden countryside with the heroine, Ruth Pennistant, living in a farmhouse that is 'nearer to the earth than most', with sagging floors and propped up furniture, very much as at Long Barn. Ruth also has Vita's duality, the Spanish blood that warps her peace of mind, and – to be brief – she marries the wrong man, Rawdon Westmacott, who is a bully and a bore. The 'right' man, Christopher Malory, goes off on a long banishment, ending up in Ephesus as assistant to an eccentric Scottish archeologist. To remind him of home he makes a garden, and realizing that the cyclamens and orchids available from the mountain pastures are not 'cottage' flowers, he writes home to Ruth for mignonette seed. The annual sending of the mignonette seed is the only link that eventually takes Malory home to Ruth and a happy ending. It is difficult not to make *Heritage* sound like a sixpenny romance like this, for the story is simple, but Vita's ability to give weight and vitality to the Kentish landscape is just as powerful as Thomas Hardy's evocation of Dorset, and this alone makes the book worth reading still. Also, she wrote it when there seemed little hope of a happy ending for her, and the symbols she so deftly uses – the pots of red geraniums on the farmhouse kitchen sill, the waltzing mice and the mignonette seed, are perfectly expressive of the seemingly fragile bonds that she and Harold believed to be the strongest of all.

And so, back to the Teheran garden in the legation compound. Harold sent immediate requests for rosemary and lavender cuttings and hyacinth and tulip bulbs. In his letter of 11 December he sketched his house, with its back to a straight wall and a semi-circular wall enclosing the garden on the west, south and east sides. The main entrance was at the west end of the plot, with a footpath directly from road to door in the centre of the south front. He wanted to start with a small formal garden at the east end, with a treillage hedge and beds of annuals; the west end was to be left for Vita's advice when she came. He allowed himself to spend £20. He soon discovered the soil to be very light, 'and I have little hope beyond rosemary, santolina and lavender – cuttings, please, my saint'.[5] He longed for Kentish clay, realized that Teheran was too cold in winter for 'hot' things and too hot for 'cold' things, and when he left for any time everything was stolen anyway! When he despaired of gardening or diplomacy he rode out of the city 'over the vast and stony plains and dried torrent beds' to a little red flag on a hill where he dismounted and sat smoking his pipe, looking down:

> I never saw a town look less like a town from a distance, every building is in a garden and no building is higher than one or at the most two stories ... it is just like an encampment in a rather sparse wood, with the smoke of the camp fires hanging lazily among the trees ... and the sweep of the plains and the bare rugged sun-indented slopes of the lower hills, a little bit sad and untidy yet there is a certain grandeur and at sunset the hills turn scarlet ...[6]

For Vita at home letters were not enough. She awaited them eagerly, every day dawning in hope (except Sunday, 'as that is a day to be blacked out of the calendar'),[7] and then she tore them open, devoured them and was left unsatisfied. She carefully packed up cuttings and sent them off, but really both Harold and Persia had to be seen for herself. After copious instructions as to travelling and what to bring from Harold, and armed with secateurs, trowels and seeds as well as her Jaeger fluffy flea-bag and two Ever-hot bottles, she set out from London on 20 January 1926 for the greatest adventure of her life.

She travelled with Dorothy Wellesley, but that didn't divert her from recording her every shift of mind as she moved across first a familiar, then an unfamiliar landscape. The record of her journey is *Passenger to Teheran*, a traveller's diary, a slow unwinding of all her sensations of journeying. It is, after nearly sixty years, the best kind of travel writing, and it tells just as much about the traveller as about the travels. She knows that she is facing loneliness and discomforts (and actually some quite alarming experiences), but she also knows that it will all be worth 'the memory of an Egyptian dawn and the flight of herons across the morning moon'.[8]

As the Pullman slides through the Kent fields she feels the dragging at her heart – and then corrects it by thinking how often she has watched this very train and the faces at its windows with a longing to be off and away. It is home which drags her heart but 'the spirit which is beckoned by the unknown'.[9] Everything begins to recede, home and friends fade, 'a pleasant feeling of superiority mops up, like a sponge, the trailing melancholy of departure'. She makes an effort of will 'and in a twinkling I have thought myself over into the other mood, the dangerous mood, the mood of going out. How exhilarating it is, to be thus self-contained; to depend for happiness on no material comfort; to be rid of such sentimentality that attaches to the dear familiar; to be open, vulnerable, receptive! If there is a pain growling somewhere in me I shall ignore it. Life is too rich for us to stick doggedly to the one humour.'[10] That, in a few lines, is the reasoning behind every escapade she had; that is the brave Vita that Harold and her friends loved.

She found Italy of her past passion wearing 'an odd contrary look' under a blanket of snow (so much for summer passions!); for her, she realized, the Lombardy Plain needed to be fresh with Star of Bethlehem and grape hyacinths or burnished with maize and vines! Egypt had been marred for her on her honeymoon by sunstroke; this time she would see every picture, inside and out. The white walls of Luxor were well suited to their magenta blankets of bougainvillea; creamy Nubian camels posed beside the Nile. Along the 'dazzling naked road' leading to the Valley of the Kings she saw a mirage of Kent – as though through the wrong end of a telescope – bright green fields full of life; but here, in the white dust: 'a hoopoe? a lizard? a snake? no, there was nothing: only the tumbled boulders and the glare of the sun.' The silence and lifelessness frightened her.[11] She paused and recorded the delicious moment between *not* knowing and *knowing* what the burial grounds of the Pharoahs actually looked like. In later years she had a childish enthusiasm for the cinema and the television, but thank goodness they had not come to blunt her mind to these experiences! It is important for us to realize that Vita's experiences were all her own, never second-hand, which is why, exactly why, they were so well learned and so effectively transformed by her. She is also a proof that poets make the best topographers; she has written pages of delight on the agriculture of the Nile valley – she betrays surprise, she is disconcerted, she who had believed that the traditions of her Sackville country were old:

> ... the very centuries shrink up, and the life of man with his beasts becomes very close. They seem to have acquired the same gait and colour through long association with each other and with the earth. In long files, flat as frescoes, they trail along the dykes, mud-coloured: the camels, the buffaloes, the little donkeys, and the man. Slouching they go, in an eternal procession; with the Egyptian genius for design, as though they were drawn with a hard, sharp pencil on the sky.[12]

The living labourers occupy her longer than the dead kings; she finds the greater nobility in the fact that those she can see patiently carting the excavated earth in solemn files look little different from their forbears who did it for the first time. One Pharaoh alone is redeemed by the tomb he gratefully gave his gardener, with its roof and walls painted with leaves, grapes and peaches like an arbour, a living arbour in a dead place.

The second stage of her journey was by boat from Port Said, via Aden to Bombay – a route she vowed never to take again. She felt she never met India, only making a flying visit to Delhi old and new – 'a red city and the genius of Akbar, a white city and the genius of Lutyens',[13] where Lutyens's assistant A. G. Shoosmith showed her Viceroy's House and the Mogul garden.[14] From Bombay another boat took her back across the Persian Gulf to Basra, and from there she travelled by train to Baghdad. Here she found, through a door in a blank wall – 'a rush of dogs, a vista of a garden path edged with carnations in pots, a little verandah and a little low house at the end of the path, an English voice – Gertrude Bell'.[15] Within a few moments the exhausted traveller felt that life was worthwhile once again, and she laughed for the first time in ten days.

Gertrude Bell was the perfect person to welcome Vita out of the wilderness, for she could offer her physical and emotional refuge of a very special kind. They had met before, in Constantinople, they had lots of people in common at home and Gertrude knew Harold and the diplomatic circuit; but here, in Baghdad, Vita appreciated, was where she belonged. They had much more in common – the place Gertrude loved most in England was her garden at Rounton Grange in Yorkshire, they were both indefatigable recorders of their adventures, and they both had the same concertina'd sense of time. For Gertrude Bell it was not so much the country she was helping to bring into the twentieth century that she adored, it was Babylon.[16] But whereas she was an English lady who found fulfilment in the East, Vita was the other side of the coin – she belonged to England, but was about to enjoy an exciting affair with the East for a time. It was very good for Vita to find someone into whom she could look as into a magnifying mirror for once in her life – they talked and talked, and planned for Vita to make a longer visit, and went to tea with the sad King Feisal. Perhaps, before they parted, Vita had read Gertrude Bell's first impressions of Persia, seen and recorded in the year she had been born:

> Oh the desert around Tehran! miles and miles of it with nothing, *nothing* growing; ringed in with bleak bare mountains snow crowned and furrowed with the deep courses of torrents. I never knew what desert was till I came here . . . Say, is it not rather refreshing to the spirit to lie in a hammock strung between the plane trees of a Persian garden and read the poems of Hafiz . . .[17]

On 5 March Vita reached Teheran at four in the afternoon in lovely sunshine [43]. To recover from her journey she gardened for Harold and wrote (she was finishing *The Land*), and when they started exploring she found *Iris persica* and little yellow jonquils. Then the serious affair began.

Vita became 'netted in the love of Persia'. She felt that other countries had things in common – they were green, submissive to man – but not Persia, Persia 'had been left as it was before man's advent'.[18] The space intoxicated her. She discovered a new standard against which her mind had to adjust, the elation and the threat of a savage and desolate endless country. To her mind, nurtured in the diminutive dips and swellings of the Weald of Kent, educated on the misty frescoes of Tuscany, Persia offered a paradox that fulfilled all the demands of her own dual and adventurous spirit. The paradox was between the country and its paradise gardens.

In a society based on uncertainty, with its consequent fatalism, and nothing to bridge the gulf between the dark ages and the twentieth century, she experienced a total suspension of belief in home, that such a country as England could exist at all, and it freed her mind. The passivity, the patient forbearance of everyday life in Persia renewed her sympathy, so that she both saw and felt things anew. All her sensations and experiences were new. She was amazed at the effect of the light – as she said, bluntly, the plain was brown, the mountains were blue or white and the foothills were tawny or purple. But these were mere words. 'Plain and hills are capable of a hundred shades that with the changing light slip over the face of the land and melt into a subtlety no words can reproduce. The light here is a living thing, as varied as the human temperament and as hard to capture; now lowering, now gay, now sensuous, now tender; but whatever the mood may be, it is superimposed on a basis always grand, always austere' . . . there was a rightness in this, the ancient bones of one of the oldest places upon earth were brushed with changing moods and shades 'like a blush over a proud and sensitive face'.[19] The quality of the light added to the unknowableness of Persia and enhanced its mystery, for she never knew if hills supposed to be 100 miles away were really so, as every cleft seemed so clearly marked, or if Demavend himself, seventy miles distant, would not at any minute annihilate Teheran with his volcanic fires. And there was delusion and coquetry, as with a veil – 'plains of strange rocks which seemed to advance in battalions, like the dreams of some mad painter . . . rocks that could materialize from an army of giant tortoises into murderous engines of war, in a setting now brown, now sick-turquoise, as the light changed again and again'.[20] And, over the next ridge, the dried-up bed of a salt lake, 'opal, milky and wide'.[21] Among the deadness, she learned, there was life; a shower of rain brought out a crop of anemones, which a day of hot sun would shrivel; but the sun brought out the tortoises and made the waste land stir.

Against Persia's timelessness Vita could pitch her sumptuous Sackvilles and even Knole, like pitching rosebuds at a bastion wall. What were a few Elizabethan intrigues and betrayals against a country that persistently walked by on the other side while beggars lay in the gutters vomiting blood or dying of starvation? What were the Sackville treasures against the treasury of Reza Khan, which she was allowed to visit, plunging her hands up to the wrist in heaps of uncut emeralds and letting the pearls run through her fingers on to a table that was a sea of precious stones . . . 'I gasped; the small room vanished: I was Sinbad in the Valley of Gems,

Aladdin in the Cave.'[22] Although, even in 1926, Teheran was touched with 'a shoddy, would-be European' appearance, Vita was lucky enough, because she was there for the coronation of Reza Khan Pahlavi [45], to see it filled with Baluchis, Turcomans, Bakhtiaris, Kurds, Lurs and Berbers come out of their tribal fastnesses into a city whose walls were hung with carpets, a city that Marco Polo would have recognized. Here was romance indeed, that banished for ever the powers of Dumas and Scott, of Raleigh and Chatterton, of dressing up and escapades.

T HE other half of Vita's Persian experience was her discovery of Persian gardens as symbols of refuge from a cruel nature. Persian gardens were the baccalaureate of Vita the gardener – before she discovered them she had merely been a grower of flowers.

She is disarming in her admission of innocence: 'Ever since I have been in Persia I have been looking for a garden and have not yet found one. Yet Persian gardens enjoy a great reputation. Hafiz and Sa-adi sang frequently, even wearisomely, of roses. Yet there is no word for rose in the Persian language; the best they can manage is a "red flower". It looks as though a misconception has arisen somewhere.'[23] Oh, wonderful Vita! Never afraid to say what she thinks, brave enough never to dissemble, to record what she sees rather than what any second-hand education has told her. This is the glory of her and the reason for the clarity of her seeing. Remember, she had been brought up in a garden that had not stepped beyond the purely functional layout, in a garden of debased and crumbling organization, that had never pretended to be great design, but was overlaid with the charm of its adored past. She had been brought up to regard the garden as just another delightful room, in a house full of delightful rooms, in a world that was hardly less delightful. In Italy, too, the gardens were lovely outdoor rooms. At the instigation of Geoffrey Scott she may have realized that the paths of sequence and the vistas of surprise at the restored Villa Medici were demanding rather more of her senses, but it was a purely intellectual realization. Her emotional senses, I suspect, were rather too busily deployed elsewhere. And she could never appreciate design on paper. Harold was for ever teasing her about her inability to understand plans – he knew she would not even understand the simple drawing he sent of his Teheran garden, and not long before she had calmly bought some fields near Long Barn, quite different ones from those she thought she was buying, because she had looked at the plan the wrong way round! And anyway, for Vita the romantic, the lesson had to be emotionally taught. Persia was a hard teacher:

> Imagine you have ridden in summer for four days across a plain; that you have then come to a barrier of snow-mountains and ridden up the pass; that from the top of the pass you have seen a second plain, with a second barrier of mountains in the distance, a hundred miles away; that you know that beyond these mountains lies yet another plain, and another; and for days, even weeks, you must ride with no shade, and the sun overhead, and nothing but the bleached bones of dead animals strewing the track. Then when you come to trees and running water, you will call it a garden. It will not be flowers

and their garishness that your eyes crave for, but a green cavern full of shadows and pools where goldfish dart, and the sound of a little stream.[24]

The realization was so stark that the satisfaction must be worth examining in detail. She discovered that the design of Persian gardens can be traced back to Xerxes and Cyrus, and that across the centuries the extreme formality had been admired and prized, so that it had become a mystical obsession. The vital irrigation rills cut the garden up into four just as the universe was cut by four great rivers; by the time they got into the book of Genesis the rivers had been given names (Pison, Gihon, Hiddekel and Euphrates) and the crossing where they met symbolized the meeting of God and man. Over the years this orthodoxy remained intact and revered, but a passionate and luxury-loving people added decoration. The enclosing walls were battlemented and ornamented with pigeon-towers and flowers and fruit were trained on them. The water channels were lined with avenues of almond trees, or, in larger gardens, pines and cypress. Arcaded pavilions were built for shade and the languishing of dusky maidens. The four grass plots sprouted spring bulbs or roses which tumbled out of their confines. It was in these gardens, as Sylvia Crowe has written, that the intellectual concept of geometry was wedded to the freedom of organic growth.[25] In other words, Vita learned her lesson in formal design through the romance of Persia. It was the only way she could have learned [colour pls. 1, 2, 3].

She expressed her realization in a very personal way. On that first trip she saw the gardens of Isfahan – Safavid Shah Abbas's pleasure gardens laid along the spine avenue of Chahar Bagh (including the dervish garden, the nightingale garden and the donkey garden) and the Hall of Forty Columns, 'a Persian pavilion at the peak of its loveliest expression' with in reality only twenty columns and the other twenty reflections in the pool. She actually described the two aspects of the historical ideal which were exquisitely illustrated, in miniature, in the courts of Seyed, the owner of a tobacco shop in the bazaar at Kum [44]. Seyed had two homes and two courts (one for his wife and one for his mistress). In the first Vita found a welcome silence and a stillness after a journey, a rectangular tank reflecting the pale sky, an oleander, a cool room with a pile of rugs to sleep on and a delicious meal of chicken cooked in pomegranate juice with walnuts, eaten in the night air.[26] And then 'Seyed had opened the book again at another illuminated page. There in the centre of the court stood the tree from which the yellow roses had been picked; a bush taller than a man, smothered in the wide, single, yellow rose that, more like a butterfly than a flower, settled upon the green. It was the magic bush of the Arabian Nights; I looked about for the Singing Fountain and the Talking Bird . . .'[27]

She also found a garden without an owner and it taught her something more. The neglectedness of Persia enhanced her sense of ownership. From a ruined garden, with peach trees in blossom and water running everywhere, 'a tangle of briars and grey sage, and here and there a Judas tree in full flower' at the foot of the Elburz, she contemplated 'ownership':

> The sense of property, too, is blessedly absent; I suppose that this garden has an owner somewhere, but I do not know who he is, nor can anyone tell me. No one will come up

and say I am trespassing; I may have the garden to myself; I may share it with a beggar … All are equally free to come and enjoy. Indeed there is nothing to steal except the blossom from the peach trees, and no damage to do that has not already been done by time and nature. The same is true of the whole country … no evidence of law, no signposts or milestones, even the road is nominal, you pass the best you can.[28]

She recalled with irritation the tight organization of the crowded island which was home – Persia added a very subtle generosity to her atavistic idea of ownership and privacy, which eventually gave her the grace to share, gave her even a talent for sharing, her enjoyment of her private world with her readers and the visitors to her garden.

And then there were the Persian flowers. She loved the sudden arrival of the spring when the desert broke into flower; she was intrigued by the Kingdon-Ward and Farrer feeling of collecting treasures to bring home. Knowing that the seventeenth-century Persians had prized tulips, iris, hyacinths and roses in their gardens, it thrilled her to find these growing semi-wild in the forgotten gardens at the foothills of the Elburz, among overgrown jasmines, almonds and peaches. She found the little *Iris persica* shooting bright green like a butterfly defying the lion of the desert, and her beloved *Iris stylosa* growing wild; she collected the scarlet *Anemone fulgens*, a pink gladiolus (possibly *G. segetum*), colchicums, the little nodding golden *Tulipa sylvestris*, the yellow and white *T. polychroma*, the flame orange *T. ostrowkiana*, a white iris with dark veins (probably *I. susiana*) the Widow Iris, *I. tuberosa*, and – most splendid of all – 'like an old and rich brocade', the yellow-splashed rich rose pink *Tulipa aucheriana*. Crown Imperials and the Persian yellow roses, *Rosa foetida persiana*, the pink damask 'Isfahan', and the *Rosa lutea*-derived 'Le Rêve' and 'Star of Persia' were always to be treasured in her gardens.

This first encounter with Persia brought Vita to an important quandary:

> Such a desultory life I lead, and the life of England falls away, or remains only as an image seen in an enchanted mirror. In fact, I lead two lives, an unfair advantage. This roof of the world, blowing with yellow tulips, these dark bazaars, crawling with mazy life, that tiny far off England and what am I? and where am I? That is the problem and where is my heart, home sick at one moment and excited beyond reason the next? But at least I live, I feel, I endure the agonies of constancy and inconstancy; it is better to be alive and sentient than dead and stagnant. Let us, I said, as we emerged from the bazaars, go to Isfahan …[29]

The shrine of her spiritual calm seems to have been the Madrasseh of Isfahan:

> … a long range of buildings, tiled in blue, enclosed a rectangular space; a long pool, with steps going down into the water, reflected the buildings; lilac and irises, in sheets of purple, seemed but a deeper echo of the colours of the tiles; a golden light of sunset struck the white trunks of the plane trees, flushing them until they turned to living flesh; and among the lilacs, the irises, and the planes strolled the tall, robed figures, or sat by the water's edge, idly stirring the water with the point of a stick …[30]

This she felt, was a psychological cloister, a place of calm akin to the desert valleys.

Vita left Persia on 4 May 1926, travelling home (with many adventures) overland via Moscow and Berlin and reaching London on 16 May. She wrote *Passenger to Teheran* during the summer. Harold continued with his garden; on a Sunday evening in September she sat down and wrote to tell him she had packed up hundreds of iris, scilla and tulip bulbs, and some *Iris reticulata* that he was to plant in a shallow bowl to flower in February – 'I want you to feel as I do when you plant them, that when they flower I shall be there.'[31] In November she sent more bulbs as Harold's birthday present, and planted a Judas Tree at Long Barn in memory of Teheran.

Her visit the following spring was not quite so magical; after some time in Teheran she and Harold left with friends for an expedition to the Bakhtiari Mountains. They saw the tomb of Cyrus, collected precious iris from the plain of Pasagardee, and visited Shiraz to see the gardens, including that around the tomb of Sa-adi, then in romantic ruin, and that of Hafiz with the slender columns of its pavilion framing a view over Shiraz. But the romantic in her found disillusion. She admitted it was churlish to 'complain of monotony in so grateful a sanctuary', but she did feel that the Persian garden was becoming monotonous; the Bakhtiaris proved a little too tough and tiresome for their rather carefree assault, and the final blow to the romance of Persia came with their visit to the Abadan oilfields and the realization that Persia's future was dependent upon such 'a hell of civilization'.

Vita and Harold left for home together; the summer of 1927 at Long Barn was to be the happiest of their lives so far. Vita's book of the Bakhtiari trip, *Twelve Days*, is regarded by many as one of the best of all travel books; yet in comparison with the brightness and wonder of *Passenger to Teheran*, it has a touch of disillusion and anticlimax. It is a requiem for her love affair with Persia. As she had written at the beginning of *Passenger to Teheran*: 'For observe, that to hope for Paradise is to live in Paradise, a very different thing from actually getting there.'[32]

5

THE CONSTANT LURE: 'THE LAND' AND LONG BARN 1927-30

The country habit has me by the heart,
For he's bewitched forever who has seen,
Not with his eyes but with his vision, Spring
Flow down the woods and stipple leaves with sun,
As each man knows the life that fits him best,
The shape it makes in his soul, the tune, the tone,
And after ranging on a tentative flight
Stoops like a merlin to the constant lure.
The country habit has me by the heart.
V. Sackville-West, *The Land: Winter*[1]

VITA finished her first epic poem *The Land* in Isfahan, on her first Persian trip, in April 1926. It is 2,500 lines long and she had been contemplating it and writing for three years. It was first published on 30 September following, and received marvellous reviews; it was reprinted in the December and three times in 1927, and steadily reprinted for the next forty years. By 1971 it had sold 100,000 copies in Britain.[2] The poem won her the Hawthornden Prize in 1927. It was therefore both a popular and a poetic success.

The Land is not pastoral poetry in the tradition of Goldsmith, Clare or George Crabbe; it does not mourn a lost Arcadia. It is the biography of a countryside, a diary of observations on country life in the early twentieth century. Vita called it a song: 'I sing the cycle of my country's year.' It is the song of her heart. 'The country habit has me by the heart' – and, wrote Richard Church,[3] 'her heart, under that discipline, works the more harmoniously with her mind. This process, a hard one which cannot be mastered merely by winning, needs time, patience and experience before it can be acquired.'

46. Vita's Kent photographed by Keith Harding in 1984. *The Land*, pp. 46/7:

> . . . but I tell
> . . . of such flowers as dwell
> In marsh and meadow, wayside, wood and waste,
> Of campion and the little pimpernel;
> Of kexen parsley and the varied veitch;
> Of the living mesh, cat's cradle in a ditch . . .

She had had the time, all those centuries of caring landowning Sackvilles had seen to that. Some of them had other cares –

> When Drake played bowls at Plymouth, and the rare
> Coach with the cumbrous spokes
> Trundled along the single clay-wet track
> To Sussex with drawn blinds, or journeyed back
> To London on affairs of state . . .[4]

– but Vita's inheritance was from those who spent time at Knole, Edward and Duke John Frederick. They had bequeathed her that rare affinity with the soil that England used to breed. She had had the endless hours of childhood and adolescence haunting the workshops, yards and park at Knole. Because she was who she was the keepers, carpenters, woodsmen and her father's steward would raise their caps, but because she was Vita they would learn that her questions were in pursuit of real knowledge of their skills and lore. When she came to write *The Land* she used an agricultural encyclopedia (a present from Harold) for her facts, but her ability to understand these facts was inbred. After the poem was published, it was said that the farmers gossiping at Maidstone market (and farmers are a grudging breed) allowed she knew as much of their ways of life as they themselves. Thirty years on from the Hawthornden Prize, Professor A. N. Duckham of Reading University's Agriculture Department wrote to congratulate her on 'an accurate and perceptive agricultural statement . . . recording the final flowering of an agricultural system' and to assure her that *The Land* was required reading for his students.[5]

She also kept her hand in, in a small way, at landowning herself. Lady Sackville had bought Brook Farm, across the road from Long Barn, in the summer of 1916. In July 1919 Vita excitedly went to a sale of land immediately surrounding Long Barn with her father, and in her best dealer's manner paid just over £1,100 for a pair of cottages and thirty-three acres; by selling the cottages and the standing timber she would recoup over half her outlay. She wrote a hurried note from Tonbridge station to give Harold in Paris the great news of her 'broad acres'. He was equally delighted, though frantic with work at the Peace Conference: 'if you can part with it send me the map – I want to see my broad acres – I hope we have not gone and flowed over into Sussex – do we have territorial access to the sea? – if we go on this way we can have an avenue all the way to 39 Sussex Square! It is a glorious acquisition – how far more important than Greece getting Western Thrace!'[6]

She therefore had the activities of her own farmyard (managed by a remarkable tenant, Vera Cardinal) to watch and her own fields to wander around on her daily walks with the dogs; but they were big dogs and she was an energetic walker, and she went much farther through the fields and orchards westwards below the ridge of the Weald's edge to Ide Hill and south towards Chiddingstone and Penshurst. She walked with her eyes open, and it is her patient observations from these walks that fill *The Land*. Pictures spring from the pages – the sheep-shearing:

> There, in a barn, with crazy doors swung wide
> Making a square of sun on dusty floor,
> The shearer sits, in shepherd's borrowed smock . . .

And she used her ears, and patiently inquired the meaning of the strange language of the thatcher come south from Norfolk:

> Grumbling and boasting turn and turn about,
> Having told the tally of the needed threaves,
> He mounts his ladder, pocket full of splines,
> And packs his yelms, and calls his mate a lout
> If he disturb one straw from ordered lines.

Sometimes her patience in standing and watching allows her to create word pictures that Constable could have painted: the harvest beginning:

> Scythe first the heading round the field by hand,
> Then send your reaper up the flat gold wall
> With whirling sails and clash of toppling sheaves . . .

And Turner himself would not have scorned the 'wide skies where cloudy cities travel white'.

It is her patience with the timeless régime of the seasons – to which she knew that great and small had to submit – that sets the pace of *The Land*. These days we seem to want everything, especially in our gardens, instantly – Vita knew, and especially in her gardening, that everything must come in its due season, and she watched a farming world where that was still true. We have become arrogant about such things; she was deeply humble, trusting and needing to trust because of her Sackville melancholia, in the 'recurrent patterns on a scroll unwinding', the 'classic monotony, that modes and wars leave undisturbed'. *The Land's* eloquence unwinds from the dark and cold of winter through the sowing season, birth of new stock, sheep-shearing, haysel, harvest, ploughing, threshing and hedging and ditching to cider-making and hop-drying in the oasts. She felt she was enough of a gardener, having bent 'some stubborn acres to her will', to understand the uncomplaining patience that endures the rainy dark, and sleet, and frozen red hands of winter; she has clearly seen the stars at dawn and 'the shifting munching cattle in the dark' of their aromatic stalls, and knows that of such weariness and care is a 'tired contentment born'. The excitement of spring does not delude Vita the countrywoman:

> Look, too, to your orchards in the early spring . . .
> There seems an enemy in everything.
> Even the bullfinch with his pretty song,
> And blue puffed tits make havoc in the pears
> Pecking with tiny beak and strong;
> Mild February airs
> Are full of rogues on mischievous wing . . .

Summer's harvest is hardly less fraught with dangers:

> Look to your stooking, for full many a field
> Of hearty grain and straw runs half to waste
> Through heedless stooking, and the proper yield
> Leaves half its measure to the rook and daw.

Only the autumn, for which Vita always seems to have a special affection,[7] seems to allow joy in toil:

> A holiday from field and dung,
> From plough and harrow, scythe and spade,
> To dabble in another trade,
> To crush the pippins in the slats,
> And see that in the little vats
> An extra pint was wrung . . .

The Land is no sentimental city-dweller's song; it is sharply seen and keenly felt *and* understood.

And yet she had the experience to stand back, and sometimes allow herself to be a poet as well as a gardener and countrywoman. She makes delightful, perhaps unconscious, references: the lonely shepherd on the downs (written from her walks above Rodmell with Virginia Woolf) is a pure echo of W. H. Davies, and the song of the reddleman, who

> Dyed in his scarlet dye,
> Leans like the Devil on the gate,
> And grins when children cry

is so Hardyesque, so much Diggery Venn from *Jude the Obscure*, that it must have been a joy to Vita, as much as it is to us, to find him still alive and living in post-war Kent.

Why was *The Land* so popular? I think there are three main reasons. Firstly, because of its realism and unsentimentality. Vita was evoking her countryside, a countryside in which she undisputably belonged, to early twentieth-century generations who had lost theirs, and who had become absorbed into city lives. They had a fond affection (perhaps a yearning) for the rural lives that had been their father's or grandfather's, and were concerned about what was happening to the countryside; the Council for the Preservation of Rural England was founded, by popular demand, in 1926, the year *The Land* was published. Secondly, Vita dealt neither in sentimental rubbish *nor* in intellectual over-viewing, and writing about landscape and the countryside suffered rather too much of both. The Bloomsberries might well have sniggered that it was 'poetry in gumboots', but none of them could have written it. She bridged a void between Victorian sentimentality and the daunting, horrific brilliance of Eliot's *The Waste Land*, which had been published in 1922. If, to Eliot, April was 'the cruellest month', Vita went to great lengths in *The Land* to plumb the depths of the countryman's wisdom, vigilance and cunning that allowed April to be beaten at her own game. But that is as much as she did then, and her formal and considered reply to Eliot has to await *The Garden*.

The overwhelming reason for *The Land*'s success may well be its sheer beauty. There are several exquisite poems within the poem, and *The Beemaster*, with memories of Constantinople joined to conversations with the village beekeeper, who tended the skeps in the Apple Orchard at Long Barn, is one of the best:

> And when you plant your rose trees, plant them deep,
> Having regard to bushes all aflame,
> And see the dusky promise of their bloom
> In small red shoots, and let each redolent name –
> Tuscany, Crested Cabbage, Cottage Maid –
> Load with full June November's dank repose;
> See the kind cattle drowsing in the shade
> And hear the bee about his amorous trade,
> Brown in the gypsy crimson of the rose.

The whole poem is ringing with Vita's love of flowers: wild flowers

> . . . in the meadow and the marsh
> Make rings round Easter; kingcup, marigold,
> And the pale orchis dappled like a dobbin;
> Buttercups a thousand fold
> Wearing their cloth of gold among the hay
> With clover and the little eye of day.

With her perfect balance between practical countrywoman and perceptive poet she weaves a perfect countryside where the farmer and the conservationist would both be happy; it is a countryside that works, and finds contentment, and magic in the occasional surprise, like the field of fritillaries:

> Wandering through the embroidered fields, each one
> So like its fellow; wandered through the gaps,
> Past the mild cattle knee deep in the brooks,
> And wandered drowsing as the meadows drowsed
> Under the pale wide heaven and slow clouds.
> And then I came to a field where the springing grass
> Was dulled by the hanging cups of fritillaries . . .

The most beautiful piece of *The Land*, possibly the most colourful and richly beautiful piece of poetry that Vita ever wrote, is the passage beginning 'She walks among the loveliness she made . . .', describing an island garden inlaid with spring flowers and hung with blossoms, woodbine and briar roses. The 'she' in question is Dorothy Wellesley, to whom *The Land* is dedicated, and the island garden so deliciously described is that of Sherfield Court, at Sherfield-on-Loddon in Hampshire. Dorothy was Vita's truest friend of the Long Barn years. Physically she was Vita's opposite, 'slight of build, almost fragile, with blazing blue eyes, fair hair, transparently white skin'; emotionally they had much in common, for Dottie was a natural rebel,

93

The Land: Vita's Kent photographed by Keith Harding in 1984.

47. *(above) The Land*, p. 87:

> How slow the darkness comes, once daylight's gone,
> A slowness natural after English day,
> So unimpassioned, tardy to move on . . .
> . . . The twilight lingers, etching tree on sky;
> The gap's a portal on the ridge's crest;
> The partridge coveys call beyond the rye . . .

48. *(opposite above) The Land*, pp. 98/9:

> But now the swoln fulfilment of the trees,
> Coloured and round,
> Demands another order: nimble boys,
> Reared ladders, bushel baskets on the ground,
> And pick, pick, pick, while days are calm and fine.

49. *(opposite below) The Land*, p. 104:

> But he, the master, climbs the ladder stair
> To the upper loft, where silence and pale peace
> Hold volatile lease;
> The upper loft, where mountains on the floor
> Of sapless flowers, sap robbed flowers, swell
> Bulky and weightless, ashen as fair hair
> Beneath a lamp, ashen as moonlit corn,
> As stubble newly shorn . . .

50. Vita's sitting room at Long Barn, where most of *The Land* was written.

'a fiery spirit with a passionate love of beauty in all its forms, whether of flowers, landscapes or works of art'.[8] They were also friends and travelling companions as husbands and wives – Harold and Vita first knew Lord Gerald Wellesley[9] in Constantinople, and for the following fifteen years wherever the Wellesleys went the Nicolsons were not far away. Vita and Dottie especially shared their poetry and gardening; they gardened together at Sherfield and at Long Barn, they went nursery hunting and garden visiting together, and during her most highly-charged romantic muddles Vita found a retreat in the rambling Georgian house with pink thatched gazebos added to its long frontage to the lazy channel of the Loddon. Sherfield Court's water comes actually as a surprise, for it seems to be sharing a hill with St Leonard's Church, and the suddenly revealed island garden with its delicate bridges and blowing tulips is entirely man-made.

If Vita had other loves, who merged into their castles or Elizabethan manor houses, Dorothy Wellesley's aura was demure, rose pink brick and Georgian. In the spring of 1928 Dottie gave herself real and enviable substance by buying Penn's Rocks on the fringe of Ashdown Forest near Groombridge, actually in the old Sackville parish of Withyham. She paid £10,000 for the house in its park of 250 acres – 'I wish we had seen Penn's in 1915,' cried Vita to Harold, as she realized that it was the park and garden that made her really covetous. The sedate little Georgian facade of Penn's looks out on to a park bursting with dramatic outcrops of primeval rocks – on her second visit Vita took pots of orange lilies, placed them against the rocks and pronounced the effect delicious; from then on she was captivated by the carpets of bluebells followed by even more desirable carpets of lilies-of-the-valley; she helped Dottie with the formal garden – an avenue of cherries underplanted with iris in the old walled garden is almost certainly Vita's design, and she worked hard at clearing trees and rough jobs. On hearing the news that her pet spaniel Pippin had been killed on the railway line it was the trees in Penn's woods that felt her bitterness.[10]

VITA AND HAROLD returned from Tcheran in May 1927; on 16 June Vita went to receive her Hawthornden Prize. To celebrate she spent the money on 'her Hawthornden' – a planting of hazels and poplars in Long Barn's wood. Persia and poetic success gave Vita renewed energies – or at least so one would suppose from the long list of amorous escapades which give the summer of 1927 more than a touch of Whitehall farce, as described by Victoria Glendinning in *Vita*.[11] The fact that it was also a very happy and successful summer with Harold and Long Barn's garden perhaps puts things into perspective; both Harold and Dottie Wellesley understood 'their Ophelia' and they knew they 'could only be very sweet to her'.[12] Harold had informed the Foreign Office that he did not want to go back to Teheran, but he accepted Berlin and left on 23 October. Vita lost her enthusiasm for gardening, knowing that what she planted would not be seen by the most important pair of eyes: 'I've been planting bulbs all morning, grape hyacinths mostly in the woods; but will Hadji see them? no, he won't! not unless he gets tired of being *rond de cuir* before April . . .' it's really pathetic the way I go on planting early bulbs and never see them. Nothing but an incorrigible optimism keeps me at it . . .'[13] She went out to Berlin in December and hated it. That city was to represent a very bleak period in their lives. Harold felt that everything about it was third-rate, and he kept on saying how he hated the exhibition of other people's vices, particularly as he seemed to be in constant demand from his friends as a guide to Sally Bowles land.

On Monday 9 January 1928 Vita wrote to Harold: 'Look at the above address – Mar has given herself a treat and slept at the cottage' – she had dined at Knole, put the children to bed, said goodnight to her father and fled, with her dogs, down to Long Barn. She went happily to sleep in her own room and awoke at six; she looked out to a faint mist but a clear sky 'with an enormous planet hanging over the woods all lovely and serene. I felt happier than I have for a long time.'[14]

But in the following days Lord Sackville became more and more ill, and he died on 28 January. Vita collapsed, and Harold, summoned home in haste, took charge of the funeral arrangements. On 2 February he returned to Berlin, and Vita and Olive Rubens went over to the chapel at Withyham to say goodbye. Vita remembered the carpet of flowers, the whole chapel smelling of narcissus and lilies

51. Harold at the window of Vita's bedroom, summer 1929 – in a bower of 'Madame Alfred Carrière', the old noisette climber with blush-white flowers which was one of the first roses Vita planted.

– it was lovely, but she couldn't feel that her loved Dada was there. He was gone, and so, of course, was Knole.

In the following weeks another visit to Berlin, but mostly her garden, pulled her through. Among worries over Knole, quarrels with her mother, which made her feel she had lost everything – father, mother and Knole – it was a constant relief to work in the garden in the company of the boys (Ben was fourteen, Nigel was eleven), who were writing a book. She re-started the flower-sending – a 'Mrs Sinkins' pink, a rosebud, catmint, sweet william – in a cigar box: 'tell me how they last – all my love is packed with them and that will last'.[15] On 16 May she confessed to Harold:

> I allowed myself a torture-treat tonight. I went up to Knole after dark and wandered about the garden. I have a master-key so I could get in without being seen. It was a very queer and poignant experience, so queer and so poignant that I should almost have fainted had I met anybody ... I had the sensation of having the place so completely to myself that I might have been the only person alive in the world, and not the world of today, mark you, but the world of at least 300 years ago. I might have been the ghost of Lady Anne Clifford. I have long resisted the temptation to get out the motor and drive

up there, but tonight it was so strong that I couldn't and wouldn't resist it any longer. Darling Hadji, I may be looney but there is some sort of umbilical cord that ties me to Knole – oh! ghosts, Dada, Knole, B.M., but not us, my love, not us, not us and the cottage. Mar.[16]

Harold came home for Whitsun and Vita and the boys went to stay with him at Potsdam in the summer. But mostly 1928 seems lost in a miasma of painful partings, regrets and sorrows, tensions over Harold's future career, and the death of his father, Lord Carnock, in November.

Trench deep; dig in the rotting weeds;
Slash down the thistle's greybeard seeds;
Then make the frost your servant; make
His million fingers pry and break
The clods by glittering midnight stealth
Into the necessary tilth.[17]

IT WAS hard gardening that had to compensate, and Vita probably worked harder physically in these last years at Long Barn than she did ever again. If the garden fulfilled all her dreams it must have looked as I shall now try and describe it; I have no way of knowing (nor do I think has anyone else now living) if Long Barn was ever this beautiful, but it certainly was in Vita and Harold's eyes, and that is enough. I propose to do as Vita did, and armed with a secret key and invisibility, steal down the hilly track at the end of Weald village and enter the little court. It is a perfect late May afternoon, with that lovely golden light that accompanies 4 o'clock, and (I take a leaf from Lady Sackville's book) all the flowers are magically in bloom!

The little court is filled with sun and cherry blossom on its walls. There is 'a truly magnificent bay tree' (Vita's words) in a pot, and in smaller pots at its feet there are rusty and flame tropaeolums (*T. peregrinum* 'Canary Creeper' and *T. speciosum* 'Flame Flower'), which she had brought home in triumph from an expedition to Suttons at Reading with Dottie Wellesley the previous year. Over the leaning porch tumbles Miss Jekyll's 'La Guirlande' rose – it fills the court with its orange scent and winds demurely round a decorative lead downpipe (snatched from Knole's workshop?) and a water butt. Through an iron grille and open gateway on the right is a glimpse of the box hedging of Vita's garden [52], with orange lilies (*L. tigrinum*) peeping over, and beyond are the Lombardy poplars blowing in the lower garden.

I enter the house down a long brick paved passage which is dark in contrast to the blaze of light from the garden door at the other end. On the right is Vita's (empty) sitting room – Persian rugs on a polished wooden floor, dark oak furniture, chintz covers, and open windows bringing in the scent of the ceanothus and another favourite rose, 'Madame Alfred Carrière' (which they insist on calling 'Mrs Alfonso's Career'!), the white noisette climber on the wall outside.

52. *(opposite)* The little box-edged parterre, with orange lilies and kniphofias among blue lavender, anchusas, delphiniums and scabious, outside Vita's writing room window; orange rock roses and azaleas cover the bank and steps. This photograph was taken in the summer of 1931, the last summer the Nicolsons lived at Long Barn.

53. *(above)* The garden of Long Barn, summer 1931, viewed from the door of the Big Room. There is a clump of rosemary at the door, a section of the iris border on the top of the retaining wall, and the borders flanking the terrace steps are filled with lupins, iris, and an abundant edging of *Stachys lanata* spreading over a crazy-paving mowing strip. Beyond are the lower levels of the garden, the Lombardy poplars blowing in the breeze, and the fields and trees of Vita's 'cool and candid Weald'.

At the end of the passage the garden door gives on to the brick terrace; there are generous clumps of rosemary beside the door over which I draw my hand, as Miss Jekyll liked to do, and the terrace is cluttered with an oak table, rejected chairs and coffee cups and glasses. There is lots of *Kalmia latifolia* (which Vita had recently excitedly discovered) along the foot of the house walls, with pink tulips springing

54. Vita, Ben and Nigel on the terrace steps at Long Barn, August 1931. The garden has the look of the heavy green of high summer and the old roses are over.

from the trailing leaves of *Iris stylosa*. Because of the magic there are still some 'rolled purple umbrellas' left – an excuse for not criticizing the gardener that they have not yet been tidied! The walls of the Big Room face due south, and they are crowded with a peach, the roses, 'Madame Delville' (affectionately known as 'Colette') and 'Hugh Dickson' growing in its 'food of the giants way', with great arching sprays cut to break into flower. Also against the walls, on brick pedestals, are Vita's treasured sinks overflowing with saxifrages, dianthus, soldanellas and thymes,[18] most of which she found at Colonel Hoare Grey's nursery near Cranbrook which she had recently discovered.[19]

The terrace is scattered with pots of orange tulips. Down the four rough brick steps and across the upper lawn I am conscious of the long march of mixed irises that rise from the top of the retaining wall in front of the Big Room; below them the wall is covered with aubrietas, pinks, valerian, cistus and lavenders, with the irises from Persia and pink tulips at their feet. This upper lawn is edged with the columnar Irish yews and more clumps of rosemary; at the far end of the house on the left more steps rise to the rose gardens outside the end windows of the Big Room and the windows of Harold's writing room. I will look at the roses in a moment, but my attention has been caught by activity on the tennis court, behind its hedges of pink and white thorn which Vita has planted around the wire, along with lush scatterings of madonna and martagon lilies. The seemingly deserted house and terrace are explained – the occupants are immersed in their tennis. Vita, in a low-waisted cream silk dress, white stockings and shoes and a red silk scarf around her head, the slight and fair Dottie Wellesley in white trimmed with pale blue, Vita's languid, sandy-haired cousin Eddy Sackville-West, come down from Knole, and the small, precise neatness of Raymond Mortimer – they make a foursome of exact contrasts. I don't think Harold was ever too keen on tennis – he is probably reading in his writing room!

In front of his open window are the rose beds, revelling in the dappled shade of a healthy mulberry tree. The beds are filled with salmony and red hybrid teas – the pinkish gold 'Betty', bright satin 'Caroline Testout', warm white 'Killarney', bright pink 'La France', crimson red 'Richmond', Ladies 'Hillingdon' and 'Ashtown' and others, all undercarpeted with catmint, rosemary and lavenders. Against the house 'Wedding Day', with creamy yellow buds and full white blooms, weaves round Harold's windows and up to the eaves along with the velvety crimson China climber 'Cramoisie Supérieure' and the rosier crimson 'Fellenberg'. In the borders at their feet are orange lilies and scarlet penstemons with an edging of white pinks.

Victory shouts from the tennis court make the lounging dogs rise and bark, and the white pigeons flutter; there is a fluttering too, of turquoise and gold, in the cage of budgerigars set against the south corner of the Big Room. Because of her childhood at Knole Vita had always felt that birds are essential to a garden; she would have liked lots of really exotic budgerigars, but had recently found them priced at 30 guineas a pair in the Tottenham Court Road, and had reluctantly turned away from the shop![20] The first white pigeons were brought to Long Barn in 1928 – 'All the pigeons are let out now,' she reported to Harold[21] – 'and they seem well contented only instead of sitting on the Big Room they sit in it!'

A pigeon flutters to the lawn beneath my feet as I come down from the rose garden and cross the upper lawn to the second flight of steps leading down to the second terrace lawn which Vita proudly calls the Pleasaunce. This flight is also marked with a pair of pots sporting purple violas, on brick plinths that Vita and the boys amused themselves building in August 1925 and marked with their names and the names of the dogs. The Pleasaunce is quite stylish; it is surrounded with box hedges and the grass is neatly cut; but it is not over-tidy (Vita's gardens never were), and pansies, pinks, sedums and even London pride and lots of thymes occupy odd patches of soil and creep round the edges of the steps and terrace walls. From the Pleasaunce a third flight of brick and stone steps leads down to a narrow green terrace and there is a fourth flight to the lowest level of the garden; the landing is a brick path which runs the whole width of the garden from east to west – across it are the raised brick-edged beds of Lutyens's Dutch Garden [55]; on the far right are the poplars at the foot of the raised parterre outside Vita's windows, and on the extreme left the matching avenue of poplars leading into the 'Delphic grove' or wild garden. Along beside the path, below the retaining wall of the Pleasaunce, is a long border of shrubs enjoying the fairly damp clay here – *Kalmia angustifolio rubra, Philadelphus coronarius, Osmanthus fragrans, Pieris japonica, Paeonia lutea* and

P. delavayi. I walk to the far end of the shrub border and climb the grass bank to look more closely over the box hedges and Vita's garden; here is where she tended the orange and blue colour scheme described on page 67 – a succession of tulips, lilies, roses, anchusas, scabious, delphiniums and gentians with generous annual additions of nemesias, scarlet verbenas, phlox and orange gladioli.

The raised brick beds of the Dutch Garden were for softer colour schemes, carefully planned. She dreamed up delicious mixes – a blue bed of 'Blue Jay' gladioli, *Meconopsis wallichii* and *Eryngium amethystium*, with white lilies and white snapdragons, all edged with 'Mrs Sinkins', and another of delphiniums, anchusas, *Commelina coelestis* and *Linum narbonense*, edged with lobelia. Her grey and pink scheme was for pink gladioli, *Lilium speciosum* 'Jelpomene', *Gypsophila paniculata*, lavenders, and edgings of pink violas and pink tulips. The schemes went on through grey and salmon, grey and orange, grey and yellow, and grey, purple and blue. Two of the brick-edged beds were for herbs (Vita was no cook and it did not occur to her to have them nearer the house), and there was a comprehensive collection – bergamot, pink balm, thyme, salvia, pink marjoram, sweet cicely, southernwood, hyssop, chicory, woodruff, basil, marjoram, vervain, peppermint, tarragon and rue. And everywhere there were generous edgings of lavender (Old English and dwarf French), for Harold would not have considered travelling without his Long Barn lavender bags and *pot pourri*; the latter was his particular speciality and he was constantly chiding Vita to keep collecting the petals and oiling the mix!

On the left of the Dutch Garden a honeysuckle arch led through the hedge into the Apple Garden, an old orchard to which Vita had added plums ('Victoria' and 'Black Diamond') and 'White Heart' cherries. 'Paul's Scarlet Climber' and 'Lemon Pillar' were encouraged up the old apple trees, and bee skeps sat in their shade surrounded by *Iris persica*, fritillaries and crocus, followed by clumps of tulips, deep blood-red hollyhocks and creamy delphiniums. The first gardener, Cooper, had been followed by the enthusiastic and exact Barnes – 'the sort of unslops that does everything with a garden line and spirit level' – *very* unlike Vita herself! Barnes, to her great joy, had straightened and edged the path through the Apple Garden, and here she planted dozens of the coppery pink hybrid tea 'Betty Uprichard', whose wonderful scent she adored and which she loved to cut for the house.

The lowest and farthest part of Long Barn's garden was the damp, wild wood. Here there was already a very wet area, perhaps a pond, when she came, and her first treatment was Mundsteadian. Bog bean, arums, loosestrife, mimulus and pink astilbes were planted at the water's edge, with surrounding banks of scarlet azaleas and drifts of *Iris sibirica*. Then she introduced forget-me-not and honesty – 'Blue and claret – nice?' – a mixture she was very proud of, and she teased Harold about his assumptions of pure chance:

> Now, look here, Hadji, the silver birches – we have been lucky, you say, but was that position for them carefully thought out? – lucky indeed! He always does that – he says: 'I say Mar what a bit of luck those orange tulips coming up just there where they show in that gap in the Apple Garden' – Lucky, indeed! Monster! I shan't tell you about the

1. *(above left)* The foothills of the Elburz: '... imagine you have ridden in summer for four days across a plain; that you have come to a barrier of snow-mountains and ridden up the pass; that from the top of the pass you have seen a second plain, with a second barrier of mountains in the distance, a hundred miles away; that you know that beyond these mountains lies yet another plain, and another; and that for days, even weeks, you must ride with no shade, and the sun overhead, and nothing but the bleached bones of dead animals strewing the track ...' (*Passenger to Teheran*).

2. *(above right)* A ruined garden near Quanat: '... then, when you come to trees and running water, you will call it a garden' (*Passenger to Teheran*).

3. *(right)* Bagh-i-Fin: the design of Persian gardens can be traced back to Xerxes and Cyrus. Across the centuries the extreme formality had been admired and prized until it had become a mystical obsession. The vital irrigation rills cut the garden up just as the universe was divided by great rivers.

4. Long Barn and its garden in 1980. This view is from the Dutch Garden, looking up the terraced slope to the original cottage on the left, and the barn added by the Nicolsons on the right.

5. *(opposite above)* Avebury Manor, Wiltshire. The Nicolsons visited Avebury for the first time in 1924 – 'How I want it,' wrote Vita. As well as its ancient stones and antique interiors the Manor has a lovely old garden with a yew walk, long, paved and narrow, such as Harold would eventually create at Sissinghurst.

6. *(opposite below)* Rodmarton Manor, Gloucestershire. The Hon. Claud Biddulph's Arts and Crafts revival house was actually begun just before the First World War by Ernest and Sydney Barnsley and their craft community. Both house and garden must have presented Vita with a pastiche of all her own antique tastes; this present-day corner of the garden is crowded with clipped and pleached greenery and trough gardens, all her favourite features, but somehow in need of a touch of classical control.

7. Stokesay Castle, Shropshire. 'Wonderful, wonderful Stokesay,' wrote Vita, 'it launches itself forward like a ship.' It was one of her favourites among her countrywide 'collection' of castles, and she visited it at every opportunity.

8. The Cumbria/Yorkshire border country near Brough, Lady Anne Clifford's countryside. 'I love the hills and wild roads my old sport Lady Anne used to bump over,' Vita wrote home to Harold, while she was absorbing the atmosphere which she wanted to write into her introduction to *The Diary of Lady Anne Clifford*, published in 1923.

honesty and forget-me-not – it is a cloud of pink and blue – if you saw it you would say how lucky it elected to grow together just above the pond.[22]

The wood had young red chestnuts, poplars, willows and wild cherry, a walk of hazels underplanted with narcissus and coloured primroses, with musk roses 'Aurora' and 'Cornelia', *Magnolia stellata*, lilacs, dogwoods and a constantly changing picture of flowery incidents – a patch of dark blue *Anemone blanda*, drifts of clear blue *A. appenina*, lilac stars of *A. hepatica* and lavender flowers of *A. nemorosa robinsoniana* in the shade; lilies of the valley, gentians, scillas, fritillaries, pink and orange primulas and martagon lilies – the flowery cavalcade from Sherfield Court had come marching home to Long Barn.

A ND SO the garden must have flowered in 1929, a year of great heights and deeps. Vita started sending flowers to Berlin with the earliest daphnes and iris, and by April she could manage hyacinths, tulips and narcissus. (All was well provided the diplomatic bag didn't get delayed!) Everything was being organized for Harold's homecoming in June. On 22 May she reported that the nightingales were in full blast and she had spent the day visiting her new gardening friend Colonel Hoare Grey – 'the country around Goudhurst is looking absolutely divine'. On the 26th the 'swimming pool', the former pond which had been converted (much against Harold's better judgement) with £100 from Vita's poetry broadcasts, was inaugurated by Ben and Nigel; two days later Vita was writing: 'Darling, I think the garden is more lovely this year than it has ever been before.' At the end of May she heard that her Uncle Charlie and his American wife Anne had moved into Knole and were immediately thinking of selling the Hoppner painting and the silver furniture. On 3 June – 'the roses are getting ready for Mr Nicolson'; 5 June – 'Oh dear, the greenfly, I must Abol before Hadji comes!' She went 'officially' to lunch with Uncle Charlie and his daughter Diana and found the familiar setting – the sitting room, vases with pink flowers, the fire, Booth the butler, and her uncle's footsteps sounding just like her father's – all too much. She came home in the rain, in tears, and had to stop the car because she could not see to drive. Harold arrived on schedule in mid-June but was called back urgently to Berlin a week later. The garden *was* looking lovely and in the language of the Mars he sent his regrets:

> ... over and over again he has told her that it is a real joy to him that she should be there when it is lovely and that what he would really mind is (i) if it were not lovely and (ii) she were not there when it is – but she goes on feeling guilty about me feeling that it isn't fair that it should be a garden full of roses. My darling, revel in it as much as you can – that is what I want – and if your love of it is as intense as possible some of the enjoyment will cross the North Sea and steal among the shadows of the Herrenzimmer.[23]

Before Vita went off flower-hunting above Val d'Isère with Hilda Matheson she confessed her feelings about Knole:

> ... my voluntary exile from Knole is very curious – I think about it a lot – it feels exactly as though I have had for years a liaison with a beautiful woman, who never, from force

of circumstances, belonged to me wholly, but who has for me a sort of half-maternal tenderness and understanding in which I could be entirely happy. Now I feel as though we have been parted because (again owing to force of circumstances and through no choice of her own) she had been compelled to marry someone else and had momentarily fallen completely beneath his jurisdiction – not happy in it, but acquiescent. I look at her from afar off; and if I were wilder and more ruthless towards myself I should burst in one evening and surprise her in the midst of her new domesticity. But life has taught me not to do these things.[24]

From her walking expedition in Switzerland she went to meet Harold briefly for a few idyllic days, and they parted on 4 August on Cologne station. It was the bleakest parting that even they had ever had; she sat in the hotel lounge, trying to write, staring at the hurrying passengers, ordering food she did not want so that she could stay out of the rain, biting back her tears; from behind her came the softly mocking strains of 'Velia, Oh Velia', and in the cavernous roar of loneliness that only a large and crowded concourse can produce she felt, as she said, like a widow and not very merry. Harold had decided to give up the Foreign Office, but what was he to do? Could he be foreign editor of *The Times*? could he go into politics? he could work for Lord Beaverbrook! Vita had been trying very hard. She went home to a miserably wet Long Barn and lumbago which prevented her from gardening. At the end of September Harold went home briefly to accept the job with Lord Beaverbrook, and returned to finish out his Berlin stint. Vita found him a London flat at 4 King's Bench Walk in the Temple, and busied herself furnishing it. There was a momentary flush of excitement in November when Bodiam Castle, 'beloved Bodiam',[25] came on to the market, but it was priced wildly out of their reach at £30,000. In December Harold came home from Berlin and the diplomatic life for the last time. There could now never be another Christmas at Knole, so they spent it at Long Barn and were happy.

On 1 January 1930 Harold started work as a columnist on the *Evening Standard*; his biographer and friend James Lees-Milne describes this moment as 'the great divide' in his life. He had given up a profession he at least believed in for something which very, very soon was to fill him with disillusion. As he struggled with his new London life, week-ends at Long Barn at least remained a consolation to him. For Vita, only half resigned to the loss of Knole, it was rather too much like living next door to a lost love. In March they heard that the next door farm had been sold and was to become an intensive poultry farm; they were offered the fields adjoining the garden at what they considered was an inflated price, or even the whole farm for £21,000, which was out of the question. It seemed that the cruel force of circumstance was now attacking their last refuge. Where were they to go?

55. The raised flower beds, the Dutch Garden designed by Sir Edwin Lutyens and Harold Nicolson on the lowest level of Long Barn's garden, viewed through the arch of the Apple Garden entrance. Again photographed in the summer of 1931, they sport the most successful achievements of Vita's apprenticeship in gardening.

6

THE CASTLE AND THE ROSE
1930-39

A tired swimmer in the waves of time
I throw my hands up: let the surface close:
Sink down through centuries to another clime,
And buried find the castle and the rose . . .
And here, by birthright far from present fashion,
As no disturber of the mirrored trance
I move, and to the world above the waters
Wave my incognizance . . .
Beauty and use, and beauty once again
Link up my scattered heart, and shape a scheme
Commensurate with a frustrated dream.
V. Sackville-West, *Sissinghurst*[1]

I T WAS Dorothy Wellesley who spotted the advertisement for a sixteenth-century
castle in Kent, and it was she who took Vita and Nigel down to look round. On
4 April 1930 Harold wrote in his diary: 'Vita telephones to say she has seen the
ideal house – a place in Kent near Cranbrook.' The next day they all went down,
Harold and Ben catching the train to Staplehurst for the first of countless times. His
next diary entry reads: '. . . we get a view of the two towers as we approach. We go
round carefully in the mud. I am cold and calm but I like it.'[2] Vita had already fallen
'flat in love', she knew her home when she found it – was not this tower the very
image of that at Bolebroke, were not these courts the very pattern of Knole, was
not this the home of Sir Thomas Sackville's wife Cicely Baker, surrounded by walled
spaces of the kind of garden she knew so well, among the Wealden fields she loved?

She transferred the feeling of seeing Sissinghurst for the first time to Evelyn
Jarrold, the heroine of *Family History*, who is taken to the home of her lover, Miles
Vane-Merrick:

> The lane widened, and the fan of light showed up a group of oast-houses beside a great
> tiled barn; then it swung round on a long, low range of buildings with a pointed arch
> between two gables. Miles drove under the arch and pulled up. It was very dark and cold.
> The hard winter starlight revealed an untidy courtyard, enclosed by ruined walls, and
> opposite, an arrowy tower springing up to a lovely height with glinting windows.[3]

56. Sissinghurst: the kitchen garden and the Tower as they found them – June 1930.

Evelyn goes on to discover the old orchard beyond the tower, the cottage that had once formed part of the original castle ('only a cottage, but in its mullioned windows it preserved traces of grandeur'), how the sunshine enriched the old brick walls with a kind of patina that turned them pink, how the tower sprang 'like a bewitched and rosy fountain', how there was a peace within those high brick walls and how the view from the top of the tower was of the fields, woods and hop gardens of Kent. All this – the cold, the peace, the touch of grandeur and familiar forms – this is why Vita fell 'flat in love' with Sissinghurst Castle and remained so for the rest of her life.[4]

On 6 April Harold and Vita went back again. Harold wrote: 'My anxiety had been that the main wing would be too narrow to build in. But we measure and find that we get 18 feet. We then go round the buildings carefully and finally walk round the fields to the brook and round by the wood. We come suddenly upon a nut walk and that settles it . . .'[5] But by the 13th and another look he was not so sure – 'It all looks big, broken-down and sodden.' The next day he brightened, and ten days later assessed the situation:

> My view is (a) that it is most unwise of us to get Sissinghurst. It costs us £12,000 to buy and will cost another good £15,000 to put in order. This will mean nearly £30,000 before we have done with it. For £30,000 we could buy a beautiful place replete with park, garage, h and c central heating, historical associations and two lodges r and l. (b) That it is most wise of us to buy Sissinghurst. Through its veins pulses the blood of the Sackville dynasty. True that it comes through the female line – but then we are both feminist and after all Knole came in the same way. It is for you, an ancestral mansion: that makes up for company's water and h and c. It is in Kent. It is in a part of Kent we like, it is self-contained, I could make a lake and ride – we like it, but we have to be quite clear about the obligations thereof – are there any charges on the place? We must make it clear to Beale that we cannot buy it if it is going to be a drain on our income . . . everything must be covered by certain lettings . . . no optimism, we must know the worst . . . we better have immediate possession of . . . the Tower, Bosky's cottage and the other cottage . . . in fact the emplacement of the old castle as bounded by the moat and the bit of the park field necessary to make a square of the existing holly hedge plus the lake field and the field adjoining the lake . . .[6]

Eventually even Harold admitted to being excited – they decided to buy and the acceptance of their offer was confirmed on 6 May. What they had actually bought was an agricultural slum. Sissinghurst had remained the great house of the Bakers until about 1750. It was then used as a prison for French prisoners of war [57] – a ghastly place – then largely pulled down. The remaining buildings, much as Vita and Harold found them, served tenant farms on Lord Cornwallis's estate from the latter half of the nineteenth century. George Neve was the tenant of 767 acres of Castle and Bettenham Farms till 1903, then the property was sold to Barton Cheeseman. Harold went to the London Library and found a 1912 photograph of it with the entrance range covered in ivy, the arch bricked up and a large pond beside the drive. Sissinghurst had been sold again in 1926 to William Wilmshurst, who

57. 'Sisingherst Castle . . . dedicated to the Officers of the Militia, engraved from a Drawing taken on the Spot By an Officer 1760'. At this time it was a prison for French prisoners of war.

had died in 1928; John Wilmshurst had put it back on the market, where Dottie had found it. It is odd now to note that on the survey particulars it is Castle Farmhouse with its ten bedrooms and 'well matured grounds with lawn and rhododendrons' that was thought the gem. Other assets mentioned were the 'picturesque old buildings' containing cottages, a brew house and stabling for twelve horses, a bailiff's house (in want of immediate repair) and the central gateway and towers in a passable state of repair. 'I understand that Mrs Nicolson proposes to occupy this' – was the amazed final comment.[7] Apart from the raggle-taggle of buildings Vita and Harold found endless vegetable gardens and a vast accumulation of rubbish – rusty iron, old bedsteads, old ploughshares, old cabbage stalks, old broken-down earth closets, old matted wire and mountains of sardine tins, 'all muddled up in a tangle of bindweed, nettles and ground elder'.[8]

They paid £12,375 for this ruin and Castle Farm. Throughout that first summer they made working visits, sleeping at the George in Cranbrook or the Bull in Sissinghurst village; they picnicked and worked in the garden and generally supervised discoveries and building works. Castle Farm was let to Oswald Beale, who became a stalwart friend to the Nicolsons over the years.[9]

The sardine tins must have caught Vita's imagination, for she apparently served sardines up for picnics, much to Harold's disgust, and he sent them, the clayey mud, the temperamental water supply and Vita's rosy view of their slum into an hysterically funny eternity in a broadcast in November 1930. If it wasn't his imagination, they had actually spent their first night at Sissinghurst in the bailiff's house (South Cottage) feasting on Harold's pet hates – the said sardines, soup from a tablet, cheese wedges and tongue (tinned), beside a boy-scout fire with one candle and cold water for the washing-up; our hero fumbled from catastrophe to

58. *(left)* The tower at Bolebroke, ancestral home of the Sackvilles at Buckhurst in Sussex, which in appearance and date is so like the tower at Sissinghurst.

59. *(right)* Vita's tower at Sissinghurst, as they found it in June 1930.

catastrophe while Vita (Edith) swanned serenely through. It was certainly Vita who would have laughed most.[10]

The first priority was Vita's tower [59] – it was hers of right, for a very similar tower at Old Buckhurst [58] had been the refuge of Anne Torrell, wife of Sir John Sackville, in Henry VIII's time. The first night they 'officially' spent at Sissinghurst was on camp beds in the upper room of the Tower on 18 September 1930. South Cottage was ready next, and when the furniture from Long Barn was moved over they slept there for the first time on 6 December.

Vita's earliest joys were those of the treasure hunter – what the prosaic farmers had left around as useless was often a treasure to her. Not, I hasten to add, the sardine tins and old earth closets, but beneath the heaps there were remnants of Sir John Baker's castle, chunks of carved stone and bits of Tudor fireplaces. A hoard of the latter was found in an underground passage – '... was it where Bloody Baker Hid Slaughtered Mistresses?' asked Harold. 'If so he would scarcely have gone to the trouble of putting in a fireplace every three feet!'[11] The last thing they wanted to do was to destroy the magic of Sleeping Beauty's castle, so they discovered it, revealed it, piece by piece. The ivy came off the rosy brick walls, the ugly lean-tos were stripped away, the courtyard was emptied of rubbish, levelled and seeded to become a green court, and the entrance arch was opened. Some of Vita's first plantings were around the arch; she planned a colour scheme of coral, white and green and planted *Chaenomeles japonica*, sweet bay, *Magnolia grandiflora*, and her

60. *(above left)* Sissinghurst: the north wall of the Rondel Garden looking towards South Cottage – the site of the present herbaceous border – in June 1930.

61. *(above right)* Sissinghurst: The entrance court, June 1930 – the arch is still blocked up.

62. *(below)* Sissinghurst, June 1930: the sixteenth-century barn as they found it. They considered moving this building to form the north boundary of the entrance court – but were more than likely dissuaded by their architect A. R. Powys, who as Secretary of the Society for the Protection of Ancient Buildings would have strongly opposed such an idea.

63. *(left)* Sissinghurst, March 1931: Vita starts digging the border in the south-west corner of the Tower lawn (the doorway was subsequently removed).

64. *(right)* Sissinghurst, August 1931: Ben and Nigel on the wall in the corner of the courtyard beside the Tower – the ground shows signs of Vita's first irises.

first two rarities – *Myrtus tarentina* 'Jenny Reitenbach', and *Plagianthus lyallis* (now *Hoheria lyalli*), with grey leaves and white flowers in July. The porch was called Alex's Porch, after Alex le Fossard who lived in the rooms above. Later Vita found another treasure, an enormous stone sink upside down in a pigsty, with the legend attached to it of being Wat Tyler's footbath – she rescued it, placed it on brick piers outside the Big Room and filled it with gentians, lithospermums and *Omphalodes luciliae.*

Despite Harold's dislike of his journalism, 1930 was a year of some success; Vita published *The Edwardians*, and Harold's book about his father's world, *Lord Carnock*, subtitled 'A Study in the Old Diplomacy', unleashed a few sensations and much favourable comment. After a late summer holiday with the boys Vita returned to Sissinghurst in October: 'I am writing from our castle, as you see I am terribly happy here . . . it is an incredibly lovely evening and the sunset from the top of the tower was a poem, all yellow and black. Hayter[12] has cleared the Moat Walk and a lovely wall has come into view . . . the east end is perfect but the west end is very bitty.' The discovery was so exciting it was worth a second bulletin: 'The moat wall is going to be very superb. They have uncovered its foot a bit and I think there is no doubt that there was originally water there too. There are lovely big stones at

65. Sissinghurst, summer 1932: they have moved in – Harold and Ben are sitting on the moat wall, which is bedecked with Bagatelle vases (looking somewhat out of scale), and Vita's lovely wall has been fully revealed. The view she (as photographer) is taking is the view Dionysius has, across the moat and up the moat walk to Sissinghurst Crescent.

the foot of the piers. The piers are going to be lovely ...'[13] Clearing the Nuttery revealed that the trees were in avenues; Vita made a first planting of narcissus here as a bow to William Robinson (whom she had visited at Gravetye[14]), and added foxgloves which Harold collected from the wood in an old pram. Also, as he had dreamed, he supervised the damming of the Hammer stream to make his lake; the dam cost £125 to build in December 1930.

1931 was the year of Harold's entanglement with Sir Oswald Mosley's New Party, and the consolation of Sissinghurst was much needed. South Cottage's garden was arranged on its simple crossing with brick paths around the edges and a hedge of briar roses on the orchard side – was it not, as McNed had said, that every house should spring out of a briar bush? On South Cottage's walls Vita planted the noisette rose 'Mme Alfred Carrière', which nearly took the cottage over, and the climbing hybrid tea 'Madame Edouard Herriot', the yellow lantern-flowered *Clematis tangutica*, *Lonicera fragrantissima* (creamy flowers in winter) and *Lonicera trigophylla* (golden flowers in July). *Bignonia grandiflora* and *Chaenomeles superba* 'Knaphill Scarlet' also wreathed South Cottage – it was a veritable bower.

Vita revelled in the space for climbing wall plants that Sissinghurst supplied. She planted the climbing rose 'Richmond' on her tower, with clumps of rosemary at its feet, and roses and figs on the courtyard walls. The Tower lawn had already been enclosed with a single yew hedge on the orchard side, and the Bishopsgate wall (adorned with the plaque of three Greek bishops that they had brought from Constantinople) made the fourth side. It was planted with the rose 'Fortune's Yellow', *Abutilon vitifolium*, a ceanothus, rose 'Emily Gray' as a companion for sweet bay, and a large flowered *jackmanii* clematis, 'Gypsy Queen'. These were later joined by a precious *C. armandii* Harold brought from La Mortola. Ben and Nigel had slept in the renovated Priest's House for the first time in April, and the whole of 1931 was filled with working visits, when they worked very hard and Vita got progressively more excited about it all. In the September she was given her first contract for gardening journalism – 'Madam: I understand that you are prepared to contribute to this journal a weekly article containing hints to the amateur gardener.' The journal was the ill-fated *Action* (the New Party's paper) and the editor was Harold. Vita did several contributions for which she was never paid.[15]

The Nicolsons actually moved into Sissinghurst on 9 April 1932; it was not an auspicious time. Their castle was a considerable drain on their income, and Long Barn (the chicken threat having faded) was still to be maintained;[16] Harold, having given up journalism and Mosley's politics, had no job nor expectation of any and found it frustrating trying to convince Vita that they were poor. But as more of Lady Sackville's discarded treasures (including pairs of the fabulous Bagatelle vases and the statue of a Bacchante) arrived he appreciated the paradox:

> ... Louise during the day has been spreading out the carpets Vita brought from Streatham. They are moth eaten but superb. It is typical of our existence that with no settled income and no certain prospects, we should live in a muddle of museum carpets, ruined castles and penury. Yet we know that all this uncertainty is better for us than dull and unadventurous security. After dinner we discuss the front at Sissinghurst. We decide to plant a wall of limes, framing the two gables and the arch and following on to a popular avenue across the fields. That is our life. Work, uncertainty and huge capitalistic schemes. And are we wrong? My God! We are not wrong![17]

He spent the summer at home writing *Public Faces* and *Peacemaking 1919* and they really settled in.

In July the first aerial photographs of the castle were taken, which enable us to look back and see just what they had done. The photographs also illustrate Harold's quandaries about design. The approach is still only through a ramshackle farmyard – though the arch has been opened there are only muddy tracks across the grass towards it. The entrance range of buildings is still cottages on the right and stables (the Big Room has not been started) and the brewhouse on the left – the awkward angle of the range that Harold was to curse is clearly shown. Inside the courtyard the marks of the clinging cottages can still be seen on the walls, and the ground looks level and green with a gardener reassuringly walking back to his wheelbarrow beside the flower border. The roses and figs seem to be making their marks on the walls, but Vita's first border planting of bush roses, lilies and pinks looks a little

66. Aerial photograph of Sissinghurst taken in July 1932, after it had belonged to the Nicolsons for two years. The entrance arch has been opened up, but the entrance range of buildings is still cottages on the right and stables on the left. The courtyard has been cleared and grassed, but has not yet been closed on its north side, where what will be Delos is filled with rows of vegetables. Vita, who has left her car outside the entrance arch, is standing outside the Priest's House with (probably) Hilda Matheson – they are looking up at the aeroplane! The Priest's House garden has been set out in the form of the White Garden it will become, and a single row of yews has just been planted along its eastern boundary, continuing to enclose the lower lawn. In the top right of the photograph the kitchen garden, as it was called, is still filled with vegetables, but the garden of South Cottage has been set out and Vita has started planting.

67. Summer 1933: Harold and Vita in the garden of South Cottage.

overgrown. The courtyard has not yet been closed at the northern end; they debated building a wing for themselves across here (or even, having moved one barn before, using Sissinghurst's splendid barn to fill this gap!), but decided it would be too expensive. The next idea was for a covered loggia which would also house Vita's birds – but more of that later. On the north side of the garden is the Priest's House, then home for Ben and Nigel, with the bare outline of a rose garden; what is to be Delos is uncompromisingly filled with rows of cabbages, and more cabbages seem to fill the unhappy rectangle that is the kitchen garden (and was called so until the Rondel was made) on the south side of the garden. South Cottage, with its unsquare cottage garden, is where Vita and Harold sleep and Harold works. A single yew hedge has just been planted to enclose the Tower lawn and the Priest's House garden, and beyond it is the wild orchard where paths have been cut and daffodils planted.

It was in the spring of 1932 that Harold faced up to the quandaries of his design:

> Vita and I measure the Kitchen Garden to discover how much paling will be required to make it square. I fiddle about with this vista problem. Obviously what would be good in a teleological sense would be to put the end of the main nuttery walk at the end of a main vista running from the new angle of the Kitchen Garden, past the cottage garden and thus perspectively to what is now a gate into a field but which one day will be a classic statue erect among cherry trees. Only this cuts angularly across the holly hedge in our own little cottage garden and fits obtusely with the rest of the design. That is what is such a bore about Sissinghurst. It is magnificent but constantly obtuse ... disturbed by these considerations we weed the delphinium bed. A sedentary occupation which gives us the reward of finding one or two delphiniums sprouting among the crowsfoot. It is very odd. I do not like weeding in any case. I cannot get a job and am deeply in debt. I foresee no exit from our financial worries. Yet Vita and I are as happy as larks alone together. It is a spring day. Very odd.[18]

He had to give up the idea of a single vista – though on the rough canvas with which he was working it could not have looked so impossible as it does in today's neat garden. He used the obtuse southern boundary cleverly to make his Lime Walk (planted in 1932) to tie the Nuttery and kitchen garden together. When the Moat Walk was cleared they could see that it was not parallel with anything either and was shaped like a long thin coffin. The shape was disguised by the bank of azaleas that glow in spring and autumn between the Moat Walk and the Nuttery. The Moat Walk was given its desired dignity by a beginning in a semi-circular space surrounded originally with acacias which they jokingly called Sissinghurst Crescent (after, I think, some new town planning that Harold had been looking at). The vista from the crescent ended with their much-loved Dionysus on his plinth across the moat.

The aerial photographs must have helped, but Harold did his planning from the top of the Tower and his actual setting out with sticks, balls of string, tape measures, and usually Nigel as staff man with a scarf on the end of a bamboo cane. It was by means of Nigel that Dionysus found his correct place. Harold's sister Gwen St Aubyn was on hand to help with the kitchen garden, and to give Harold moral support as well: 'Measure the central path in the Kitchen Garden and Gwen helps me. Finally Vita refuses to abide by our decision or to remove the miserable little trees which stand in the way of my design. The romantic temperament as usual obstructing the classic.'[19] He tried again but 'came up against artichokes and Vita's indignation' – and retired sadly to weeding. Later they had a discussion about women's rights!

Harold, of course, won in the end, and the kitchen garden was transformed into the sublime Rondel Garden of exquisite geometry and luxurious plants, now contained within box boxes. Perhaps Vita went away and reflected that Gravetye, the garden of the plantsman she most admired at that moment, William Robinson, also had 'one of the prettiest bits of formality imaginable'. Though Miss Jekyll may have been her first influence, Vita had increasingly turned to Robinson in her last Long Barn years and his influence pervades the whole of Sissinghurst. He had written to her [68] to say what intense pleasure *The Land* had given him and inviting her over to see his woods and the source of the Medway, of which he was the 'happy owner'.[20] He had talked learnedly throughout the visit – she enjoyed the lunch but a terrifying ride, lurching and heaving, through the woods in his caterpillar-car apparently wiped all his wisdom from her mind. However, she must have turned to *The Wild Garden* and *The English Flower Garden*, for the way she mixes her borders and beds, the succession of hardy flowers after bulbs, the pansies and pinks she put with her roses and especially the planting of Sissinghurst's orchard

68. William Robinson wrote to Vita in appreciation of *The Land* and she visited him at Gravetye in 1927 or 1928, when he was nearing ninety. Despite a terrifying, lurching journey around his woods in a 'tank-like machine', she was fascinated by his knowledge and found him 'an admirable old man'. She wrote her tribute to him in 'Gardens and Gardeners', published in *Country Notes*. The narcissus under the hazels, her wild orchard with roses scrambling in the trees, flowers growing from ruins and walls, are all Robinsonian themes from *The Wild Garden* which were practised at Long Barn and transferred to Sissinghurst. His letter to Vita is reprinted below with a transcript.

Madame,

I have read '*Land*' with interest and pleasure and venture to write now as to a big gap in your Kent pictures – the woods of the near Sussex. I have a large area of oak and other woods here grown in the forest way preserving themselves, nourishing themselves, with none of the ceaseless labours of the rich land. Kent land is too good to plant in forest, and so we have more of wooded land here. I am the happy owner of the source of the *Medway* at Mill Place Farm and should be glad to show the sylvan scene to you any spring or summer day, and hoping you will please excuse this note.

Ever yours faithfully,
W. Robinson.

9. Montacute, Somerset: the perfect marriage of flowers and antique stones in the courtyard. In 1948 Vita was asked to create planting schemes for these borders, but, sadly, her schemes have not survived.

10. Cold Ashton Manor, near Bath: the genuine article in the manor house cult, owned by Lt. Col. Reginald Cooper, a Foreign Office colleague of Harold's in Constantinople. Vita referred to it as 'a lovely little grey house', and it was another one that she coveted.

11. *(above)* Kiftsgate Court, Gloucestershire: Vita admired this contemporary of Sissinghurst. She and Mrs Muir shared many gardening tastes, especially their love for old roses, and recommended plants to each other, but Kiftsgate rejoices in a lovely hillside site that is very different from Sissinghurst's.

12. *(left)* Cranborne Manor, Dorset: the herb garden. It was during the postwar years, when Sissinghurst and Vita were first famous, that the Marchioness of Salisbury (then Viscountess Cranborne) began to replant this old and lovely garden in the Sissinghurst manner.

13. *(opposite)* Cranborne Manor: spring flowers in the Church Walk.

14. The Green Court at Knole.

15. The courtyard at Sissinghurst.

Beauty, and use, and beauty once again
Link up my scattered heart, and shape a scheme
Commensurate with a frustrated dream.
                                        (Sissinghurst, 1931)

are very Robinsonian. But if Robinson was pervasive there was also a cavalcade of rather more direct influences in the dozens of gardening friends and experts who homed in on Sissinghurst even from these earliest years. The first of these was Colonel Hoare Grey, who lived less than ten minutes' drive away and who must be credited with both the suggestions and the supply of most of the rare and more precious plants that were now coming to Sissinghurst. He would have found in Vita a gardener after his own heart (he had very high standards and rather grandiose taste), and neither his ideas nor his prices would have daunted *her*! (It is surely with Colonel Hoare Grey that the pursuit of the excellent which both Harold and Vita adopted as the motto for Sissinghurst's plantings began?) She would have needed to go no farther than his Hocker Edge nursery for the *Plagianthus lyallis* (which he refused to call *Hoheria lyalli*), the *Schizophragma hydrangeoides* 'Siebold' planted in the courtyard, *Abutilon vitifolium* 'De Candolle' and *A. megapolamicum* 'St Hilaire', *Tricuspidaria lanceolata* 'Miquel' with crimson urns of flowers, and the *Mutisia retusa* 'Remy' – which were all part of her newly sophisicated taste. And his alpine catalogue offered her treasures for her sink gardens – the forget-me-not blue *Omphalodes luciliae*, dozens of rare gentians, *Lithospermum prostralum*, *Ozothamnus obcordatus*, the rock *Penstemon venustus*, the crimson *Dianthus* 'Mozart' and *Androsace carnea laggeri*. From now on the winning and the keeping of such precious jewels, the spinning and the weaving of a brocade of exquisite taste, was the essence of Vita's gardening ambition.

B UT it is time to put Sissinghurst into context. Apart from Vita's personal recognition of all she was looking for in a home, she and Harold were in fact following a trend rather than setting one with their seemingly eccentric escapade. Sissinghurst was no rugged fortress, but it was the echo of a dream that had come rippling down the years fairly frequently since castle building had come to a halt in mid-Victorian Scotland. Andrew Carnegie had restored Skibo in Sutherland, Lutyens had modernized Lindisfarne for Edward Hudson, William Waldorf Astor had bought Hever, Robert Lorimer had rebuilt a whole string (Ardinglas, Kellie, Lympne and Balmanno), and Philip Tilden had attended to Saltwood rather nearer home. To out-castle them all Lutyens had built Castle Drogo, starting in 1910 but not finishing until 1930. Since the war only Americans could afford such fantasies – William Randolph Hearst wanted a castle and had bought St Donat's in 1925; he had rejected Leeds near Maidstone, which was snapped up by Lady Baillie. Now the English with dreams and taste but no fortunes had to resort to manor houses, and it is really into this context that Sissinghurst comes. Vita already knew and loved Compton Beauchamp and Sutton Courtenay; she later fell for Sir Ernest Wills's Littlecote which he bought in 1922, the Jenner family's Avebury (they had already restored Lytes Cary and given it to the National Trust), and Harold's Foreign Office friend Colonel Reggie Cooper's handsome Cold Ashton Manor above Bath. This was their milieu, and it is to be noted that these houses, and many more that will be encountered, had lovely gardens that influence and pervade this book.

Of course, it was not a totally angelic movement. In 'rescuing' St Donat's, William Randolph Hearst outraged the nation by pillaging Bradenstoke Priory in Wiltshire (which Vita had visited at almost its last moment) for its stones, fourteenth-century collar beam roof from the refectory, medieval tithe barn and windows. The outrage was led by the Society for the Protection of Ancient Buildings; posters were put up in the underground, there were questions in the House. The Secretary of the S.P.A.B. was one of the Powys brothers, the architect Albert R. Powys, and he warned: 'England at present suffers much from the removal of old buildings and fittings from places where they were originally set, but it must be said that this damage to our heritage is more the result of our own population than of the citizens of the United States of America. My Society asks Mr Hearst to set Englishmen a good example... to shame them perhaps into better behaviour...'[21] Within a very short time A.R.P. (as he was usually called) was to have his own chance – for rather than choosing any of their friends as their architect for Sissinghurst, the Nicolsons chose him.

A.R.P.'s first visit was purely as a consultant in August 1932, but he was not one to do a job by halves.[22] He was known as 'Brother Positive' at home, and his most famous brother, John, described his ferocious integrity and directness of purpose and opinion, which would have been crushing had it not been for the wave 'of disarming self-deprecation' that reached out from his deepest soul. He added: '...the secret of his method was to deduce beauty from the line of least resistance in practical common sense, when he was in contact with wood, stone and bricks he lost his identity as a particular person and became All Men in contact with the works of All Men's hands.'[23] Whether they dared mention moving the barn to A.R.P. we shall never know, but the first matter discussed was the building of a wing across the north end of the courtyard. It was scrapped as being too expensive, but not before Harold had had a lecture on choosing bricks – 'Many men think', wrote A.R.P., 'that they are able to do what others cannot, and it is passing through my mind that I would be better able to recognize the capacity of the brickmaker foreman to take my idea, than you might be.'[24] Over the next few years bricks were a constant source of friction; many of them were to come from the then-working Frittenden Brickworks two fields away, and more were found by A.R.P., and they were given all kinds of attention with cow-dung dips and the like – the result being that Sissinghurst does look all of an age and not like a patchwork. There were to be endless battles, but Sissinghurst owes much of its character to A.R.P. His loggia design for the courtyard (which Vita wanted to wreathe with 'Mermaid' roses) was rejected but the existing wall was built by him, he made life for Ben and Nigel in the Priest's House a lot more comfortable, he converted the 'barracks' into the Big Room, did various repairs to the farm and its buildings and built his *pièce de résistance*, the wall enclosing the west end of the Rondel Garden. And all the time he was doing these things he was offering advice on the garden design as well. 'A great thing to remember,' he wrote to Harold, 'in laying out gardens is that the scale out of doors is so much larger than indoors; that is where many go wrong, particularly those who plan gardens in offices.'[25] Harold was very much an out-of-doors designer but he was having difficulty with the connection between the Tower lawn and the orchard. He was contemplating the planting of the second row of yews that make the Yew Walk but wondered if the entrance into the orchard should be significant in some way. A.R.P. made an elaborate suggestion for concave curving hedges towards the Tower which doubled and curved convexly towards the orchard so that the approach from the moat did not 'have something of the look of the back of a vase of flowers arranged to be put on an altar'.[26] He also suggested that the long hedge should be broken, so that it looked complete in perspective but was broken to allow views of the orchard from the Tower lawn – a device from Italian gardens that was also used successfully at Marsh Court, near Stockbridge in Hampshire, by Lutyens. When it came to the planting of the second row of yews A.R.P. was prickly: 'I notice that your yew hedges are little more than 12 inches thick. They will grow to three or five feet or even thicker. You must watch that . . . have you ever measured the thickness of an old yew hedge?'[27] Harold remained polite and assured A.R.P. that he did not think the walk would be too narrow – Hollamby the contractor had assured him there would be enough light for grass to grow and he eventually wanted to pave the walk anyway – 'Stone against yew is a lovely thing.' But perhaps A.R.P. was on to something – the entrance from the Tower lawn to the orchard *is* a very weak point in Sissinghurst's design, and perhaps the Yew Walk is a little narrow – it is for one person rather than two side by side, which has a touch of sadness about it.

A.R.P. went home and worried a little more about the Nicolsons' doings. He came back with a design for an arched wall for the north end of the courtyard, which would look good from both sides and allow for Vita's climbers and an aviary. Vita grumbled that it was too elaborate but Harold, absent in America, was not so sure – 'I think we need a touch of architecture to that wall.' Battles about 'taste' ensued. A.R.P. would not let them have diamond panes – 'they come too near to Wardour Street English' – but he sent a design for the door for the dining room in the Priest's House which had Vita screaming: 'It's simply bloody, all studded with nails, Ye Olde Tea Shoppe with a vengeance!' Just to help fuel the fire Harold threw a suggestion for the courtyard wall across the Atlantic – he wanted niches along it for the busts by the German artist Hammann that had been done for something of a lark in Berlin. These were from wax masks done of him and his friends, including Eddy Sackville-West, David Herbert, Raymond Mortimer and Dorothy Wellesley (Vita would not have hers done because it entailed her face being completely coated with wax with a straw stuck up one nostril for breathing through!).[28] Sissinghurst's 'wall of heroes' must rank with another of Harold's suggestions – that the Bassin de Neptune at Versailles would have looked rather good in the Rondel!

The north courtyard wall ended up as a plain wall and the debate switched to the paving. It is difficult to realize it now, but the level at the entrance porch was much higher than at the foot of the Tower. Harold wanted a 9-foot wide stone terrace all along in front of the entrance range of buildings, but this meant a step down from flags to grass which would destroy the effect and usefulness of Vita's 'precious sweep' of paving from the entrance arch to the Tower arch, her tribute to the Green Court at Knole. The paving of the 'terrace' and 'sweep' would meet at mean angles. Harold analysed the problem as a matter of complex diplomacy.

The paved path against the barracks is giving me a great deal of thought. The difficulty is so to adjust the level and alignment of this path (which I myself visualize almost as a terrace) both to the level and to the alignment of the existing path from porch to tower.

I do not want in any way to destroy the effect of thoroughfare which the existing paving gives. On the other hand I am aware that the levels, as well as the angles, are awkward. The extreme solution would be to level the paving to the porch, then again to level the paving for nine feet after the porch, and hereafter to allow it to diverge at an obtuse angle, and on a definite slope, to where it meets the Tower Arch. This would entail two steps, one at the edge of the porch, and another at the place (nine feet further on) where the terrace edge ends and where the West–East pavement between the yews begins to run at an angle towards the tower.

Our eventual idea is to have a terrace or path running parallel to the barracks from North Wall to South Wall at a width of nine feet. We should want this terrace to be flush with the wall of the barracks except in so far as incidental gaps were allowed for present and eventual planting. We realize that this would entail a small retaining wall if it is to be level. We also realize that a difficulty would arise at the point where this terrace met the existing paved path from porch to tower. Either the existing thoroughfare will have to be levelled up to the line of the terrace (this entailing a step nine foot distant from the porch level) or else the existing slope would be retained, thus breaking the level of the terrace and making two sharp niches on each side. We also realize that a path or terrace of this width would draw sharp attention to the facade of the barracks themselves. This would be all to the good on the section north of the porch which, once the present scheme has been carried out, would be architecturally able to bear such confrontation. On the other hand the section of the barracks south of the porch is in a most disordered state. We do not wish to draw attention to it.

Thus for the moment we wish that the terrace (nine foot from the barracks) should only be built on the North Section of the Barracks – and that we should leave the South Section without any paving.

If a terrace is built against the facade of what will be the hall and the big room we shall be able to see whether it meets the present sloping paving from porch to tower at an intolerable angle and then to decide whether we shall level up that area of conjunction in the event of our continuing the paved terrace to the south end (opening upon the flower garden by an iron-work gate).

Thus What we want to do for the moment is the following:
(1) To construct a level path or terrace of York stone nine feet wide from the existing paving which runs from the porch to tower to a point where the new North Wall strikes the Barracks.
(2) To support this terrace on a retaining wall of brick of the height desired.
(3) Not to level the existing pathway to the level of this terrace but to leave a drop between the two in order that we may see how awful it looks.
(4) Not to continue the terrace beyond the porch but to leave the south section vague in

order to decide eventually whether the advantage of having a terrace running the whole length of the terrace (*sic*) is greater than the disadvantage of having a stone base to the muddle of the barrack facade south of the porch.

(5) To treat the north end of the courtyard in purely gardening, as opposed to architectural, terms:– i.e. to have a flower and fruit bed of five foot against the wall and a brick path of three foot as an edging running down to the door which will lead to the north cottage, and complemented by a similar path across front of S. Section of barrack to the gate into the Rose garden.[29]

This time he was to lose the battle, but not before A.R.P.'s concern for his clients' finer feelings had surfaced again: 'He was rather funny about this,' reported Vita to Harold, 'as he knew you were in favour of the step or rather that you felt one to be inevitable, and said "Now, how can we persuade him? Is he, by any chance frightened of fire?" – I was puzzled by this and asked what fire could possibly have to do with it. He said "Well, you see, we could point out to him that the fire engine from Cranbrook would be unable to reach the Tower as quickly if a step were in the way, while you were burning in your sitting room."'[30] They tested the problem by laying the stones down as Harold suggested to see the best, or worst, but in the end the steam-roller came in and ploughed the courtyard, re-levelled it and it was re-seeded [69]. Harold lost his 'terrace', and they simply made the wide border against the north wall with the narrow (too narrow?) stone path leading round to the gateways into the Priest's House garden and the Rondel Garden.

69. This photograph of the courtyard, taken from the Tower in 1936, shows the compromise that was reached to accommodate both the paving Harold wanted along the front of the entrance range of buildings and the continuous path, 'her precious sweep', that Vita wanted from the entrance arch to her Tower. This solution was made impossible by changes of level, so the whole courtyard was ploughed, re-levelled and re-seeded to achieve the result pictured here.

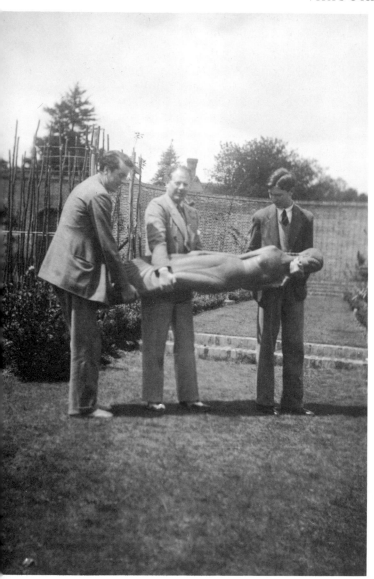

70. *(left)* Summer 1935: deciding where to put the Virgin – The Virgin, Ben, Harold and Francis Graham-Harrison in front of Powys's new west wall in the Rondel Garden.

71. *(above right)* September 1936: the paving being laid in the Lime Walk, then called the Spring Border.

72. *(below right)* Summer 1937: the newly planted yew hedges of the Rondel.

By the time all this was over it was obvious that A.R.P. was far from well, but he constantly thought about the goings-on at Sissinghurst and how he could help the Nicolsons: '... my wife grumbles because it causes me to sit silently'.[31] He was taken ill with an internal haemorrhage – overwork had overtaken him – and he died in

May 1936. He was only fifty-five. Vita wrote that he was such a maddening architect but such a nice man – 'now I shall not be able to feel cross any more every time I look at the sloping piers of the garden wall'. This wall, the west garden wall of the Rondel Garden, is Powys's memorial at Sissinghurst – it should always be called Powys's wall. Powys's wall gives form and presence to the Rondel Garden, which would have been a dismal space indeed with just a straight wall as Vita wanted. Its great semi-circular bay raises the garden to the status of a garden room of the finest pedigree – they must have realized that they were recreating the parterre of Villa Gamberaia in the textures of a colder clime. But when it was being built Vita was always so worried: 'Why so thick? Why sloped? Why not build an ordinary upright wall? The whole point of walls at Sissinghurst is that they are SLIM ... a great lumping elephant of a wall will look wrong.'[32] The situation was eventually smoothed over, she buried a 1935 penny in it, and the wall was finished off. As she admitted, with poor A.R.P.'s death she accepted it as part of Sissinghurst.

It is perhaps worth a brief moment to wonder just what would have happened had Harold and Vita had the money or desire to employ Lutyens. He was then finishing New Delhi and starting his *magnum opus*, the Roman Catholic Cathedral at Liverpool, but he did do small things (increasingly rather sad small things, such as the tombs of Miss Jekyll (1932) and Lady Cynthia Mosley (1933) and the Tennant monument at Rolvenden), and he was doing the fantasy Drum Inn at Cockington in Devon. Would he have made fantasy rather than mere virtue out of Sissinghurst's obtuseness? The old walls would have been clipped and finished in smooth cream stone, with elegant drooping curves at wall ends, stone door frames and garden doors of French lattice design. Would there have been free-standing pillars of brick and tile, classical screens (ornamented with Harold's busts?), gazebos, niches of plum-coloured brickwork that made the rosy pink exciting, circular steps and pools, and everywhere the seats with the breaking wave along their backs?[33] Sissinghurst *is* tame compared to Folly Farm or even Little Thakeham or The Hoo at Willingdon. But it *was* only a brief thought!

THUS in the thirties Sissinghurst was shaped into the Nicolson family home. It had more than a little unconventionality about it – parts were really spartan, but it was uniquely suited to the writers who lived there. Its special endearment is perhaps that it is a home *within* a garden rather than a home, as most are, with garden merely attached. Vita used to say frequently that Sissinghurst was *not* a winter resort. The lifestyle was idyllic in summer but demanded goodly amounts of English fortitude in the cold and the wet. When the faithful Copper[34] took the car to the entrance porch, Vita and Harold walked to South Cottage either via the Tower or the Rondel Garden, both routes crossing wet grass and skirting dripping plants. Presumably there was the chance of a nightcap in Harold's sitting room beside the fire, and hopefully there was a fire too in Vita's bedroom, where layers of Victorian wallpaper had been stripped (thus uncovering the fireplace) and the walls were bare bricks and the floor bare boards with a Persian rug. For breakfast they came down the Yew Walk, across the whole width of the garden, to the Priest's House dining room – the route that had also to be taken in the dark after dinner at night. As Vita said, 'it may be delightful to cross moonlit quadrangles on a warm summer evening on one's way to bed, but on snowy nights it is less agreeable'.[35] Harold also made the return journey to work in South Cottage; Vita braved the wind blowing through the Tower arch and went up to her writing room, with its one small radiator to combat the gales howling round the turret. Ben and Nigel were comfortable in the Priest's House; Ben felt that Sissinghurst was a perfect existence, and nowhere else to this day could be home for Nigel. As a family they came together over meals and for occasional gatherings, usually with visitors, in the Big Room, which was stripped of its stable fittings, panelled in oak and floored with old boards, some over two feet wide, and filled with Lady Sackville's treasures. The Big Room is Sissinghurst's only shadow of a 'show' room.

Earlier in this chapter I left them in 1932, the year they moved in: Harold was forty-five, Vita thirty-nine, Ben seventeen and Nigel fifteen. Vita's *Family History*[36] was published in the autumn; on 31 December Harold wrote: 'A lovely year for which I thank life heartily ... Sissinghurst has become for us the real home which we shall always love ...'[37] He and Vita were launched on a three-and-a-half-month trip to America, lecturing and partying in fifty-three cities and over 30,000 miles. 1933 and 1934 were both of a similar pattern – a lot of time at home writing in the summer with jaunts in the spring and autumn; Vita published her *Collected Poems* in autumn 1933 and *The Dark Island* in the autumn of 1934. In the November their senior dog, fourteen year-old Canute, had to be put to sleep, and he was buried, with sad ceremony, in the orchard. Harold was busy but unsettled; he wrote his book on Lord Curzon and spent a lot of time in America on *Dwight Morrow* – he found America alternately very exciting and very lonely. The highlight was a trip to Mexico, which he adored, sending a long and luscious description of a garden of small rooms, high walls, steep changes of level, pools and Gauguin planting back to Vita: '... the gardenias are selling like daffodils in April, there are violets, tuberoses, lilies, and in my room a great bowl of Bermuda lilies and a huge dish of violets, my dearest, how I wish you were here.'[38] As James Lees-Milne has discerned, Harold remained unsettled until the autumn of 1935, when he was elected as the Labour Member for West Leicester and found his spiritual home (apart from Balliol) in the House of Commons, where he was to be for the next ten years. 1936 was a nostalgic year – Lady Sackville died at the end of January and, a few months later, on going through her mother's belongings, Vita found the papers that enabled her to write *Pepita*. In August Harold returned to Clandeboye to research his book on Lord Dufferin, *Helen's Tower*; it made him profoundly depressed, mostly because he felt he had done so little in the twenty-five years that had gone since his last memories.[39] In the autumn of 1936 Harold became embroiled in the Abdication Crisis, and this began a period of heightened paradox wherein he became more and more involved in European politics and what we now know was the slide into war,[40] while Vita became more and more buried in Sissinghurst and the endless quiet days. During the long week-ends their two worlds met and they were serenely happy. The long week-ends were essential to both of them.

Vita left Sissinghurst less and less; her London season slipped into three hectic days around Christmas and she became a fat and indolent country lady. She hated dressing up in skirts, and perpetually wore her uniform of corduroy breeches and boots mixed with the most beautiful silk blouses and her rope of huge pearls, with cardigans hand-knitted from the wool of her own Jacob's sheep. 'Another quiet day at Sissinghurst' creeps more and more frequently into her letters; she had indeed, it seemed, slipped into the life that fitted her best, and her work (for now she did not write much though she gardened very hard) – her garden – repaid her by becoming uncompromisingly beautiful, rich and serene.

Those last summers before the war were when the visitors really started to come – there were requests from Women's Institutes, antiquarian societies, and a party of Baker relatives, and on 1 May 1938, at the suggestion of Mrs Christopher Hussey at Scotney Castle, the garden was advertised as 'open' on the yellow posters of the National Gardens Scheme for the first time. There is no doubt that in the eyes of those who saw it Sissinghurst was at its most beautiful then, in the face of war. Imagine it, with its vistas direct but not quite fulfilled, its pavings crisp and new but the exception rather than the rule, its beds and borders overflowing in a perfect delicate partnership between flowers planted and those arrived by chance, and over all an easiness and ease that comes from nature and the gardener working in a harmony of mutual respect. In the first of the pair of Bagatelle vases by the entrance the ram's horns are wreathed in purple violas; the rosemary in flower tumbles across the path; through the arch, past the carefree Irish yews, is the vista to another arch, another pair of vases and the blossom in the orchard beyond. The courtyard is serene and pretty with pots of lavender and more violas, but one feels there is a lot going on overhead; gables, chimneys, turrets and weathervanes rise into the blue, and the rather vivid (and new[41]) Sackville flag in black, red and yellow flies in the breeze. The grass is newly cut, but gently so by the old machine pulled by Gracie Fields the pony in her leather boots.[42]

In the Rondel Garden the tiny rondel is but a green toy (but the earliest of the Rev. Pemberton's hybrid musk roses, 'Danae', *was* in bloom on 1 May 1938 and the glossy fountains of her sisters were getting ready too); the iris spikes and flowers of purple and gold pressed over the grass paths, and inside the east wall of the garden the herbaceous border is a model of expectant neatness at that happy moment *just* before staking is necessary. In Harold's Lime Walk the edges of the new and narrow Montessori path are awash with a hundred shades of blue and yellow, muscari, primroses, scillas and white-winged jonquils; his newly acquired oil jars and terracotta pots are filled with red tulips. The Nut Plat, as Vita now likes to call it, is that never-to-be-forgotten sight of the rainbow polyanthus carpet edge to edge. The moat is cool and still and slightly overgrown. The orchard has paths cut through nodding grasses and fritillaries and is noisy with birdsong and blossoms in all shades of pink. It is just becoming the wild garden of their dreams – wide green paths with

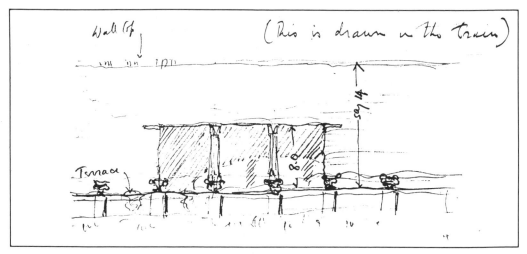

73. The Nicolsons' architect, A. R. Powys, spent much of the last eighteen months of his life worrying over what was happening at Sissinghurst and how he could best help two people he had become very fond of: ''Tis odd – or may be 'tis odd – how every now and again some work or some human relationship takes a hold of me and goes on talking in my head,' he wrote to Vita on 27 March 1935. More of his ideas were used than he is usually given credit for – this sketch is contained in a letter about the north wall of the entrance courtyard, where he wanted to include 'a cave' with classical supports for outdoor dining – it is essentially the Erectheum, subsequently built in the corner of the Priest's House garden.

74. The Erectheum as a lunch venue: June 1937. Vita and Ben are with Harold's sister, Gwen St Aubyn, and her daughters Jessica and Philippa.

bosky banks and tangles of wild roses, with drifts of iris, narcissus and white foxgloves 'but not real garden stuff'. There was of course no White Garden to draw the gasps, only beds of roses and delphiniums – planted for the later effect of the Tower seen rising from their spikes. The last picture is of Delos – in Vita's words – 'small irises come through mats of aubretia and thyme, and the myrobalam plum trees overhead are white with blossom' that tumbles on to the ranks of old stones, treasures from Sissinghurst and treasures from Clandeboye.[43]

There are only two more things that need to be said here. The first is that Vita was by now something of an expert on roses. Her mentor at this time was the epicure and expert Edward Ashdown Bunyard,[44] with whom she loved to talk about roses and good things to eat. A notable lunch she had regaled him with in January 1937 consisted of Indian corn on the cob, woodcock on a croûton with pâté de foie and truffles, Clos Vougeot 1911 and a cigar – 'then we went out and talked about roses for the rest of the afternoon. I ordered recklessly.'[45] Edward Bunyard was full of enjoyable wisdom on vines, peaches, mangetout, apple cucumbers, yellow fruit tomatoes, sorrel, red cabbage, aubergines, squashes and pumpkins – both the growing of them and the enjoying. To Vita unusual vegetables were a *very* enjoyable hobby; Sissinghurst was also very fruitful – besides apples for eating and for cider, pears, crabs, quince and all soft fruits, she would have been very disappointed if she had not had at least one of their own figs, nectarines, peaches or bunches of grapes in the silver fruit bowl every day. To return to Mr Bunyard: it must have amused Vita greatly to be able to show the author of the classic book *Old Garden Roses* a rose he did not know, for Vita had found, among the brambles and nettles, the vigorous suckers of an old rose that produced the most dramatic flowers – plum-coloured petals, almost maroon, with magenta crimson edges and pinky magenta reverses and golden stamens. It was decided that it was a *gallica*, 'Rosa des Maures', and it was given the name 'Sissinghurst Castle' and blooms there still.

The last words in this chapter belong to Harold. On 8 June 1937 he wrote to Vita:

> ... never has Sissinghurst looked more lovely ... Farley[46] has made it look like a gentleman's garden, and you with your extraordinary taste have made it look like nobody's garden but your own. I think the secret of your gardening is simply that you have the courage to abolish ugly or unsuccessful flowers. Except for those beastly red-hot pokers which you have a weakness for, there is not an ugly flower in the whole place. Then I think, si j'ose m'exprimer ainsi, that the design is really rather good. I mean, we have got what we wanted to get – a perfect proportion between the classical and romantic, between the element of expectation and the element of surprise. Thus the main axes are terminated in a way to satisfy expectation, yet they are in themselves so tricky they also cause surprise. But the point of the garden will not be apparent until the hedges have grown up, especially (most important of all) the holly hedge in the flower garden. But it is lovely, lovely, lovely – and you must be pleased with your work.[47]

1 October 1938 was their silver wedding. Harold did nothing because Vita didn't like that sort of thing, but wrote in his diary: 'I say a little private prayer of thanksgiving to Demeter, who I feel is the most appropriate person to receive it.'[48]

7

THE WAR AND 'THE GARDEN' 1939-45

> ... I tried to hold the courage of my ways
> In that which might endure,
> Daring to find a world in a lost world,
> A little world, a little perfect world,
> With owlet vision in a blinding time,
> And wrote and thought and spoke
> These lines, these modest lines, almost demure,
> What time the corn still stood in sheaves,
> What time the oak
> Renewed the million dapple of her leaves.
> V. Sackville-West, *The Garden*[1]

T HE paradox of the new-born Sissinghurst's blossoming in the face of war symbolized a feeling common to all those who loved their countryside and gardens or just peace itself. The soldier poet Henry Reed later gave the symbol its lilt of terror:

> Today we have naming of parts. Yesterday,
> We had daily cleaning. And tomorrow morning,
> We shall have what to do after firing. But today,
> Today we have naming of parts. Japonica
> glistens like coral in all of the neighbouring gardens,
> And today we have naming of parts.[2]

He spoke for the thousands of young men drilling on village greens or town squares and the thousands watching them, as well as for some who would come to drill in

75. *The Garden: Summer*, p. 112:

> And set the axis of your garden plan
> In generous vistas reaching to a bourn
> Far off, yet visible ...

Vita's 'precious sweep' of the pathway from the entrance to the Tower and beyond. The vista is temporarily closed by the hayrick made from cutting the courtyard and Tower lawns.

This series of photographs (75–81), taken by Christopher Hussey, comes from those taken for articles on Sissinghurst by Vita which were printed in *Country Life* on 28 August and 4 and 11 September 1942; they therefore illustrate Sissinghurst both in wartime and as a background to *The Garden*.

the courtyard at Sissinghurst. For Harold and Vita the paradox was different but not less apt; Harold would not have to go to war but he was a fighting politician, and he was fighting in the thin ranks that shared the despair of Anthony Eden with the policy of Appeasement and mistrusted the Munich Agreement. Throughout the last half of 1938 and the first half of 1939 he was only ever at Sissinghurst for the briefest week-ends, but as he stared out of his South Cottage window waiting for the right words to come, or paced the Lime Walk (and perhaps occasionally did some weeding), the garden bore the brunt of his deepest fears. He examined his motives over and over again, but at the bottom of them all he feared that Hitler had a blatant cause and a belief – we would but be fighting to preserve the *status quo*, 'which was neither so noble nor inspiring'.[3] His private *status quo* was in front of his eyes, basking in the sun, white lilies and yellow musk roses, the dappled carpet of the primroses beneath the hazels, M. and Mme Pochard and their young flotilla rippling the moat – how could these fragilities, which were all the world to him, be worth a world war?

Vita embodied the other half of the paradox, and from her seclusion at Sissinghurst she was gathering strength. Her intention to submerge herself into her little world, into 'her birthright far from present fashion', had been clearly enough notified in her poem *Sissinghurst* in 1931, and now she had done it. There was probably much of Virginia Woolf's own depression in her bitter description of the fat and indolent country lady with tomato cheeks and black moustache that no longer cared for books or poetry and 'only kindles about dogs, flowers and new buildings' ... But undeniably Virginia must have felt the loss of the vibrant, aristocratic Vita of her fascination. It was also partly true, as Victoria Glendinning has written, that after Lady Sackville's death in early 1936 and the writing out of the Spanish gypsy side of her personality in *Pepita*, the 'English conservative side' of Vita's nature could take over and allow her to become a middle-aged English lady.[4] Vita, however, was worth rather more than jams, pickles and charity bazaars; she had come full circle from the calm and stolid girl with 'deep stagnant gaze' whom Violet Keppel had met when she was ten, the Vita who talked wholly of dogs and rabbits, but she had learned a tremendous amount in the circling. Was it not merely that this new Vita, who grew as Sissinghurst grew in the 1930s, had asserted values that were rather different from those of Bloomsbury sets and drawing rooms? The actual building and beginning of the castle and the garden was the basis of all her thoughts and doings up until that summer of 1937; Harold's 'thank you' letter to Vita for his garden, their garden which had so enchanted his West Leicester constituency ladies, and his admission that they had got what they wanted in their alliance of classical lines and romantic flowers, seemed to mark the end of the building phase. Vita settled within herself and into her routine. During the first three months of 1938, however, she became increasingly ill with recurring gastritis which was complicated by pleurisy. The cause was diagnosed as lead poisoning, traced to the apple crusher that made Sissinghurst's house cider. Cleaned out and slimmed down, she came home from hospital just in time to supervise the great *'travaux publiques'* necessary to get ready for the 800 visitors of that first official opening on 1 May 1938. She was also armed with Kingsley Martin's request for regular 'Country Notes' for the *New Statesman*, and it is in the first of these pieces, 'A Country Life', that she explains herself:

> Living in the country as I do, I sometimes stop short to ask myself where the deepest pleasure is to be obtained from a rural life, so readily derided as dull by the urban-minded. When I stop short like this, it is usually because some of my metropolitan friends have arrived to ruffle my rustic peace with the reverberations of a wider world. They ask me if I have seen this or that play, these or those pictures, and always I find myself obliged to reply that I have not. This makes me appear, and feel, a boor. Then after this most salutary visit they drive off, back to London, and the peace and the darkness close down upon me once more, leaving me slightly disturbed but on the whole with an insulting sense of calm superiority.[5]

She was certainly not oversure that she was right – her letters to Harold are recurringly on the theme of Oh, what a dull and quiet life I lead, the things I talk about must bore you when your life is so exciting – but 1938 and the growing inevitability of war cured her doubts. She was forced to believe in everyone doing the best they could: '. . . if one means to be a good little sweet pea (in your phrase),' she wrote to Harold, 'one must be the best sweet pea one can . . .'[6] Vita's best was to fight for the world, the little world, that she believed in, both for Harold's support and for the inspiration of a wider world, and she did it the only way she could, in prose and poetry. Her *Country Notes* and *Country Notes in Wartime* were the first salvos of her war effort, and they are in the first rank of centuries of writing about the English countryside.

Vita had never been one to go around with her eyes shut, but now her perception was sharpened to a pitch and what she saw with her eyes she spotlighted with an equally intense inward vision. 'I suppose the pleasure of country life lies really in the eternally renewed evidence of the determination to live – if you have a taste for such things, no amount of repetition can stale them.'[7] She had her taste for such things. The first lambs, the pushing crocus, the new shoots of hornbeam that banished the dead leaves from the hedge, such things were now her inspiration and her satisfaction and they filled the routine of her quiet days.

At Sissinghurst breakfast was at nine; if she had done as she so often chided herself for doing and gone back to sleep after waking with the dawn chorus, she would emerge from South Cottage only in time to wander through the orchard on the way to breakfast. At this first viewing of the day it was the smaller miracles that caught her eye – the economy of the witch hazel, 'little bunches of yellow ribbons, with the ends snipped short and a maroon button at the base' of each bunch. They had the spare precision of a Chinese drawing that exactly suited the brown earth and grey sky – 'They have style.'[8] She loved the naked beauty of winter, the wild wet skies and bare trees and cart ruts full of water in January – which she regarded ideally as the month for thick shoes, the dogs at her heels and the wind in her face.

After breakfast she saw her post, then retired to her Tower to write, coming down well in time for some fresh air and another look round before lunch at one. February frost kept her amused, she traced the leafy veinings on her window panes with the tip of her finger, which sent 'correspondent filaments of cold up the veining of one's arm',[9] and then wandered down to the moat: '. . . there is still a film of ice over shady stretches of water, so thin that by midday the breasts of the ducks cut with a brittle tinkling sound through it like miniature ice-breakers.'[10] She cheerfully endured winter (with Sissinghurst's generous gulps of fresh air between meals, its draughts and exposure to north-east winds) in the cause of her soul, until 1 March. After that she got very impatient for spring, and of the two things that would make her get up really early, one was to catch the fair delusion of spring; to find the clear light of a spring dawn and the first delicate flowers standing out with peculiar brilliance – blue anemones, minute narcissus, inch-high saxifrage, with their 'childish heads' lifted to the roughest weather. The other thing that ensured she would be out first was fresh snow; with the uncertainty of our vacillating winter and spring around March and April she found an answering contrariness, often regretting that moments of 'such fantastic beauty' as this were gone for another year:

> There was the moment when the aviary full of brightly coloured parakeets turned into a cave of snow, the purest snow driven against the wire netting, making a roof and walls of simple whiteness. Against this whiteness the blue, yellow, and green of the birds showed up with such brilliance that they might have been flood-lit. No painter but Van Gogh could have splashed them on to canvas.[11]

Sissinghurst afternoons were for quiet writing in winter and visitors to the garden in summer. After tea about fourish, and the visitors with luck discarded, Vita would either work in the garden (the gardeners left it to her alone at five) or take the dogs for a walk. Her large alsatians were perhaps the most in evidence of Sissinghurst's residents; they were completely devoted to her, knowing that their freedom depended upon her being there and that the screwing of the cap back on her fountain pen was the signal to be off! She wrote several pieces about the characters of her dogs. She was capable of being the most sentimental dog-lover over their abilities (Martin could manage the door catches himself), she was amused by them, and she was also captivated by their beauty – the pale and silvery puppy surveying the landscape from a window 'like a ghost dog mounting guard in the casement of some rose-red Pre-Raphaelite manor'. Her dogs were her most constant companions. She walked them down to the lake and in Roundshill Park Wood and back again, and it was probably often their discoveries that gave her her copy.[12] She, or they, encountered the earth-pig, with leaves and bits of moss from his winter sleep home still on his prickles – 'his ancient and truly indigenous appearance unchanged since he walked with Piltdown man'[13] giving him a dignity that neither badger nor rabbit could share – certainly not the rabbit, 'that upstart foreigner who claims, with more justification than most of our aristocracy, to have arrived on these shores with William the Conqueror'.[14] They found a shrew 'with a fury of energy enough to do credit to any dictator' and a mole with very sharp teeth – 'as you will learn if you attempt to pick him up' – which perhaps she tried to rescue from the dogs, getting her fingers bitten in the process!

Her entrenchment emphasized her squirishness, and expressed itself in her attitudes and her land hunger; if this was compensation for Knole, which she now hardly ever saw, at least it was put to creative use. Castle Farm, which they had bought with the castle, included the fields beside the drive to the road and those beyond the orchard and the farmyard to the north-east. But Vita liked to walk on her own land and she was a good walker, needing space; she felt that stocks and shares were boring and that the family trust funds put away for Ben and Nigel would be much more enjoyable used for, and would not be at all threatened by, buying land. Her first purchase was forty acres of fields and young orchards adjoining their Bettenham boundary, which included a long stretch of the Hammer stream and a chain of ponds, and gave her a good two-hour walk without going off Sissinghurst property. On the strength of this she wrote a short piece called *Buying a Farm*, in which she admitted that her 'absurd pleasure' in owning land came simply from her love for fields and orchards 'so much that I want to feel them safely mine'. This ancient healthy attitude was then as rare as frost in May, and her further concern 'that all hedges shall be properly slashed, laid and trimmed in a workmanlike manner, nor the size or shape of any field be rendered different without my consent' marks her as one of the vanishing breed of caring landowners. In November 1940 she bought another 110 acres at Brissenden, farther north still, for £5,000, and they could walk a little farther. Then, immediately, she got very excited over Hammer Mill Farm on the other side of the Biddenden to Sissinghurst village road, which had lots of woods and orchards. Old maps had told her that the original Sissinghurst estate had been 2,000 acres – with Hammer Mill they would have recovered almost 950 of them. Harold was indulgent – 'Bless you, my dear chatelaine, I love to feel that more Kentish land passes under your wise and understanding control' – but also practical: he warned her not to go above 1,000 acres as land owned above that figure might well be nationalized. Sadly, Vita had to forego Hammer Mill (the price of £12,000 was far too high) and that was the end of her spree.

But her little world had become larger, and her scope was extended. She used to go up and talk to the gypsies when they came to cut hazel in Roundshill Park Wood, and her daily *tours de propriétaire* were definitely to keep an eye on who was working where and what they were doing, even though the farm management was entirely in the hands of Ozzie Beale. She would walk up to the woods with the timber merchant, bargaining as they went. He wanted Scotch pine and tentatively inquired whether she would sell the stand that had set itself on that hill. He loved trees, that was why he worked with them; he was rather relieved when she flatly refused, and understood that some things were 'beyond business'. On that basis they agreed on lesser specimens that could go, to be planked for him and lopped and topped for cordwood to be carted home for Sissinghurst fires. The picture was completed on a winter's day when Vita watched the hunt from her Tower:

> ... they found their fox ... when to my delight he had the sense to bolt straight into my own private woodland where the hunt is forbidden to follow ... I reflected, not without pleasure, on what my neighbours must be saying about me. Nothing would disturb the fox now, so long as he remained where he was, nothing worse than the big waggon lumbering down to bring in the cordwood for my fires.[15]

Understandably, that timber waggon was one of her favourite sights, and she paints it as Brueghel would have done – lumbering 'across a picture as black and white as a photograph after the first fall of snow, the team pulling sturdily, the men trudging alongside, their upright whips drawn delicately against the sky'. In just those two images she had summed up her countrywoman's understanding – the men and the horses were earning a living, her wood was keeping her warm and providing an escape route for the hunted fox; she knew full well that he was the same fiend that she had caught coming up to the garden at noon the day before after her chicken, but she had very definite views about 'live and let live' and 'fair game'.

These she had got from her father, Lord Sackville. He had hated blood sports, deer shoots in particular, but had not had the courage to stop them, for they paid a lot of wage packets. She remembered how they would stand, he with his gun at the ready, and with an unspoken understanding between them of what was to be done.

> We both liked the woods; we liked the sounds, the bracken, the birches; we never talked much; even the dogs stayed quiet – then ... would come the sound of the beaters, then the suspense, then peering round the tree trunk the first elegant head, the bright eyes, the tiny horns, the active arrested hooves, searching for escape down the familiar ways. Then he, – taking apparently careful aim, – would fire and a scamper of feet would follow. How had he managed to miss? The fruitless report must have scared all deer for a mile round. Yet he was generally considered as a very good shot![16]

Much the same behaviour attended their fishing expeditions, when after much preparation and a very brief struggle the small, cold prey was returned from whence it came. In memory of happy times with her father Vita made an expedition to London to buy herself a fishing rod. Home again, with a calm warm evening, bats and flies about, a happy sort of evening to pull a trout, she went down to the lake and found herself confronted by a large wet sheep.

> The poor thing had been driven into the water by a dog – my own dog, suddenly gone gay. Fortunately it was also one of my own sheep, one of that unusual horned variety known as Jacob's sheep, so that I need feel no sense of guilt or apprehension towards an injured farmer. I did, however, feel a sense of responsibility towards the animal itself and rowed towards it in a spirit of rescue, discovering then (not for the first time) how very difficult it is to help animals in distress, so profound and instinctive is their mistrust of one's good intentions. Alarmed by my approach it made efforts to swim, and indeed did very nobly as a swimmer, crossing the lake as I rowed after it, swimming desperately in the effort to escape me whom it took to be yet another enemy. I caught it up on the farther shore, where it stuck in the shallows, enabling me to lasso it neatly round the horns with the boat's painter; I had no other rope, so had to sacrifice the painter with my knife. We sat contemplating one another, the sheep and I, I still wishing to fish but

entangled instead with this poor tiresome creature, unwillingly looped to it by a rope, faced by the need of getting it safely back to land. It looked at me with vacant eyes; seldom had I seen so unhelpful a victim. We stared at one another, and as we stared it sank lower and lower, getting wetter and wetter, until its fleece billowed out like a Victorian bathing-dress filling with water, floating on the surface in woolly flounces half buoyant, half sodden. Its long tail drifted on the surface behind it, an absurd sausage. I tugged at the rope hoping to tow it back to shore, but the beast, apparently intent on frustrating my friendly purpose, wrapped its forelegs round a stump of old willow and could not or would not be budged. I sat back in the boat thinking how ticklish a problem it was ever to help people out of their private difficulties, the sheep meanwhile continuing to contemplate me with the same vacant unhelpful eyes. I tugged again; rolled up my sleeve; sank my arm to the elbow; grasped the all too muscular forelegs; succeeded in unwinding them from the stump; and eventually rowed off with the sheep in tow, a ludicrous rodeo that ended in landing the most unexpected fish I ever caught.[17]

VITA could be very funny about places she really loved, and had an ability to laugh at herself. But the lake, the lake that Harold had made as his first dream fulfilled at Sissinghurst, had always delighted them both. For Vita it had revealed

> ...a whole region of wildlife I had never known before: water birds, water insects, water plants and the general peacefulness of water life. There are few things to compare with this tranquillity ... whether at dawn, midday, sunset or midnight, whether spring, summer, autumn or winter ... few things so well adapted to repair the cracked heart, the jangled temper or the uneasy soul. The very reflection of trees in the water suggests how true and untrue life may be ... solid oak – mirrored reflection – the one no more convincing than the other ...[18]

The lake was many things to her, and she went there often, sometimes regretful of feeling so far removed from the world, but always reassured that its beauty was right. The lake was also where she met another adversary, the lordly Jack Heron. She had become very cross with his indiscriminate strewing of her mangled trout on the lake banks. The locals were at a loss to know why she didn't shoot him and looked at her pityingly; she had contemplated shooting and *paying* the £5 fine to square her conscience, but it did not dispose of her conviction that if the law troubled to protect the heron it meant that he needed protection and she would regret it if he disappeared. In the end she did nothing and lost interest in fishing; 'live and let live' posed constant dilemmas that kept her thinking, rather as some of her escapades had done.

Besides being beautiful the Sissinghurst estate was also supremely productive; fuel, flowers, vegetables, fruits, honey, eggs, milk, fish and fowl, sheep and home knitteds. Vita must have been very early in the fashion for Jacob's sheep – the romance and mystery of them undoubtedly appealed to her, with their supposed descent from the 'ringstreaked, speckled and spotted flocks' which Jacob had tended in the land of Laban and the crusaders had brought back from the Holy Land. But she also liked them for their hardiness and for the pleasure of watching them being shorn so that the wool could be sent off to Scotland for cleaning and dyeing. Even more exciting was the return package of orange, green, red and purple bundles, which were then knitted into cardigans for her and jumpers for the boys.

Those same Jacob's sheep who gambolled in the calf orchard and delighted the garden visitors in May 1938 were putting on their first winter coats when Sissinghurst was being fitted up with a gas-proof room (the Big Room with asbestos sheets over the windows and the cracks in the door filled with putty) and the residents were being fitted for their gas masks. Vita wrote of a 'calm resignation' in being part of a corporate body called England, 'not merely England but all those whose ideals and principles are at the moment similar', and the strings of her being tuned to a pitch – she hoped that they would not snap. In her Country Note she recorded September 1938 going down

> in a slanting golden sun, touching our familiar landscapes with a light so rich and mellow as to preclude all suggestions of irony. It seemed, indeed, inconceivable that devastation should fall suddenly on such a scene. Looking across the harmless, sunlit hills, the mind rejected the concept of violence ... We dug trenches in the orchard ... This sudden hasty burrowing into the earth struck one as truly horribly uncivilized: man seeking refuge from an enemy under the peacefully ripening apples and pears ...[19]

Even in winter Sissinghurst persisted –

> Last night was so beautiful – a very clear sky with stars and a full moon. The Pleaides were perching like a flight of birds on the weathercock of the tower, white mist was rising from the lake cutting off everything but the tops of the trees in the wood. I went down to the lake and the swans sailed majestically towards me. As usual, I had not bread.[20]

On 15 February 1939: '... it has been so lovely again today, I walked up through the wood and the primroses were coming out' ... On 27 February: 'I have discovered a pink magnolia which we simply must have – in a hundred years hence someone will come across it growing in the ruins of the tower – the tower having been brought down by high explosive bombs in 1940 and say "someone must have cared for this place".' She kept Harold going with her love and her insistence on the beauty of it all, and, of course, his flowers went back with him after every week-end and were renewed throughout the week – 15 March from him: 'I see all the lovely flowers around me that you sent and I think of the spring and I feel sorrow in my soul that the world should be so safe for lunatics.' Throughout the summer the tension mounted, and the sadness; in July they started air raid rehearsals at Sissinghurst – '... it all seems so crazy as though the human race has lost its reason – then, irrationally I go out and consider the regale lilies and feel better or encouraged.' Harold felt wretched about the real world but perfectly happy about his inner world – 'Sissinghurst alone with you always puts me back fair and square upon my assiette.' He instructed her to have the Buick ready always, with food for twenty-four hours, and to take her jewels, the diaries, some clothes, Gwen and the Coppers and escape to Devon, should Hitler invade Kent. Vita decided she would not leave and miss all the flowers, and of course she never did. (However, they had their suicide pills from a Swiss doctor friend in case the Germans did come.) In

August Vita described the belated haysel: '... all crops seem to come to fruition at once: the corn, the apples and the hops. These things happen every year but this year one notices them more keenly than usual ...' And on that fine September morning she walked down the path to where Harold was sitting outside South Cottage in the sun, and said 'It has begun.'[21]

Her first reaction was one of protection towards the Sissinghurst world; both her prose and later her poetry have a special value, written from the home front at the moment when it seemed certain that the fields of Kent would be Hitler's invasion path to London, and those same fields and gardens lay submissively beneath the mistakes and casualties of the battles overhead. In that first autumn of terrible suspense she wrote of the blackout:

> I could imagine nothing more desirable and mysterious than these black secret nights, were it not for sinister intention behind them. I suppose that one should not allow the intention to impair one's appreciation of this new beauty of the starry night. The moon has gone, and nothing but stars and three planets remain within our autumn sky. Every evening I go my rounds like some night watchman to see the blackout is complete. It is. Not a chink reveals the life going on beneath those roofs, behind those blinded windows: love, lust, death, birth, anxiety, even gaiety ... Alone I wander, no one knowing that I prowl ... I might be a badger or a fox ... I think of all the farms and cottages spread over England sharing this curious protective secrecy where not even a night-light may show from the room of a dying man or a woman in labour ... The blackout is inconvenient to the men drying the hops – I stroll round to the oasts and find one door left open beneath the shadow of the stageing. They have hung a green silk scarf over the central lamp so that the glaucous light of the under-seas tinges the lime-washed walls to the very colour of the hops themselves. War brings an unforeseen strangeness to these small interiors of illumination.[22]

Her England seemed to hang suspended during the heat haze of that glorious summer of 1940, waiting ...

> ... day after day of sunshine ... There is a softness about the air, a scent of musk and hay, a scent borne from the great white lilies to the tumbling roses. It has seemed for weeks as though the weather must break ... the monotony of beauty has married itself to the suspense in which we live. Only a few sharp showers have interrupted our anxiety about the drought. A countryman expressed himself as one coining a new proverb ... 'Hitler and the rain will come together.'[23]

> In these days I find, one readily interprets the happenings of Nature into symbolism. One clings to the permanence and recurrence of Nature. It is a calming and reassuring thought ... yet Nature is a nasty cruel thing. I had an example of it when I watched a small horrifying sight: the wounded frog mesmerized by the power of the adder's head which kept shooting out at it – not daring to turn to me for rescue – I thought of Roumania and Greece, with the spiteful tongue shooting out towards them.[24]

> I know the other morning when I awoke, aroused not only by the first square of dawn beyond my window but also by the thrum of engines overhead, I looked out on a world so fair that the grief attendant on that hour dissolved into what was almost a rejoicing in

the union of tragedy and beauty. It suggested a mythological marriage between light and darkness: the pale nymph of the English dawn lying still virginal and unravished before the Wagnerian wooing of Wotan. A thin and milky mist drifted across the trees, a huge pale lemon moon still moved suspended in the morning sky. A few stars still showed ... those few great stars which had travelled from darkness into daylight seemed to me symbols of the faint home persisting into dawn. The weak had extinguished; the strong remained.

I should like the German war-lords to be swallows on the wire observing our panic-stricken rural population. The morning begins without interruption. One is allowed one's breakfast in peace. Then towards midday the local siren goes off, setting up its banshee plaint across the fields. The English genius for understatement has already given it various nicknames: Moaning Mollie, Wailing Willie, Tiresome Timmy ... people engaged in their normal occupations of harvesting, hoeing, fruit-picking, cock their ears for a moment to listen, and then say, 'there's that thing again' and return to their ploy ... We do not pay much attention to the cyrene in the country ... then the planes arrive. They fly overhead in a great flight like geese, and people looking up from the fields wonder vaguely whether they are Germans or ours. We then observe that one goose has become detached from the flight and that two fighters are tumbling round in the summer sky. Machine guns crackle. The goose wavers in its flight; it banks, it sinks; it is wounded; its great wings flap; we hear it has come down at Appledore ten miles away. The air-warden was a naturalist – to her the dog-fights were 'just like butterflies' so far removed from reality.[25]

The gardening papers have all been urging us not to neglect our flowers in favour of our vegetables ... man cannot live by potatoes and onions alone! There is much to be said for this argument, though the more practical man might reply that sufficient beauty may be found supplied by Nature without cost or labour in a copse crammed with bluebells, wind-flowers, foxgloves with a dash of wild crab and honeysuckle thrown in amongst the shadows of the wood. True. We need but walk out into our woods to find compositions of loveliness which no gardener can rival ... [but our shrubs and trees represent] not only years of careful cultivation, but also the endurance and knowledge of wandering botanists in distant and difficult countries [and we cannot let these go].[26]

Because I was restless and had no desire to seek the sleep which would certainly have eluded me, I went down to the lake where the black water gave me a sense of deepest peace ... the moon gave no reflection into the darkened waters. The only things which gleamed and glowed were the water-lilies, whitely resting on the black pool. Taking the boat out, I cut the milky stalks of the lilies in the moonlight, and as I did so, drifting aeroplanes appeared over the lake, chased by the angular beams of searchlights, now lost, now found again; now roaring out, now silent, traceable only by their green and red lights sliding between the stars. A fox barked at them, like something in a fable curiously up to date. I tried to compose the fable for myself, something which would combine the fox, the lilies, and the white bodies of the young men up there aloft, but nothing neat would come to me although in that lonely hour I felt that they were all invested with an extraordinary significance. I remembered how many years ago, I had first seen an aeroplane flying by night ... like a planet broken loose ... this time it was with a different dismay that I watched the lights above, the fan-like sticks of the searchlights, the tumbling acrobatics of the pursued. The fox barked again, and carrying the inert lily buds I made my way across the field. The homely weapon of the scythe shone all along the blade where I had left it hanging among the fruit.[27]

On this basis and in these moods Sissinghurst adapted to the war. Harold came home for snatched week-ends when he could; the able-bodied had all gone, and Vita was left ruling a little world of women, children and landgirls. Her white pigeons, like magnolia flowers, flew off she knew not where and her precious budgerigars could not be fed; the lawns and the orchard were left to grow and cut for hay, and the weeds took over the flower borders. The army used her Tower as a lookout; Ben and Nigel became a prey to danger. In December of 1940 she agreed to meet Violet, who was home for the war, and her emotional security was shattered; this, combined with Dorothy Wellesley's alcoholism which had taken her beyond Vita's help, and then Virginia Woolf's suicide in March 1941, brought Vita to the end of her first campaign. Poetry was all she could turn to now ...

> Yet shall the garden with the state of war
> Aptly contrast, a miniature endeavour
> To hold the graces and the courtesies
> Against a horrid wilderness. The civil
> Ever opposed the rude, as centuries'
> Slow progress laboured forward, then the check,
> Then the slow uphill climb again, the slide
> Back to the pit, the climb out of the pit,
> Advance, relapse, advance, relapse, advance,
> Regular as the measure of a dance:[28]

Most of Vita's major works of fiction, non-fiction and poetry were written especially for, or because of, another person or place. Her dedications, whether to Harold, her mother, Knole or an unidentified lover, hold the keys to nearly all her writings. *The Garden* is the exception. She wrote *The Garden* for herself. There is an interesting comparison with Richard Jefferies that I would like to draw here: Edward Thomas, considering the vivid word pictures of country life in *Wild Life in a Southern County*, written when Jefferies was in his early thirties, says:

> All through the book he sees things ... as they are, without tinge of pastoral or other sentiment; he mentions his dreaming in summer, or standing to muse in an early spring night ... but he mentions it with no dimmest hint as yet of what those dreams are to bring forth, and he is silent as to what he dreamed or mused. The importance of those brief mystic moments may not yet have come home to him, or he may have felt that the dreams had no place in such a book. He remembers his shooting, and bird watching, and roaming, and his talks with farmers ... And he waits.[29]

Vita too was in her early thirties when she wrote her word pictures of country life in *The Land*; she had thought she could follow her observations up with her dreams and had started her poem about gardens six months after finishing *The Land*. But it

76. *(above) The Garden: Winter*, p. 57:

> Neglect may hold a beauty of her own;
> Neglected gardens in these years of war
> When the fond owner wandered as a ghost
> Only in thought . . .

The garden of South Cottage.

77. *(opposite) The Garden*, p. 14:

> Yet shall the garden with the state of war
> Aptly contrast, a miniature endeavour
> To hold the graces and the courtesies
> Against a horrid wilderness.

The break in the herbaceous border and the gate on to the Tower lawn.

would not come and she too had to wait. Jefferies, under the pressure of ill-health and poverty, managed his dreams in his autobiography *The Story of My Heart*, published after four years of waiting; Vita, with her health beginning to worry her (especially pains in her back) but with the greater pressure of war, wrote her dreams, all her 'beliefs and unbeliefs' into *The Garden*.

The Garden does have a dedication, a poem in its own right, dedicated to Vita's friend of these years, Katharine Drummond, who was the wife of General Lawrence Drummond of Sissinghurst Place. Katharine Drummond was a lady of indomitable spirit and youth, and she was a great gardener, even though she was confined to a wheelchair when Vita knew her; Vita found in her the maternal wisdom, the secret of the art of growing old with grace and without bitterness, that she felt she could not grasp herself. In a way Mrs Drummond had taken on some of the roles of Knole:

> You loved me too, as I like to think;
> I felt your love as a benediction
> In tranquil branches above me spread,
> Over my sometimes troubled head,
> A Cedar of Lebanon, dark as ink,
> And grave as a valediction.[30]

The whole of *The Garden* is a dialogue between practical and fantastical things, between reality and dreams, a sort of shuttlecock diplomacy between Vita's outer experiences and inner thoughts. She jumps straight in with her wellington boots, into the compost, dung, blood and bones that serve 'the digger and his clod' and are the foundations of garden beauty; then, by the end of the stanza, she has lifted the sense by introducing the robin that perches where he can watch every gardener . . .

> . . . for limitations rule
> Robins and men about their worms and wars,
> The robin's territory; and man's God.

That word 'God' carries all the weight of the preceding sixteen lines (which run without a full stop) and it is a recurring device in the poem. She weaves hard work and good husbandry with a constant emphasis on how necessary they are to hold the balance of grace and courtesy against the wilderness, and how therapeutic they are for dispersing fears and nightmares; *but*

> The gardener half artist must depend
> On that slight chance, that touch beyond control
> Which all his paper planning will transcend;
> He knows his means but cannot rule his end:
> He makes the body: who supplies the soul?

The Garden is a poem of many facets – of memories, dreams, good sound advice and good gardening taste, but it is also Vita's search for a belief. She returns immediately to the theme of the blackout, but this time she turns it into herself and her darkened room:

> A tomb of life not death,
> Life inward, true,
> Where the world vanishes
> And you are you.

> War brings this seal of peace,
> This queer exclusion,
> This novel solitude,
> This rare illusion,
>
> As to the private heart
> All separate pain
> Brings loss of friendly light
> But deeper, darker gain.

But that is the bravery of the deepest, darkest despair, when one has to cling to some hope. As the long winter draws on, and Nature's darkness allies itself to the blackout, the two become merged into an even darker threat:

> It is not Winter, not the cold we fear;
> It is the dreadful echo of our void,
> The malice all around us, manifest . . .

The Garden is also a poem *of* belief, a belief in the eternal renewal of life and hope. With daylight comes the colour of life, lichen-covered roofs 'Green in the rain but golden in the sun' – and she is able to return to her dreams. Her gardener's dreams are of the colourful hopes of the new catalogues –

> Fantastic, tossed, and all from shilling packet . . .
> An acre sprung from one expended coin,

– of apple blossom in an orchard of flowers, of the gardens of Spain and of Persia:

> . . . where the thin canal
> Runs in transparency on turquoise tiles
> Down to the lost pavilion.

She dreams of the plant collectors – Forrest, Farrer, Fortune and Kingdon-Ward – travelling in the lonely mountains, on the eaves of the world, and she remembers Pharoah's gardener come at last to his long Paradise in his painted tomb.

But, dreaming done, she comes down from her room to face the world, and prepare the most beautifully written 'Things to do in the garden' ever – for her poem is also that. Never to be forgotten, outside her Tower door, was the Box of the Dead – the labels that were no longer required, a constant reminder of sad failure, and a constant intimation to do better. There was the frost to be put to best use, and there were winter treasures to be discovered – witch hazel, *Viburnum fragrans*, her beloved Algerian iris (*stylosa*, which I really refuse to call *unguicularis*! – her little mauve rolled umbrellas) and *Crocus tomasianus*, 'Lavender cups of tiny crockery'. There was the beauty of the snow to be enjoyed, and the damage of the snow carefully repaired when the thaw dripped, there were the first crocus, Lenten roses, daphne sprigs and violets to be collected for offerings, and the endlessly desirable annuals to be planted – so much to be done, until suddenly – 'March tips over, as a watershed' . . . and Winter . . . 'Seemed finally and desperately dead'.

WHEN Vita came to spring in *The Garden* she had waited for over ten years since Eliot's *Waste Land* and was prepared to wait no longer to make her reply. It was her reply to the whole school of politically depressed poets of the twenties and thirties – she knew Eliot, Spender and Auden, and she neither could nor would subscribe to what she felt were biased emotions. In *The Garden* she quotes (with profuse acknowledgement) Eliot's stanza beginning 'April is the cruellest month' in order that she may strike back:

> I would sooner hope and believe
> Than dig for my living life a present grave.
> Though I must die, the only thing I know,
> My only certainty, so far ahead
> Or just around the corner as I go,
> Not knowing what the dangerous turn will bring,
> Only that some one day I must be dead,
> – I still will sing with credence and with passion
> In a new fashion
> That I will believe in April while I live.
> I will believe in Spring,
> That custom of the year so frail, so brave,
> Custom without a loss of mystery.

In spring she walks beside Harold's borders, nostalgically named Unter den Linden, which he had vowed to make the loveliest spring garden in the world (and would do so after the war), and finds the windflowers, anemones, the Lady Tulip, the Glory of the Snow, scillas, grape-hyacinths

> running between the cracks of paving stone
> In rivulets of blue . . .

and remembers where she has seen them in their native lands. She walks on, into the nuttery, where the harlequin primroses are washing in a tide 'down the colonnades of Kentish cob'. And then it's back to work again – sowing drifts of larkspur and forget-me-not, attacking the weeds, seeing to next year's biennials, dealing with moles and caterpillars, pruning, tying and staking . . . with finally a little time to enjoy the tulips. Ever since Vita's first orange tulips had sprung so successfully beside the terrace at Long Barn, both she and Harold had come to adore them and indulge their adoration; tulips fascinated her mythological mind, she loved their exotic foreignness, the fact that Shakespeare *never* knew them, that they had wandered out of the East as the treasures of Dutchmen with strange names and found their way into the paintings of Brueghel and Rembrandt. In her poem she welcomes the Princes of Orange and Austria, the plum shot crimson 'Couleur Cardinal', the elegant Darwins, the Rembrandts and Bizarre 'in broken rose and white' and the 'Green flounced with pink, and fringed, and topple heavy' Parrots. Part of her private war effort had been to indulge in buying thousands of bulbs in the first year of the war as a sign of hope – her tulip cavalcades blew in the orchard,

78. 'A quantity of fine old stones lying about in odd corners ... had to be collected and assembled somehow, so they were placed together to form rough terraces along a path, where they make an unconventional sort of rock-garden ... inspired by the island of Delos, where the ruins of the houses have left precisely this kind of little terrace smothered there by mats of the wild flowers of Greece' (V. Sackville-West, *Country Life*, 11 September 1942, p. 508).

the South Cottage garden and the Lime Walk, and more would be added to their number when Harold really took over the Lime Walk after the war.

June brings the roses and irises in the Rondel Garden into bloom. This garden of Sissinghurst, with its Italian form and ordered spaces, filled with fountains and cascades of roses that tumbled over the blades of the iris leaves, was the fulfilment of her most daring dreams. She had a real and gentle affection for the pale dog-rose and its fellows – 'The candid English genius, fresh and pink' – but her desire was for a flower of very different colour and character – the rose's true character ...

She's a voluptuary; think of her
Wine-dark and heavy-scented of the South,
Stuck in a cap or dangled from a mouth
As soft as her own petals. That's the rose!

These roses of such dangerous beauty were those of crimson, wine, magenta, violet and purple, the crimson velvet *gallica* 'Tuscany', the red-indigo robed 'Cardinal de Richelieu', the purple and lilac Old Velvet moss 'William Lobb', the damask 'Ispahan', 'Rose de Provins', and the dark red, almost black 'Souvenir de Docteur Jamain'.[31] They were massed above the iris blades like dripping blood; they signified to Vita, with their long associations with love and wars, that beauty could survive, and that was her belief. But was there anything more to believe in? Roses had so long been part of the ceremony of the Church, she remembered Easter Day in St Mark's, Venice, when a rose-red robed cardinal bade her pray – but who to?

Those blood-red roses floating in the pool,
That blood-red lamp above the altar slung,
Were they identical, or I a fool?

Poor brave Vita, godless, wanders into July which is too heavy, too rampant and too lush. She does not like her garden then (and indeed, she invariably left Sissinghurst at this time) and her thoughts wander far away, while she carries on her tasks in the wartime garden from whence there is no escape. She turns the summer of war in the countryside into poetry – the 'craters in the simple fields of Kent', the brute reality that tumbles from the sky into their little world, the sound of guns borne on the wind from France, their shared worries about their sons, the scurrying like beasts to earth when the siren wails, and a rare beauty born of hideous war – the searchlights that pattern the sky at night:

And see, at meeting apex, how they hold
A wide-winged dove, a crucifix in gold.
Is it a dove, soft-feathered? or a plane
Tiny with murder? or a wooden Cross?
    A dove, a plane, a Cross, amid
The meeting beams at their convergent vane?

Yet again she returns to the gardener's persistent war and her particular enemy, the wasp. Having sung the praise of bees and their world in *The Land*, she had always been fearful that she would be reduced to less lovable beasties for *The Garden*, but an unfortunate chance – a wasp sting that affected her very badly – gave her good reason to face the 'little dragons of the summer day'. She treats them

79. *(above)* The hybrid musk and 'old-fashionable' roses – 'It was thought that the place lent itself kindly to their untidy, lavish habit: there was space in plenty, with the walls to frame their exuberance...'

80. *(below)* '...and consequently they may be found foaming in an unorthodox way in the midst of flower borders...' (V. Sackville-West, *Country Life*, 11 September 1942, pp. 508/9).

81. *The Garden: Summer*, p. 106:

> Plant box for edging; do not heed the glum
> Advice of those unthinking orthodox
> Gardeners who condemn the tidy box
> As haven for the slug, through winter numb.

The newly planted box edgings, the lavender border and almond trees in what was to become, after the war, the White Garden. In the background are the Priest's House and Erectheum. The Virgin is in her former place at the end of this vista (she was moved to the White Garden after the war).

justly, rather as D. H. Lawrence did *The Snake*, and honour is equally assuaged. In convalescence we can picture her, sitting beneath the vine pergola they had called the Erectheum, outside the dining-room door of the Priest's House:

> Green vine-shade; sweet airs breathe; leaves lift;
> Tendrils in tenderest of shadows drift.
> Dog, on the dappled ground your dappled body lay.
> Black sun, black bumble-bees, black grapes;
> Slim carven columns wreathed in vine;
> My little world of gently stirring shapes;
> Summer, the corn's last standing day.

She fills the rest of summer (when she obviously is recovered) with advice on the planting of hedges – *not* privet, laurel or macrocarpa, but box, yew and roses, cydonia (which she had seen at Ian Davidson's garden at Brandon), and cherry-plum (*Prunus cerasifera*). She recommends vistas and living water in your garden; this piece is in the best tradition of William Mason's *The English Garden*, but it is the only part of Vita's poem that is.[32]

Autumn in *The Garden*, autumn at the end of the war, brings a tired peace, with moments of fiery beauty: blue smoke drifting across brown woods, the 'fervour of azalea/Whose dying day repeats her June of flower', the motley pink and yellow of the medlar leaves (which she picks to set against the oak panelling of the Big Room), and the rich, fat yellow hanging fruits of medlar and quince.

> All's brown and red: the robin and the clods,
> And umber half-light of the potting shed,
> The terra-cotta of the pots, the brown
> Sacking with its peculiar autumn smell . . .

Yet after the slow pacing of the season, faced with the dread of winter when she is tired and afraid of growing old, can she still believe in, and hope for, spring?

Vita had started writing *The Garden* in the winter of 1939/40, and she had only been able to pick it up fitfully during the war years. Though on the surface she was busy enough protecting her little world, putting on a brave front for Harold and generally keeping going, she was in fact becoming more isolated and nervous and more afraid that the arthritis in her back would disable her. She took the bombing of Knole in February 1944 as a personal injury, she (quite naturally) grew increasingly fearful that Ben or Nigel (both in the army) would be captured, wounded or worse, that Harold would meet with an accident of some kind, and her anxiety meant that she could rarely write. *The Garden* was left unfinished; she seemed to reach the depths of her depression in the winter of 1944/5, and being Vita, it was brought to a head not by damage to a person she loved, but to a place; in summer in *The Garden* she had written the following elegy for the lake, her last refuge:

> Now will the water-lilies stain the lake
> With cups of yellow, chalices of cream,
> Set in their saucer leaves of olive-green
> On greener water, motionless, opaque,
> – This haunt of ducks, of grebes, and poacher herns.
> Now is the stillness deeper than a dream;
> Small sounds, small movements shake
> This quietude, that deeper then returns
> After the slipping of the water-snake,
> The jump of trout, the sudden cry of coot,
> The elegaic hoot
> Of owls within the bordering wood, that take
> The twilight for their own.
> This is their hour, and mine; we are alone;
> I drift; I would that I might never wake.

On 19 December 1944 she wrote to Harold:

> Darling, I went down to have a look at the lake and to see if it was doing anything wild. It wasn't. I went out of a sense of duty because I have lost all pleasure in the lake, and, indeed, in the woods, since the soldiers came and invaded them and robbed them of their privacy I so loved. I shall never love the lake or the woods again in the same way as I used to. You didn't understand when I minded the tanks cutting through the wild flowers. I mind about this more than you would believe. It was a thing of beauty now tarnished forever. One of the few things I had preserved against this horrible new world. I wish I could sort out my ideas about this new world – I feel that one ought to be able to adapt oneself and not struggle to go back to and live in an obsolete tradition – all this makes me very unhappy . . . and my back worries me . . . I don't mind it hurting but the weakness it brings to my limbs worries me – I used to be so strong but now I dare not make a rash movement . . . I feel that I and the lake and the woods are all damaged and spoilt forever. I mind very much. Our lost youth in fact. The lake and the wood are sort of symbols to me of what I feel about myself – it is selfish of me to tell you all this and, indeed, I have been concealing it from you so far as I could, but often all you are is the person I love most and I think I am the person you love most so I tell you. If only I thought I could write good poetry I should not mind anything, but even over that I have lost my conviction.[33]

Having sunk to the depths she pulled herself up again, and returned to practicalities; out of duty she wrote her book about the Women's Land Army. On 7 May 1945 they hoisted the flag again on the Tower for the first time in five years, Ben and Nigel duly came safely home, and life seeped back to Sissinghurst. Harold lost his House of Commons seat in the General Election of 1945 and was dreadfully disappointed; Vita *had* to revive. In the autumn of 1945, as she worked in the garden, the poetry came again:

> My mood is like a fire that will not heat;
> There's touchwood and a chequer-board of peat;
> The sturdy logs laid ready, sere and dry;
> The match-box, and the chimney swept and high;
> There's all the setting for a roar of flame
> But love and poetry are but a name,
> And neither will my fuel burn, nor I.
> . . .
> Get hence, damp mood, as musty as the shroud,
> Such sulky torpor suits no spirit proud;
> Come, flame; come, tongue of courage; scorch me, sear;
> I'll risk the burning to regain the clear
> Fangs of returning life as sharp as fire.
> Better, I swear, to be consumed entire
> Than smoulder, knowing neither zest nor fear.

She *will* believe in spring. She will be willing to get her fingers burned. This is not merely an avowal in an emotional sense, it is much deeper, it is the essential courage of her character re-asserting itself, refusing to assume a veneer and determining to

82. Sissinghurst in wartime – landgirls and schoolchildren at a farm sale in front of the castle.

remain vulnerable in order to be creative. But where was her creativity to go? She finished her poem and waited nervously for publication. *The Garden* came out in May 1946, and was reprinted in November and again the following May. It pleased Edith Sitwell (which pleased Vita), but did not spark many notable reviews; it did win her a £100 Heinemann Prize, which she spent on azaleas for the Moat Walk. But she knew that it did not count with her fellow members of the Poetry Committee of the Royal Society of Literature (besides Edith Sitwell they included Henry Reed, George Barker, Dylan Thomas and Louis MacNeice), and she never published another poem.[34]

Whether she realized it or not, she in fact turned her creativity elsewhere – into an alternative struggle; 'I feel that one ought to be able to adapt oneself [to this new world] and not struggle to go back to and live in an obsolete tradition' was what she had written in her despair, and her feeling was true. But her way would not be to write the poetry 'of a society invented by beach boys and supported by girls without girdles'[35] – which she could not do; nor could it have been her way to rush off and become a social worker in a northern city. If the world of poetry had left her, rather than she leaving it, she still had the graces and courtesies of her little world, especially of her garden, to share. More people than those who read poetry would come to bless her name and thank her for the delight which she brought to them as they struggled with post-war Britain. Perhaps it was a blessing in disguise that *The Garden* was not such a success after all?

8

VITA'S ENGLAND

Thus I do love my England, though I roam.
Thus do I love my England: I am hers.
What could be said more simply? As a lover
Says of his mistress, I am hers, she mine,
So do I say of England: I do love her.
She is my shape; her shape my very shape.
Her present is my grief; her past, my past.
Often I rage, resent her moderate cast,
Yet she is mine, I hers, without escape.
V. Sackville-West, *The Garden: Winter*[1]

To PEOPLE tired and saddened by war, harassed by ration books and utility coupons for their every need, with little or no transport to go out in and nowhere in particular to go, gardens were a great and necessary consolation. With war damage and neglect to be repaired, the joy of growing flowers to be rediscovered (or discovered by the thousands who had come to gardening by way of 'digging for victory' vegetables), and the pride of that first bunch of sweet peas or that neat, weed-free gravel path to be won, gardening became something of a craze. Sissinghurst too had to be revived from neglect, a task that was started immediately after the war ended, but the revival of her garden, and her *Observer* articles from 1946 on that made it a beacon in the lightening gloom of the fifties, must be seen against the wider context of Vita's post-war world. She had lost her literary society (only Virginia had really kept her in touch with it anyway) and was now 'nervous' of clever people, but she could enter the gardening world without a qualm, with her reputation as a poet (she was awarded the Companion of Honour in the New Year's Honours of 1948) and with her garden to support her. To follow her there is a fascinating journey and one that is absolutely necessary to complete the balance of her life.

Her first Expert friends (Vita regarded them as capital Es), Edward Ashdown Bunyard and Charles Hoare Grey, had now left the scene (Bunyard had died in

83. *(above)* Hidcote Manor: Major Lawrence Johnston's English garden as Vita knew it, a garden of immaculate vistas and spaces made with 'living barriers' – hedges – 'which do much to deepen the impression of luxuriance and secrecy,' she wrote.

84. *(below)* Hidcote: the Bathing Pool Garden, one of the features of architectural severity that made Major Johnston's taste so different from the Nicolsons' – his extremes, of severity and of lavishness in planting, and his courage to indulge them, were what Harold and Vita admired.

1938, and Colonel Grey had sold Hocker Edge Nursery – which the Nicolsons had considered buying with the proceeds from the sale of Long Barn – and moved north to Yorkshire at the end of the war), but others had been steadily drawn to Sissinghurst. Vita was (she never denied it) flattered by their interest, but she was content to stand back and listen: '. . . if you want real highbrow talk commend me to three experts talking about auriculas – Bloomsbury has nothing on it, I couldn't understand half they said – they mentioned Mr Middleton as Lytton Strachey, Tray [Raymond Mortimer] and Virginia might mention Warwick Deeping . . .'[2] This was Vita describing a visit from Clarence Elliott, the collector of mountain plants,[3] and Captain 'Cherry' Collingwood Ingram[4] in 1941, and it was the first of many such scenarios. In her turn she was an enthusiastic Fellow of the Royal Horticultural Society, singing its advantages in an *Observer* piece – its journal, the fortnightly London flower shows, the share of free seeds from Wisley garden, entrance to Wisley and to the Chelsea Show – and then (not realizing how experts *love* publicity) wondered that they made such a fuss of her! She went to lectures and gave them, met friends and experts, and beautifully records her capacity for wonder at one particular February show, when after a busy day in London she went to Vincent Square to dine – 'Imagine, Hadji, the flower show had shut to the public at 6 and the huge Horticultural Hall was all lit up for members of the horticultural club and there wasn't a soul there – I had purposely arrived early – the scent of the hyacinths was almost too much and the beauty and absolute stillness of the flowers, slightly queer in their colours under that artificial light is a thing I shall never forget . . .'[5] It ranked, she said, 'very high in the good moments of my life'.

She enjoyed her 'garden open' days and the wider gardening fraternity coming to Sissinghurst, though she grew impatient with the merely curious. Having joined the 'yellow book' company she did her bit for the National Gardens Scheme,[6] and wrote enticingly of her fellows with names like Heronden Eastry, Bevington Lordship, St John Jerusalem, Castle Drogo, the Isle of Thorns, Magna Carta Island and the House in the Wood:

> Nor is this all. At Tinker's Corner, for instance, you are offered tea *and music*; Bickleigh Castle provides floodlighting and a moated Saxon chapel, modestly adding '*romantic interest*', which one can well believe. Little Whyley Hall somewhat startlingly tenders not only cups of tea but big-game herds. You can see Shelley's birthplace and Rudyard Kipling's house. You will be given 'strawberries if ripe' at Kempsons in June.[7]

Sissinghurst's visitors came in increasing numbers – stray walkers, roving architects, childhood friends now grown up with families of their own, coach parties from women's institutes and gardening clubs from all over Kent and Sussex and farther afield; though coach loads of 60+ at a time morning and afternoon were a little daunting (she contemplated training Rollo her alsatian to perform as sheepdog), on the whole she and Harold adored their visitors as long as they were in turn appreciative. Harold remembered happily how they strolled down through the orchard one fine Easter Sunday morning and chatted to youth hostellers who were happening by on the other side of the moat, and Vita warmed to Jacquetta Hawkes, who wrote of 'the curious and lovely place in which you live', feeling that she had really understood and enjoyed her visit. And in turn, the visiting experts and her other friends with gardens were pleased to have visits from the châtelaine of Sissinghurst – these visits were a pure pleasure for her, for they were journeys into a world that held no fears.

Apart from returning compliments, she was also doing her homework for the National Trust. Harold had joined the Trust's Council in 1944, and Vita became a founder member of the Gardens Committee in 1948, along with Lord Aberconway, the Earl of Rosse, David Bowes-Lyon, Sir Edward Salisbury and Dr H. V. Taylor.[8] She was very regular in her attendance at meetings (usually quarterly) up until the year before her death; James Lees-Milne remembers that she was very quiet and shy, but when she was questioned 'her opinions were forthright and absolutely to the point'.[9] The Committee's chief work during her years was the inspection and recommendation (or otherwise) of the gardens that were offered to the Trust or that it was felt were important enough to be acquired. She was closely involved with the acquisition of Hidcote Manor, Bramham Park, Rousham, and Westonbirt and Winkworth Arboretums, and with the care of Charlecote and Montacute, very keen that they should be managed for the best enjoyment of their visitors, and she never got involved in the arguments.

And so to her journeys – her composite journeys made up of most of the interesting places she saw over these post-war years. She loved to turn westwards in late July and August when England turned to gold; she loved driving (a beloved Austin had replaced the wartime Buick and was in turn replaced by an 'upstart' but very enjoyable Jaguar). The westward road was a symbol of freedom which she passed on to Rose Mortibois in *The Easter Party* – Rose was driving fast, on the road which 'if she pursued it far enough would take her right down into the depths of England, down into Gloucestershire and Hereford, and into Wales, until she came to the outer edge of the island and ran off it . . .'[10] Vita pursued the old A4 (how she would have loved the motorway) impatiently through Reading, along the Kennet valley to Newbury, and at last into the open downs. Just beyond Hungerford she turned off right, then left into the south drive of the Wills family's Littlecote House; as she came over the crest of the hill she could not but gasp at the panorama of the pink brick Tudor house set among its soft hills – 'lovely beyond all dreams'; in the great hall, surrounded by the buff coats and firearms of Colonel Popham's garrison for Cromwell, is the painting by Thomas Wycke that captures the same view in the late seventeenth century – it is immediately recognizable. In the large garden of walled enclosures, flower borders and a tranquil trout canal that is a tributary of the Kennet, '*such* a garden', I imagine she would have dearly coveted the sundial which tells the time in Ispahan, Aleppo, Charlestown and Littlecote.[11]

Beyond Marlborough is the country of her novel *Grey Wethers*,[12] in which her treatment of the landscape is most Hardyesque and powerful. Avebury itself [colour pl. 5] is perhaps the star character:

... strangers to the country, coming unawares upon this singular encampment, were at first amazed; but presently there crept into their minds the sense that the whole country traversed by them had been, in a way, but the natural preparation to precisely such a mysterious and secluded path of human habitation. They recalled the straight white road driven across the Downs; the pits of poor, blanched chalk; the shaven clumps of beech, like giant ricks, upon the skyline; mounds and barrows; the perfect cone of Silbury Hill, which, rooted in its great antiquity, had forced the Roman road to deflect from its course; the primitive shapes surviving in the White Horses cut as landmarks upon their flanks. Above all they would recall those strange monuments of English paganism, the sarsen stones, hewn by Nature and transported by man to be the instruments of his superstition, left where they had fallen, singly or in rings, obscure in a fold of the Downs, or reared to accord with the eternal procession of the heavens in the gaunt majesty of Stonehenge.[13]

In this mystical setting she made the gentle little grey Avebury Manor the home of her heroine, Clare Warrener: 'they saw Miss Clare emerge presently from the gates of the Manor House, with their glimpse of garden, lawn and cedars, riding astride her pony ...'[14] Vita had first seen Avebury Manor in 1924 – 'how much I want it' she had written – and she and Harold returned several times. It is still just their kind of house – with panelled bedrooms, Jacobean furniture, beeswax, roses and lavender, its topiary garden almost Florentine in the afternoon sun – and something more: if, when Harold saw it in the 1920s, he had walked to the far end of the garden, he would have found the long yew walk, paved, with a statue at the end ... if so, then Avebury is one of the places that contributed directly to Sissinghurst.

From Avebury it is only a few miles north and west to Bradenstoke Priory, where now only the crumbling walls sleep in the waving grass at the end of R.A.F. Lyneham's runway! The old road through Chippenham, the A420, though, still has the feeling of being so old that would have captivated Vita – the farming life of centuries seems to have but lightly passed by, the sheep bleat and the cockerels still crow to each other across the valley in the morning sun. Vita looked in at magnificent Corsham Court and romantic Lacock, as most do who pass this way, but her real goal was one of the most exquisitely sited houses in England, Colonel Cooper's 'lovely little grey house', Cold Ashton Manor [colour pl. 10]. This hamlet of Cold Ashton *is* the school, the church and vicarage, the manor and the farm, all lined along a ridge looking south to Bath over the green dips and hills of St Catharine's Valley, shadowed with the indents of eternal sheep paths. It is after balmy Bath that Cold Ashton lives up to its name, and the manor provided a welcome refuge on a wet August afternoon with 'late tea beside a roaring fire in a deep shadowed, whitewashed hall with flickering glimpses of sculptured oak and moulded stone'.[15] Reggie Cooper was a friend of Harold and Vita's from Constantinople days, and he had restored the glamour of Cold Ashton's seventeenth-century youth – they could explore by candlelight through this house of symmetry and severity, of interior vistas through brown-grey oak-panelled screens, through the buttery, parlour and solar, all sparsely furnished with good Jacobean, Stuart or Georgian furniture – the essence of good taste in the manor house cult.[16]

Next morning, wakened by farmyard sounds from over the wall, Vita could have watched from her window as the early sun gradually warmed the grey stone walls, steps and arches of the formal garden filled with topiary yews and fading summer flowers.

From Cold Ashton she was more than once tempted west to Berkeley Castle, 'savage, remote, barbaric, brooding like a frown across the jade-green watermeadows towards the hills of Wales . . .'

> How far is it, my lord, to Berkeley now?
> I am a stranger here in Gloucestershire,
> These high wild hills, and rough uneven ways . . .

Some of the fascination of Avebury had been for its romantic associations with Pat Dansey (to whom *Grey Wethers* was dedicated), whom Vita met there; but much of Pat Dansey's attraction was surely that she lived in Berkeley Castle – the combination of Shakespeare *and* barbarity being irresistible to Vita! In 1954 she was delighted to be asked to advise on what to do with Berkeley's garden – 'terraces falling away beneath towering walls and buttresses, apparently constructed of porphyry and gold' – before the castle was opened to the public. She felt Berkeley had to be simplified: 'Make a broad green walk, quiet and austere, to be mown once a week. And on no account smother the walls with climbers. Whatever there is must be special and choice.'[17] It was, she said, a counsel to be applied to all gardens, whether majestic or modest! She admitted that her taste in gardens never remained static, but was it by the mid-fifties becoming more severe?

From Berkeley she turned inland towards her beloved Cotswolds, first stop Rodmarton Manor, off the Tetbury to Cirencester road. Rodmarton [colour pl. 6], with its long cool façade curving round an enchanted green, is a house of the greatest beauty and simplicity. It is a twentieth-century house, built in centuries-old hand-crafted traditions within the framework of the fellowship of arts and crafts: the architect Ernest Barnsley and his friends had finished it in 1926 to perpetuate their Morrisian dreams into a century which they felt would discard such values. Rodmarton is therefore a genuine fake and I suspect it worried Vita. By the time she reached Daneway in the village of Sapperton a few miles away, she expressed her disappointment. Daneway is an old Cotswold manor, and was the original base for Ernest Gimson and the Barnsleys and their furniture-making community, but by the time Vita saw it after the Second World War it had been restored by the architect Oliver Hill. Hill had a dual nature too, and was flamboyant with it – he was able to design convincingly in any number of styles, 'the kind of architect,' says Margaret Richardson,[18] 'who drove a Chrysler at 50 m.p.h. in the 1930s but made his own envelopes'. Daneway had a studied opulence, a perfection of bare floors, dried flowers, oak furniture, and the glossiness of a design magazine: it was 'set in a beautiful garden; but tucked in a secluded arbour and approached by a narrow path was a small, bright blue swimming pool'.[19] Vita's countrywoman's mistrust of artifice finally rebelled. She would have understood Hill's love of fast cars, but his facility for turning her genuine world into a cult, into an art form, would have frightened her. No wonder she was nervous of clever people!

But when a clever person put wholehearted energies into a garden it was a different matter, for gardens belong to people, not styles. Such a garden was that of Hidcote Manor [83, 84], and such a person was Major Lawrence Johnston. The crumbling manor house had been bought by Mrs Winthrop, Johnston's mother, in 1905, and he had started to make his garden directly influenced by the Edwardian achievement that married formal design to luxuriant planting. Johnston had all the talents required – he had had architectural training, he was a keen botanist and plant collector and collected many of his own rarities from the mountains of China and Africa, and he had 'immense energy, optimism, foresight and courage', and the money to pour into his garden. Into his two gardens in fact, for he also had a villa, La Serre de la Madrone in the Val du Gorbio above Nice, which is where he went to live after the war. Many people think that Hidcote and Sissinghurst are alike, and that Vita must have been influenced by Hidcote. They may have grown alike in recent years, but when they were both the fresh expression of their makers they were correspondingly unalike, and I think the differences can still be discerned. When she wrote her description of Hidcote for the *R.H.S. Journal* in 1949, Vita said she first went there 'many years ago', with Major Johnston as her guide – he 'had sent me off with a huge bundle of syringas saying "Take your chance of these . . . you may hit on some that will do" – he was right. I took my chance, and now have some fine kinds growing in my garden'.[20] She had been to Hidcote in 1947, but it seems likely that 'many years ago' meant before the war. Even so, it would have been *after* the bones of Sissinghurst were finished. The pedigree of Sissinghurst is, I hope, now becoming clearer, but, as Vita said, the pedigree of Hidcote was Johnston's talent and courage. He had only a fine cedar, two clumps of beech and the remnants of the old manor garden among high and windy fields when he started. Having given his plant-collecting tastes full rein in the south of France, he seemed to give his architectural sense first flush at chillier Hidcote; it is a garden of immaculate vistas of sky, clipped hedges and rolled grass walks, of architectural severity even in the Stilt Garden and the Bathing Pool Garden, with little softening, and almost of whimsy in those tip-tilted pavilions. He had no restraining walls but used living barriers – hedges – 'which do much to deepen the impression of luxuriance and secrecy', noted Vita. She revelled in the brave variety of his hedges – the 'flatness' of yew mixed with shining holly, and a harlequin of a hedge of beech, yew, box, holly and hornbeam 'like a green and black tartan'. Within his hedged spaces he planted . . . and planted, and planted and planted . . . incessantly for over forty years – 'this place is a jungle of beauty; a jungle controlled by a single mind'. Johnston was untrammelled by English conservative planting traditions (he was born in Paris of American background) – there were to be no logical drifts or Jekyllian sequences for him – his was a free and bountiful and capricious planting of whatever caught his fancy. My guess is that much of this came from his plant collecting but much also from Norah Lindsay, for it was just what she was practising at Sutton

Courtenay before Johnston started at Hidcote, and she was his constant companion in gardening during the twenties and thirties. Plantings that especially caught Vita's eye were:

> ... a narrow path running along a dry wall; I think the gardener called it the rock garden, but it resembled nothing that I have ever seen described by that name. At the foot of the wall grew a solid mauve ribbon of ... *Campanula portenschlagiana bavarica* and this, of course, after the Hidcote principle, had been allowed to spread itself also into brilliant patches wherever it did not rightly belong. Out of the dry wall poured, not the expected rock-plants, but a profusion of Lavender and wands of Indigofera; there was *Choisya ternata* also, and some Cistus ...

> ... a raised circular bed round a Scotch Pine, foaming with rock roses of every shade, a lovely surprise, as light as spindrift, shot with many colours the rainbow does not provide...

> ... I recall a colony of Primula Garriarde under a north wall ... those plants were as big as the largest lettuces. I blushed as I looked at them, remembering my own poor starved samples...[21]

The lessons of Hidcote as Vita saw them were never to be content with second or third best but always to choose the *best* variety, and that the wise gardener often lets his plants settle themselves, as they are quite common good judges of where they like to be. My reader may recall that these too were the lessons from the Manor House at Sutton Courtenay so long ago. Major Johnston had gone to live in France after the war, having intended to leave Hidcote to Norah Lindsay, but she died in 1948; he therefore started negotiations for the garden to be handed over to the National Trust and run by a management committee which included Norah's daughter Nancy Lindsay, an avid but eccentric botanist and collector, who had collected some rarities into her little garden at the cottage at Sutton Courtenay Manor. It was Nancy who showed Vita around Hidcote on her June 1949 visit, answered her questions, wrote Vita long rambling letters about old roses, and with a typical generosity offered her anything from her own collection or Hidcote's. She offered the double golden briar from Persia, *R. haemispherica*, the rare mauve centifolia 'Tour de Malakoff', an exceptional rose, and the precious maroon 'Nuits de Young', as well as a tall blue iris, *I. spurea*, which Vita coveted in Hidcote's Old Garden, and any old double primroses, or old pinks such as 'Painted Lady'. In this way Vita gathered her treasures.[22]

Lessons and treasures of a different kind awaited a village away at Mrs Muir's Kiftsgate Court [colour p. 11]. Mrs Muir was an early exponent of the highly textural planting of great elegance but rather less flower that has since become the mark of professional planting designers of the later twentieth century. Her smooth paths were a foil for gunneras, grasses, acanthus, day-lilies and rodgersias. But she also loved old roses, and Kiftsgate has its own rose, *R. filipes* 'Kiftsgate', with masses of creamy white scented flowers, a vigorous climber which likes shade and is happy up trees and found its way to Sissinghurst's orchard. Mrs Muir's other roses were those Vita especially loved – mixed with golden and grey shrubs they made parts of her garden like a brocade with their crimsons, rosy purples, mauves and lavenders. Vita also coveted Mrs Muir's *Philadelphus* 'Sybille'; they had many tastes in common and admired each other's gardens immensely.

Time and again Vita wrote at the end of a happy day – 'I do love the Cotswolds.' She visited Stanway, the home of Lord Wemyss, a house that spent its summers in a 'deep slumbrous green' that never failed to capture its visitors and drew from Cynthia Asquith, who was brought up there, the admission that she loved it 'precisely as one loves a human being ... loved it as I have loved very few human beings'.[23] Vita would have understood. She stayed at the Lygon Arms in Broadway, of course, and saw Sezincote – 'less exotic' than expected. Then she headed westwards and northwards along another favourite road, across Worcestershire and into the Marches and Wales. She adored this patch of countryside – Ludlow with its 'jolly castle' surrounded by a ring of pollarded limes and a close of houses, mixed Georgian, outrageous black and white and mellow stone; she loved the fantastic Feathers Hotel, tea and muffins at de Grey's and listening to the talk of the lilty voices that are so nearly Welsh. She discovered, through an invitation to spend the night there, Ludstone Hall, at Claverley, west of Wolverhampton (the nearest she ventured into the Black Country). Ludstone is an exquisite Jacobean house of red brick with pretty shaped gables, in the soft meadows of a well-treed valley. It has a knot garden set for *Alice in Wonderland*, with spades, clubs, hearts and diamonds in box, and, at the time of Vita's visit, Mr and Mrs Rollason were making their large wild garden. Vita was enchanted.

Back west of Ludlow, where the sun spattered the patchwork of the Clee Hills, she went on to Stokesay Castle [colour pl. 7], where she found a companion soul – 'Wonderful, wonderful Stokesay' – in this fortified manor house that launches itself towards one like a ship. From Craven Arms she would drive up Corve Dale below Wenlock Edge, where the ribbons of cloud hang above Brown Clee Hill and where a sense of well-being still pervades an unpressurized agricultural countryside. Black and white Much Wenlock amused her, and then it was on to Shrewsbury and dear Hilda Murrell's Portland Nursery. Vita was a good customer to Hilda, who remained a gardening friend for the rest of Vita's life, and with whom she shared a passion for old roses.[24]

From Shrewsbury she set out for Wales, once to stay at Chirk Castle, and at least twice to Llangollen to view the memorials to the Ladies, Sarah Ponsonby and Eleanor Butler, who are quasi-royalty in their own town and were not unimaginative gardeners; they enjoyed a shrubbery of lilacs, laburnums, yews, filberts and wild white cherries, with banks of yellow crocus, drifts of wood anemones and primroses, and wild white convolvulus persuaded to clamber through the powdery blue foliage of their cedar. She found the Snowdonia landscape suitably 'Turneresque', the Pass of Llanberis 'magnificent', and was caught by the drama of the slate – 'great black bowls of slate spilt down the mountain sides'.[25] But the required paradox to wild Wales was the Aberconways' Bodnant garden, with its flowered terraces looking out on to the mountains and wooded glen. Lord Aberconway was an ideal gardening friend. Harold and Vita spent long hours being happily walked around the garden and the woods, the propagating houses and the nurseries; Vita and Lord Aberconway talked eucryphias, which fascinated her, and Harold and Lord Aberconway talked auriculas. Generous parcels of auriculas came from Bodnant to Sissinghurst – they were Harold's particular post-war passion.

In 1952 Harold was able to fulfil his long-held wish to take Vita to Ireland; they took the ferry from Holyhead with the car and arrived in Dublin to begin their nostalgic pilgrimage. The first stop was Powerscourt, where the young Duke of Dorset had been killed hunting in 1815. Harold had long admired this amazing baroque garden, visions of Schönbrunn and Versailles and the plan of Villa Butera in Sicily[26] brought home to an Irish hillside, with its orgy of statuary – painted Pegasi, Apollo and Diana, Hector and Andromache, Triton's Fountain and the familiar Bagatelle vases (these probably bought from Sir John Murray Scott by the 8th Viscount). Vita may have had mixed thoughts – if the young Duke had not been killed, he just might have shared the gardening tastes of his friend the 6th Viscount and done this to Knole! She was most fascinated by the convincingly medieval folly, like a pepperpot, built in 1910, 'filled with mortars and ancient arms up to the crenellations, covered with lanterns hung from brackets and surrounded by historic cannon, cannonades, cannon-balls, old chain shot, gyves and cressets which alternated with an astrolabe and a clepsydra, a water clock used by the ancients . . .'[27] – especially when a silver version of this turned up for use at dinner!

Next morning they began a lovely day, going first to Old Conna Hill at Bray, Phineas Riall's gothic mansion overlooking the mountains and the sea with its dell planted out with the contents of its conservatory. Old Conna Hill has the first *Cordyline australis* to be grown out of doors in our northern islands, wonderful mimosa (*Acacia dealbata*) and *Eriobotrya japonica* (loquat) – 'lovely myrtles and an immense mimosa', wrote Vita. After Old Conna Hill they went to view the Powerscourt waterfall, then on to Uplands at Roundwood and the nursery of a character in a 'suit of grass green tweed', Ralph Cusack. One wonders if there was as much laughter on that visit as there was from her tower room when Cusack's catalogue arrived; there was more than a touch of William Robinson about this wonderful man who kept his customers in order:

> I am writing this introduction to my catalogue *after* having spent weeks compiling it, and not, as on other occasions, *before* the task is done. Consequently I want to tell you that before I got to the end of it I was heartily weary of all the superlatives and enthusiastic descriptions, the unceasing search for new adjectives to praise my bulbs. But – and it is a vitally important but – I do not and cannot subtract or alter a single one of them. For how else can one describe these plants but by superlatives. I have grown 90% of them here in my garden and seen their beauty, and as each name came along in the list it vividly recalled the rapture with which I saw them, the dark wet days of winter in which they glowed, the flashing spring sunlight in which they revelled, the all too rare summer noons in which they basked. Thus I do not retract an iota, for I cannot . . . it is your job to pick out those you fancy *you* would like most . . .[28]

Vita fancied *Narcissus watieri* from the Atlas Mountains, *Muscari latifolium* (reminiscent of a beautiful arum) and *M. tubergenianum* from north-west Persia, and she was unable to resist Cusack in full flight on *Milla biflora*: '(It is difficult to compose oneself sufficiently to describe it, but here goes!): In form it is the acme of perfection: six petals, three of surpassing elongated symmetry, the intervening ones different in shape, with a beautiful kink near the base ... the whole flower a lovely star, of brilliant snowy white, reminiscent of a microphoto of snow's crystals.'[29] She also marked *Leucojum vernum*, the spring snowflake, *Iris reticulata* var. *krelagei* with crimson purple flowers, *I. histrioides major* and *I. chrysographes* with violet black falls veined with gold, *Crocus chrysanthus* 'E. Augustus Bowles', pale butter yellow, and 'E. P. Bowles', a slightly darker yellow; '*Camassia cusicki* (unfortunately no relation of mine!)' with pale steely blue flowers, and *Camassia fraseri* with clear blue star-like flowers. Some of these treasures were for her sink gardens, and many went into Harold's spring borders. Having Cusack's catalogue was like having a voluble and useful friend at one's elbow – he was the kind of nurseryman who puts his plants first and was totally undaunted by anyone – it must have been quite a visit.

The day ended in the peace of the Wicklow hills, watching peat cutting, then back to Powerscourt which they left next morning, regretfully, to return to Dublin. The trips to Killyleagh and Clandeboye were not a success – Harold found returning to his childhood scenes increasingly depressing, and Vita was not enamoured of the elephant's foot type curiosities at Clandeboye. But the weather was lovely and they escaped gladly to Mount Stewart, where Lady Londonderry took them round the garden in her car along with parrots, macaws and heaps of dogs; she had tropical fish and a baby alligator in her bedroom – Vita was immensely amused. Of Mount Stewart's garden she said nothing – perhaps it was difficult to appreciate it from the car, perhaps the ornamental animals (cats and kittens, dogs and dodos, horses and hedgehogs, baboons, rabbits and squirrels as well as the more usual lions and winged horses) were too much as well as the real ones? Perhaps the imitations of Villa Gamberiaia were too obvious, the pantiled gazebo which spawned a Spanish garden too raw, the laid out design from an Adam ceiling too much like artifice?

They left Ireland on the Larne ferry for Scotland – the old enclosed gardens of Lochinch Castle and the wonderful exotic Logan, the McDoualls' garden on the southernmost of the Rhinns of Galloway, which had come into the care of Olaf Hambro. Lanning Roper had been there earlier in the summer of the same year and has left an evocative description of this marvellous wonderland,[30] a mixture of the homely and the exotic – avenues of lofty dracaenas and of cabbage palms, rich with tree ferns, eucalyptus and gigantic gnarled rhododendrons and also roses and sundials and lupins, and

> one of the most delightful combinations of flowers that I have ever seen ... a mass of *Calceolaria violacea*, which was at least 5 ft tall and completely smothered with little bells, mauve without and spotted with violet within. Against this mauve background were fine blue *Meconopsis betonicifolia*, candelabra primulas in all the shades of pink and mauve, a particularly fine, rich, wine-coloured one known as 'Logan's Purple', a film of

mauve thalictrum, *Polemonium alba* and the clear apricot and strong wine-purple of violas.[31]

That would have made Vita's mouth water – but she was probably in time to catch the last remnants of the *shoulder-high* primulas that line the walks to the sea (*Primula pulverentula* and *P. japonica*), and the giant herbaceous lobelias were in bloom for her (*Lobelia cardinalis* came back to Sissinghurst, as did *Hydrangea villosa* and *Romneya coulteri*, which she proudly enthused about to Colonel Hoare Grey).

Southwards, back in England, was the old haunt of Vita's ancestor Lady Anne Clifford, where she had come first in 1922 for on-the-spot research for her introduction to Lady Anne's diary: 'I love the hills and wild roads that my old sport Lady Anne used to bump over,' she had written then [colour pl. 8]. Vita identified with Lady Anne, and it had much to do with their shared love of England – 'she was not born to be a wife and a young mother: she was born to be a great-grandmother and a widow ... the black serge and plain white wimple framing the hard old face became her more truly than the damask embroidered in gold that the tailor sent to Knole'.[32] Perhaps Vita cherished a misty dream that she would eventually come into her own as Lady Anne had done. She had 'served a long probation' through her marriage to the Earl of Dorset, who died in 1624, then banishment to Bolebroke, the Sackville dower house, then marriage to Philip Herbert, Earl of Pembroke – and all the time she never gave up fighting for her own Clifford lands. When Francis Clifford, Lord Cumberland, died in 1641, and Henry, his only son, died two years later, she was ready: she came into natural possession of the land she had fought for for thirty-eight years and started the life she loved – 'backwards and forwards over the roads of Yorkshire, Westmorland and Cumberland', the lonely roads over the fells, the innumerable bridges, over a rough wild country made 'musical by becks and waterfalls, dim with mist and shaggy as the mountain sheep that moved cropping among the boulders'.[33] Lady Anne died happy at Brougham Castle on 22 March 1676, and Thomas Gray wrote on her tomb:

> Now clean, now hideous, mellow now, now gruff
> She swept, she hiss'd, she ripened and grew rough
> At Brougham, Pendragon, Appleby and Brough.

But by the 1950s there was a gem set in Clifford country, the Hon. Robert James's garden at St Nicholas at Richmond [85]. Bobbie James was another great gardening friend, met frequently at Chelsea and R.H.S. shows, even though Vita did despair sometimes of his being 'so highbrow that hardly anything pleases him'. St Nicholas was situated 500 feet up on a southward-facing slope; it was once a monastic property, a rest house for Easby Abbey, and its medieval garden formed the base that Bobbie James worked upon.[34] The garden which he had made during fifty years was of great elegance, beautiful spaces cleanly cut out with sculptured hedges or old walls and filled with his highly individual planting – each plant being chosen for its merit and placed to grow happily *and* be part of a picture. He demanded that each plant was 'a good rent payer'. It was a garden bereft of bright yellows, which he did not think suited his northern light (he similarly thought autumn colours vulgar!), but it had Vita's favourite roses in purples, pinks and stripes – and St Nicholas's own rose, a huge *gallica*, fragrant, brilliant, graceful and floriferous. He had a wonderful long double herbaceous border, which again Lanning Roper saw:

> ... 130 yards long and 18 ft wide, backed by hornbeam hedges. The central strip of grass ends in a semi-circle with a William Kent garden bench. These borders are unlike any others I know. Planted to require the minimum of staking, there are large numbers of fine shrub roses, ceanothus, tree peonies, eleagnus, phlomis and potentillas, some of which are very large; for example a Woolly Dod is over 12 feet tall, and as much across. High plants are brought well forward to break the length and to add mystery. Plants are chosen for colour, for foliage and for fragrance. *Viola cornuta* creeps through the border like a breaking wave of mauve. Grey and silver foliage plants like artemisias, verbascums, artichokes, *Senecio greyii*, *Stachys lanata* and *Nepeta mussinii* are a foil for the deep crimson and cherry of sweet williams.[35]

The reds of his borders – *Phlox drummondii*, *Lobelia cardinalis*, verbena, alonsoa and red dahlias, penstemons and centaureas – would be at their best when Vita saw them. There were peat walls made especially to house a collection of Asiatic primulas, lewisias, ramondas, haberleas, soldanellas and meconopsis; rocks were lost in a profusion of gentians, orchids, trilliums and trailing arbutus, daphnes, ferns and violas, campanulas and dianthus. Also at St Nicholas Vita found some carefully cosseted varieties that she was to bring back to Sissinghurst – the climbing gazanias, *Mutisia ilicifolia* and *M. oligodon*, and *Berberidopsis corallina* with heart-shaped leaves and long sprays of crimson flowers – these set with *Nerine bowdenii* and *Alstroemeria* 'Ligtu' hybrids.

The road from St Nicholas came down the eastern side of England, a road first taken with Violet in an escapade of passion for which the excuse was *Dragon in Shallow Waters*. This novel of Vita's was imprisoned in the fenland bleakness that combines something of the menace of Dorothy Sayers's *Nine Tailors* with an almost Dickensian feeling for the life-dampening effect of the flat wet landscape and 'the seeping, shrouding fog' that 'favours the deeds of evil men'. Fog hangs over most of the novel, symbolizing the prison that the heroine Nan inhabits, and again the road is the symbol of freedom; Linnet and Nan can only glimpse a brighter future when they walk out on the road, and only at the very end, when they have won their freedom, does the clear sun flood the marshes. Vita and Violet stayed in Lincoln, at the now vanished Saracen's Head, full of heavy furniture and hanging aspidistras – the paradox of beauty in the whole bleak experience was the walk up those steep lanes to the ridge on which that wonderful cathedral stands, surveying its city and countryside.

On her happier, later trip with Harold they diverted to stay with the Cholmondleys at Houghton Hall in Norfolk, where Harold appreciated the Palladian magnificence but Vita was suffocated by it; once they lunched with 'Chips' Channon in his 'hideous' garden, and, perhaps most enjoyably, they went to Blickling Hall to admire the way Norah Lindsay had softened the Victorian parterre with massed herbaceous

16. Sissinghurst: the courtyard, with the wonderful long-flowering 'Allen Chandler' rose wreathed around the entrance arch.

17. Sissinghurst: the courtyard. *Solanum crispum* 'Glasnevin' on the wall next to *Magnolia grandiflora*, with *Osteospermum ecklonis prostratum* in the sink garden.

18. *(opposite)* Sissinghurst: the Nuttery underplanted with polyanthus, the company of the bright and the good, and in Harold's opinion 'the loveliest planting scheme in the whole world'.

19. *(above)* Sissinghurst: the herb garden.

20. *(centre)* Sissinghurst: the Lime Walk. Muscari, auriculas, polyanthus and a single tulip set in the paved walk.

21. *(below)* Sissinghurst: the Lime Walk. Muscari, fritillaries and tulips at the foot of one of the pleached limes.

22. *(overleaf)* Sissinghurst: the South Cottage, taken over by 'Mme Alfred Carrière', with its cottage garden planting – helianthemums, pansies and columbines, in warm, sunny colours.

plants and blurred the edges of formality with lavenders, hebes and sun roses. And once, in 1957, Vita took one of her last remaining close friends, Edie Lamont,[36] into the eastern counties:

> ... it was misty in Essex but cleared into a lovely golden day in Suffolk which was all and more than I expected ... we went through Tollshunt Darcy and across country to Layer Marney, which as you know I'd always wanted to see – it is very odd, far bigger and less ugly than I'd expected, and there's a lovely little church next door of the same date, with its tombs and all its decorations for the harvest festival – sheaves of corn, marrows, apples, masses of flowers, baskets of eggs, very charming and real.[37]

Lavenham, churches everywhere, Hadleigh and almost uninhabited country lanes 'with a red sunset on one side and a full moon on the other' all came up to expectations.[38]

Apart from this grand tour there was another route from Sissinghurst, taken rather more frequently ... I shall take it again as it would have been in those first years of the fifties, when Harold was working at Windsor Castle on his biography of George V.[39] On Sunday 14 June 1951 they went over to lunch with Constance Spry and to see the Savill Garden with Sir Eric and Lady Savill. They loved the woodland, and Harold wondered if they could copy the mix of meconopsis and primroses at Sissinghurst at the end of the moat – 'I think the end of the moat would be too hot, it is a suntrap,' replied Vita, 'I thought behind the azaleas with the sweet woodruff and the back row of azaleas they would take the place of the polyanthus after the polyanthus were over and we could make up the soil to suit them.'[40] Another guest was the young James Russell, then starting to revive Sunningdale Nursery, which Vita felt sure he would turn into something remarkable with his 'fine and erudite taste in design' and great knowledge of plants; he shared her passion for old roses and he found her many plants for Sissinghurst, including in these early days of their friendship *Agapanthus globosa*, with pale blue flowers, *Alstroemeria hachiensis* (deep wine-red flowers) and *A. perlarquinia* for the new white garden she was making. He sent her supplies of *Lilium giganteum*, the rarer escallonias and *Moorea spathesi*.

The fifties were the heyday of many nurseries on the accommodating Bagshot sands of north-west Surrey; besides Jim Russell's Sunningdale, Vita was a good customer at John Waterer's for shrubs, at Hillings' of Chobham for roses, and Jackman's of Woking. She used every opportunity she possibly could, with discretion, to print their names in the *Observer* before the eyes of possible customers, but on one notable occasion fell foul of George Jackman for suggesting that her readers should dig plants up from the wild instead of buying them! This became something of a *cause célèbre*, with Jackman's accusations that she was ruining the nursery trade followed by strong defences,[41] the most entertaining from the playwright Enid Bagnold:

> So, you have got into a pennyworth of trouble, Miss Sackville-West; allow me to take you out of it. I am your constant and excited reader, I am a yellow-fingered, butter-

fingered amateur – every match you strike in your slender column lights up in me a bonfire of next year's dreams. I take up my sword against Mr Jackman, I am astounded at him! When you describe the swags of clematis on engarlanded apple trees I send him cheque after cheque; when surfeited by the lushness of catalogues and yearly able better to resist them, you I cannot resist. Old fashioned roses, they are here in the garden, a scarlet virginia creeper swaying from the pallid forks of a dead tree, a lumbago garden of alpines grown in a sink at hip level, a lawn of thymes, why? envelopes of cheques go out every Saturday at five, especially the lawn of thymes, that happy nurseryman the thyme seller sent me as his personal shout of delight a poem of yours with his bundle. If I fail to tease out of the ground the effects you paint it is because I am stupid at it, have come to it late, but not because my cheque stubs aren't inky with the names of nurserymen and all written hotfoot and hopeful and Sunday dated![42]

The road westwards from the Bagshot sands, the A30, took Vita down to where claustrophobic Surrey opened out to the Hampshire downs, and wilder Wiltshire and her beloved Stonehenge. If it was unavoidable, or lunchtime, she would turn down that delicious road into the valley of the young Avon to Stephen Tennant's Wilsford Manor, a house haunted by the ghost of Rex Whistler and the presences still of Cecil Beaton, the Sitwells, Eddy Sackville-West and Rosamond Lehmann, the eyrie of that '*rara avis*', as Beaton christened Stephen Tennant. Tennant, a genius will o' the wisp, unsure of anything to believe in 'and he would like to love and believe in so much',[43] had the manor decorated in ice-cream colours, the oak staircase whitened and hung with fishing nets and corks, flower petals strewn on pink carpets, gilded shells on the ceilings with clumps of coral and pearl, and bunches of artificial flowers on every cushion. Lunch was also inclined to be rare – chaudfroid of chicken decorated with circus designs in sweets and cut-up fruits, accompanied by talk of Proust, Balzac, Verlaine and Greta Garbo. Vita was the recipient of Stephen's adoration – 'Oh, for the peace of your tower' he wrote, repeatedly – and of his lovely and extravagant ideas on gardening . . . but probably none of them was ever put into practice!

The A30 led farther westwards into the garden county of Somerset. Vita visited Mrs Phyllis Reiss at Tintinhull Manor, where the Queen Anne façade of this lovely stone house dominates the peaceful sequence of garden rooms, made intriguing by subtle changes of level. This garden was the perfect echo of the house. The garden rooms were furnished as exquisitely as the house, with trim box hedges, loose lavenders, flowering shrubs underplanted with tulips followed by lilies, *Anemone japonica*, peonies and bergenias in the first room, an enormous ilex surrounded with columbines, anemones and cyclamen in the second, a spring garden in the third, a pool garden, and so on. From across the pool, surrounded by clean stone and decorated with water lilies and only *Agapanthus mooreanus* around the periphery of vision, one views the full perspective of the garden – the other rooms stand aside and only the lovely façade of the house remains. In this serene setting Mrs Reiss had introduced planting ideas that Vita would not have seen elsewhere; her borders were one step beyond (or back from) one colour gardens – pale yellows, blues and whites in one, purples, mauves and stronger yellows in another; she used floribunda

85. St Nicholas, Richmond, Yorkshire: the garden of the Hon. Robert James as Vita knew it – a garden of great elegance and picturesqueness where every plant was 'a good rent payer'.

roses, 'Donald Prior', 'Break O'Day' and 'Elsa Poulsen', which spurred Vita to writing about them and admitting they were a success! But she also had many old roses in common with Vita, though she grew them with *Clematis jackmanii* trained on umbrella frames, which Vita might have felt a little forced. Tintinhull was a garden of conscious constant repetition of good plant mixes (whereas Sissinghurst was never that), with a stronger emphasis on textures and form of foliage than flowers. Mrs Reiss was an original planting designer, with greater flair than Vita in these terms, and she must have influenced Vita's post-war ideas on 'simplification' profoundly.[44]

At nearby Barrington Court, Miss Jekyll's veritable palace of garden rooms (she did the planting plans for the architects Forbes and Tait in 1917 when she was seventy-four) was still splendidly if not accurately furnished in the 1950s. At Montacute [colour pl. 9], a house after Vita's own heritage, she was thrilled to be asked to design planting for the courtyard borders in the autumn of 1948, and she wrote telling Violet proudly of her commission. All did not work out too well though, largely, it seems, through poor maintenance, for a spring drought upset Vita's schemes and Mrs Reiss, presumably because she was near at hand, took over. Vita, however, is still credited with the rose border below the raised walk, with the roses of York and Lancaster, *Rosa alba maxima, R. gallica officinalis, R. gallica versicolor* ('Rosa Mundi') and *R. moyesii, R. spinosissima lutea*, the climbing 'Souvenir de la Malmaison' and *R. rugosa* and hybrid musk roses.[45]

From Montacute she went to East Lambrook Manor to talk with Margery Fish about Dad's Favourite, Sticky Nellie, Snow in Summer, Wee Folks' Stockings, Old Dusty Miller and the totally fascinating lore of cottage garden plants. She saw Dartington Hall (finding Dorothy Elmshirst admirable but sentimental, which, poor thing, could not be helped as she was American) and continued on down into Cornwall, to Lanhydrock, Trelissick and Trengwainton:

> Huge bushes of camellia, *reticulata, saluenensis, donckelaarii*, J. C. Williams: towering magnolias lifting their heads of white or pink against the soft dark green background of *Pinus insignis*; enormous clumps of blood-red or orange berberis, flaming in the sun; fluffy yellow acacias (mimosa) trained against whitewashed walls; rhododendrons the size of cottages; blue lithospermums tumbling over grey rocks – all these were in full flower, and amongst them was the promise of things to come; pyramidal eucryphias, embothriums that would presently display their scarlet, Davidias that would hang out their strange white rags.[46]

'Not for me in south-east England, I fear,' she added ruefully.

On the way back she saw Lord Digby's magical woodland dell at Minterne, Cerne Abbas, and a garden that must have stirred most memories of all, the seventeenth-century Cranborne Manor [colour pls. 12, 13]. Here, in miniature, were the domestic enclosures of Knole dedicated to fruits and roses and herbs in an unchanged fashion. What greater compliment could the young Viscountess Cranborne (now the Marchioness of Salisbury) have paid her visitor than to decide to replant Cranborne in the manner of Sissinghurst?

On the borders of Surrey and Sussex, high on Blackdown, is Michael Haworth-Booth's beautiful garden. He wrote, in typical manner, after her visit: '. . . to be offered a rose by a great poetess as the morning sun lit up the breakfast table was a delightful experience' – in return he offered her his choicest hydrangeas, a Grayswood white which turned crimson and *H. serrata* 'Bluebird'.[47]

Once at home there were many more day visits to be made. To Glyndebourne and lunch with the John Christies, whom she found to be neither gourmets nor gardeners – 'we had stewed rabbit and a quavering caramel shape' – but she felt clever because she identified their laburnum with pink, yellow and mauve flowers

(*Laburnocytisus adamii,* a graft hybrid of laburnum and broom which originated in the nursery of M. Adam near Paris in 1925). At Lutyens's palatial Great Maytham at Rolvenden she talked gardening for long hours with Mrs Tennant, who sold silver plants reared in the Secret Garden that inspired Frances Hodgson Burnett's famous story. To Great Comp and Mrs Heron Maxwell's gift of 'ravishing' pink hellebores, and to Godmersham Park where she found the Trittons 'too beastly rich' for good taste but that Norah Lindsay had done another lovely border beginning with white and pale blue flowers and working up through pinks to flames and oranges.

THESE, then, were the gardens and gardeners that occupied Vita's thoughts and time and fuelled her *Observer* pieces. In the garden context of the early fifties her particular choice was biased towards gardens where the moving spirit was still in charge, and most of 'her' gardens would be called plantsman's gardens. Vita did not 'kindle' (to use Virginia Woolf's term) over the great historical gardens that Harold would perhaps have enjoyed more – Barry's Shrublands, Cliveden, Wrest Park, Powis Castle, Levens Hall, Chatsworth, Blenheim and Hever and perhaps Harold Peto's Buscot Park – all in great glory at this time. She was full of admiration and awe for the newer aristocracy of Leonardslee, Nymans, Borde Hill, Bodnant, Wakehurst Place, Sheffield Park, Stourhead and the exotic Tresco, as well as Sir Frederick Stern's garden in a chalk quarry at Highdown. These were the gardens she felt could be given the highest accolade, and (with of course the exception of Highdown) they are all rhododendron gardens and on the grandest scale. However, perhaps in an in-between category came their kind of gardens; most of these have already been mentioned, but they must also have seen the two Dalrymple gardens – Furzey at Minstead in the New Forest, and the House in the Wood at Bartley nearby, the latter most famous for its Bartley strain of *Primula pulverentula,* naturalized in the woodland and its deciduous azalea groves. There was also Great Dixter, where Mrs Nathaniel Lloyd (mother of Christopher and Quentin) was still in control, and they knew well romantic Scotney Castle, the home of Christopher and Betty Hussey. A rather special last garden, special for its owner, the Hon. David Bowes-Lyon, whom they both admired, was St Paul's Waldenbury in Hertfordshire [86]. Harold loved the radiating avenues and classical temples, arranged with a perfection of restraint (unlike Hever and Iford), and for Vita there was the ruined orangery covered with flowers and the old monastery pond banked with lupins. St Paul's also has a classical pleached lime arbour walk; against this classical green alley Harold's Sissinghurst Lime Walk, kept firmly clipped so that it could be carpeted with flowers, is an invention which is quite his own.

In this company of the great and visited post-war gardens Sissinghurst seems to stand out for one particular quality; shades of its design and all its planting ideas might be found elsewhere, but where else was such a comforting, intimate garden? Even in this company of the great and the good, Sissinghurst shone out for its quality of love. I think Vita would have really appreciated that this was beautifully

86. St Paul's Waldenbury when it was the garden of the Hon. David Bowes-Lyon, a much-admired friend of the Nicolsons. Harold especially admired the classical taste of St Paul's, particularly these radiating avenues.

expressed in a television script, narrated by Sir John Gielgud – 'her garden had all the unselfconscious charm which only art, love and knowledge combined can produce. There was no regimentation; nothing was forced. The impression given was that every plant in the garden was delighted to be there. She chose them because she loved them; and, perhaps, they knew that.'[48]

THERE are only two small postscripts, though important ones, to be added to this chapter. Firstly, even though she was busy with her gardening world, Vita did not forget her England. Soon after the war she began her work for the Committee for the Preservation of Rural Kent, the Council for the Preservation of Rural England's Kent branch, run by the indefatigable C. K. Chettoe ('I have a sick passion for Mr Chettoe' – how Mr Chettoe would have laughed if he had known she had written that!). Rather more seriously, she sat beneath the portrait of her father standing in Knole park in his coronation robes that hung in the County Hall at Maidstone – 'not that it was really characteristic of Dada to go walking in the park in his coronation robes' – and loved to linger there alone with him and her sandwiches while the rest of the Committee went out to brave Maidstone lunches. She would have brought to the C.P.R.K. a leavening of her real love for the landscape, the farmed landscape, of Kent, that would have moderated over-zealous preservation of the *status quo,* for she knew that cottages must have electricity and farmers must keep chickens and pigs (pylons and 'factory' farming units being high in the catalogue of country blights then); she would wholeheartedly have joined in the battles against green field development (a new town was mooted for Smarden wood), and how she would (as we *now* know) have been right.

Secondly, it was typical of her that her contact with all these famous gardeners and Experts gave her grave doubts about how much – or how little – she knew! In March 1956 she sent for a non-examination course in General Horticulture from a correspondence college at Dawlish in Devon run by a Mr Ibbett. The course was advertised as suitable for 'preliminary training' and useful for students not ready to take the R.H.S. senior examinations. She must have had grave doubts. She paid her four guineas and attended to the first lessons, but disregarded the one about vegetables 'as I have no interest in vegetables, only when they are cooked ...' She answered the questions on Muscat and Alexandrian grapes without books to show how much she did know, and Mr Ibbett gave her 8 out of 10! She does not appear to have done any more.[49] Perhaps the course details proved to her that she knew rather more than she thought? Perhaps it was a dummy run for an *Observer* article, though I cannot find that it appeared, or did aristocratic disdain prevent her being worried that the châtelaine of Sissinghurst's great garden might be caught in a position that *Punch* (who were already parodying her style of column) would have enjoyed? I think it was none of these things. I think that for moments, and there were many, she *really* doubted her own ability to be either a garden writer or a gardener. These doubts gave Sissinghurst its 'unselfconscious charm'; these doubts gave her garden's visitors the constant reminder that if they too were brave enough and tried for their dreams, even non-gardening dreams, they just might come true.

9

BLUNDERING INTO FAME
1945-54

What a perfect day it was yesterday, the pale stream of the River
Thames was gilded by the strangest alchemy and all the willows were
bursting into green: I sat in my tower looking out towards the
Chilterns and thought of our lovely garden all green and yellow and
expectant. It is, is, is a lovely garden and I was so happy on Sunday
just walking with you among the loveliness you made. I think it is the
loveliest garden in the whole world.

Harold Nicolson to V. Sackville-West from Windsor Castle, 24 April 1951

There is a nice article about roses in Country Life and quite a lot about
our garden . . . 'gardens such as Hidcote, St Nicholas and Sissinghurst
Castle' . . . I think it is funny how our rubbish dump has blundered into
fame.

V. Sackville-West to Harold Nicolson, 29 September 1954

B Y THE TIME the war ended Sissinghurst had indeed taken on its Sleeping Beauty
aspect. The visitors who came for the celebratory opening of 2 May 1945
must have seen blossom, some spring flowers and masses of ground elder, but
what did it matter? A fortnight later Vita was rejoicing in a chorus of nightingales
that was better than ever they were at Long Barn, and a balmy night with a newish
moon kept her outside until past midnight. Her little world, their precious little
world, had survived the war intact.

Harold, having lost his House of Commons seat in the General Election of July
1945, was home for much of the rest of the summer and early autumn, writing. In
November they learned that their young and energetic gardener Jack Vass was safe
after his wartime adventures, and he actually started back at work in January
1946.[1] Vita felt that she and Vass made an ideal combination – 'Vass is a gardener
after my own heart, I love his keenness and knowledge, only I think it is a good
thing to be behind him to check his love of over-neatness with my own more
romantic and more untidy view of what the garden should be . . . I couldn't wish for
a nicer gardener.'[2] When he had left for the war Vass's parting words had been a
plea to look after the hedges and the paths at all costs, even if everything else had to

87. Sissinghurst: the Rondel and its surrounding roses – clever geometry, immaculate hedges, narrow
walks and an abundance of flowers – Vita's rubbish dump now blundered into fame.

be let go; when he did return he found that Vita had managed to do this, and together they planned a re-working of the entire garden that was to take them the next five years.

During those five years (1946 to 1951) Harold and Vita's life settled into a pattern that lasted until Vita died. Harold worked at journalism, book reviews, lecturing and travelling, his committees (including the National Trust, the London Library) and his books. In January 1946 he moved into a new London home, 10 Neville Terrace, off Onslow Gardens in South Kensington, which he shared with Ben and Nigel. He was determined to hate Kensington and 'Devil Terrace' (mainly because it wasn't his beloved King's Bench Walk, which he had had to give up when it was deemed that there was room only for barristers after the war damage), and consoled himself with fantasies of a 'great Palladian garden' of terraces with a small, formal lake, which in reality came to flower beds and window boxes planned for him by Vita:

> I enclose a list of annuals from which you can compose either a yellow and orange colour [scheme] – I think window boxes demand a definite colour scheme, don't you? – or a purple mauve and pink one – you will have to buy these plants in May – I should mix wallflowers with your polyanthus – Orange Bedder wallflowers and Fire King with yellow and tawny polyantha. Must you have geraniums?[3]

The most consistent flowers at Neville Terrace were those still sent from Sissinghurst or taken back from his week-ends at home. Vita went on a carefree jaunt by car to France in the summer of 1946; she drove, Raymond Mortimer navigated, and Eardley Knollys was provisions officer. It was just what she needed. The summer at Sissinghurst was very happy with lots of post-war festivities and visitors; but Harold was sixty in November, which depressed him profoundly, and on two week-ends in the same month he found Vita, propped against a tree in the garden, crying because her back was too painful for her to carry on working. But they survived and went on to shiver through that notorious winter of 1946–7, to emerge on the other side for a happy summer with Harold at home a lot writing, bathing in the lake before breakfast under the Erectheum, writing all day and working and planning the garden, especially his spring border Unter den Linden, in the evenings. An idyllic existence. In February of 1948 he made his last traumatic effort to get back into the House of Commons at the North Croydon by-election and failed; the following autumn he started work on his biography of George V, which kept him at Windsor Castle working for long periods. *George V* was finished in September 1951 and published in triumph in August 1952.

As for the garden, the war had been a period of enforced reflection. Though they would never give up their belief in their garden as a luxurious brocade where only the best flowers grew, they had each had warnings about their health and capacities for strenuous work; Jack Vass, with his boundless energy and enthusiasm, was the only gardener Vita felt she could really trust, and though modernities such as the motor mower, the autoscythe, selective weedkillers and all kinds of new tools and gadgets (which Harold and Vita gave each other for presents) gradually crept in, there were still many time-consuming tasks which could only be done by patient hands. It took Vass and a boy three days to re-tie 'Mme Albert Carrière' on to South Cottage, and consequently weeks to deal with all the other roses and wall plants. And Vita would always have a stubborn weakness for her picturesque impracticalities – the donkey Abdul (brought home from Algeria in 1934), 'small, neat and serious' with his little weed-carrying cart, was a vital part of the Sissinghurst workforce until he finally died in 1958. There was no doubt that they both realized that post-war Sissinghurst would have to have a slightly different emphasis from their original dreams; Sissinghurst, as well as more modest patches, was to feel the chill breeze of 'altered circumstances', as the popular gardening columnist Roy Hay gently broke it to his devotees. 'Simplicity, economy of labour and materials and low upkeep costs' were the order of the day.[4] The chief post-war plantings – the herb garden, the Moat Walk and the White Garden – are ground-covering plantings that were originally done at little cost (often with cuttings garnered from friends or other parts of the garden) and they conformed to this prevailing mood. The fact that all three draw gasps of astonishment for their beauty proves just how sensible was their concept and how, with her characteristic generosity, Vita well understood that 'low upkeep' could never be 'no upkeep' (as we now seem to expect).

But there were concepts that were symbols, of a value above all practical considerations, and these had to be protected and enhanced. The immediate task when work really started was to cut the weeds in the nuttery; this was a bow from Vita to Harold (perhaps to make up for North Croydon and for losing his adored London home at King's Bench Walk). The nuttery's glorious carpet of polyanthus – symbol of all that was bright and good – was the first priority for restoration.[5] Then the courtyard and Tower lawns were ploughed up and re-seeded, and after such violent acts as these Jack Vass set about removing the plants, stripping the elder-ridden soil and replanting the Rondel flower beds. He moved on to the Cottage Garden, but only after consultations with Harold for whom this had an 'elective affinity', even though Vita did the planting. Neither Vita nor Vass touched the Lime Walk, which was in Harold's sole charge and looked after by its own gardener, Sidney Neve, who worked slowly but well and was paid by Harold. The Lime Walk, his Unter den Linden spring border (there were some good things to remember about Berlin, as he discovered when he went back in September 1948 and found 'a nightmare fusion of the recognizable and the changed, just as if one were to come upon Knole in ruins upon Salisbury Plain'[6]), which he called 'My Life's Work', was his great post-war achievement in the garden. He had written from Leicester in the midst of that disastrous General Election campaign of 1945: 'I am determined to make M.L.W. the loveliest spring border in England and then to make the Nuttery what it was before. If I succeed in this I shall die happy.'[7] And, apart from a sad look back to a land before a war that he never wanted to be fought, there was another reason for his spring border: on his fiftieth birthday, in 1936, still in that other land, he had thought of his life as 'an alpine meadow patinated with the stars of varied

179

(a) The plan for the head of the Lime Walk, around the statue of the Bacchante for the years 1953 to 1955. The plan is drawn on the right-hand page and the notes were added on the left-hand page:

To do 1953 for 1954
- Fill up at A A A with denticulata and myosotis pulling myosotis in front of denticulata
- Fill up B B B with more myosotis
- Yellow hellebore for blank C C C
- I need something very showy opposite entrance
- C C C is bang opposite entrance and must have Crown Imperial

Notes for 1955
- Gaps beneath the medlar
- More allioni and fritillary for B B B
- Crown Imperial for C C C
- Probably tulips for D D D   (Order all these)

Notes taken in 1955 for 1956
- Blank under medlar especially between two posts
- Blanks were marked in red. Pretty good really.
- Crown Imperials very good
- Gaps at crosses

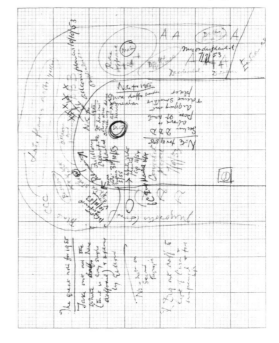

(b) This is the second sketch in the notebook for the same area at the head of the Lime Walk for the years 1956 to 1958. The notes on the left-hand page read:

Ideas for 1956
- Copy to left of path Anemone salmonea under broom
- The Crown Imperial lutea is very lovely and late. Get some more
- Denticulata to be concentrated at entrance and swamped by snake irrigation
- Put some mertensia in
- Put more violets in cracks
- Why not a sacred patch for auriculas?
- Get more Tulipa Tarda in case they die off
- Get some cuttings of the yellow wallflower near the cottage

For 1957
- A – Pegged area at path corner to be wholly replanted (Verbena Laurence Johnston planted 12/5/56)
- B – Gap where pegged between tulips and omphaloides
- C – Rather sparse

For 1958
- Clusiana (Tulipa clusiana) planted to right of path at //// Apl 13 1957
- The circle pretty good now but polemonium has not come up (April).

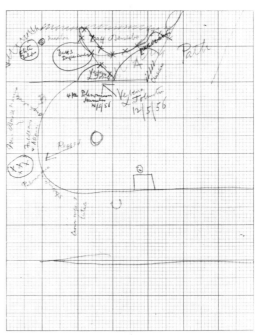

flowers. Would I feel happier if I had stuck to a single crop of lucerne or clover? No.'[8] It hardly seems necessary to add that the Lime Walk was also untouched by thoughts of simplification or economy.

In fact it is the most lavishly recorded of Sissinghurst's gardens, with its maker's efforts set out in meticulous detail in notebooks, started in 1947 and continuing through until the late fifties [88]. Harold's Life's Work had an allowance, it benefited from his constant scouring of the R.H.S. spring shows through these years for new and better varieties, and from his Saturday afternoon weeding sessions. He came to terms with weeding, which he found worthwhile here, though on one notorious occasion he poisoned Vita's carefully nurtured compost heap with the addition of M.L.W.'s entire crop of celandines! One can picture him, after an afternoon's weeding, poring over the squared paper pages at his desk in the window of his South Cottage sitting room. He is armed with blue and red biros, lead and red pencils. He plans out the Lime Walk, numbering the trees 1 to 15, marking in what is there, what has flowered well, and making notes of suggestions for replacements and additions for next year. His notebooks are a cavalcade of ideas: small crowds of the loveliest daffodils, 'Mrs R. O. Backhouse' the pink daffodil, *Narcissus bulbocodium conspicuus* the 'Hooped Petticoat', and jonquils – 'about the jonquils,' he had written to Vita before the war,

> you have no idea how I love them. I never thought of them much before – little meagre yellow things that I was never allowed to pick, then in an orgy of recklessness you put at least 7 jonquils into my Monday bouquet, and they smell out the whole Strand and across the river to Oxo, they shout in thin little voices ... and the whole of spring and Sissinghurst settles on King's Bench Walk.[9]

There are the delicate soft chrome yellow *Tulipa batalinii* mixed with Sparaxis 'Fire King', Anemone de Caen and a patch of modest little myosotis, though probably a pink or even yellow variety; he loved cottage tulips, 'Couleur Cardinal' and 'Cottage Beauty', the frail Lady Tulip *T. clusiana*, the old 'Clara Butt' and new from Peter Barr[10] 'Inglesworth', 'Rembrandt', 'Annie Laurie' and 'James Wild'. Lime tree no. 7 North was a 'museum piece' of success surrounded by *Anemone fulgens*, jonquils and dog's tooth violets; an Etruscan vase was filled with *Iris pumila* and a jar from Ravello with *Clematis macropetala*, its delicate tendrils and violet blue flowers tumbling over the jar. Dwarf iris and muscari ran between the paving stones, and *Gentiana acaulis* and even *Genista januensis*, the winged Genoa broom, were planted there; he cherished old varieties of polyanthus, especially yellow ones, a clump of *Omphalodes luciliae* which Vita gave him from her sink garden, and moisture-loving *Primula denticulata*, which grew in this dry place because Neve had strict instructions to swamp them with snake irrigation. *Iris pumila*, the omphalodes,

88. *(opposite)* Harold Nicolson's sketches for the Lime Walk from his 'My Life's Work' notebooks. He numbered the trees 1 to 15 North and 1 to 15 South and made plans for the sections between each tree in this way.

fritillaries, daffodils, *Tulipa robinsoniana* and *Anemone solomonea* between Limes 4 and 5 North made 'a very pretty section'; he coveted Barr's Parrot tulips, 'enamelled like Battersea china', and sometimes at the flower shows he ordered rashly, two or three dozen of something, assuring Vita that half would be for her. Vita, in turn, kept him informed of M.L.W.'s progress when he was away: 'I have just been on my daily tour of inspection,' she wrote when he was in Greece in March 1952,

> not very much is happening owing to the lack of sun, but lots of little noses, many of which I don't recognize – two of your *Kaufmanniana* tulips at the foot of the statue are showing colour and two Dog's Tooth Violets are open – they are all silent witnesses to Hadji's industry on happy afternoons. The primroses look well and there are lots of little cups of crocus between the paving stones – I wonder if you planted them or if they are self sown or a bit of both. I am not sorry things are so late because there will be quite a nice bit when you come back. Everything is quite incredibly tidy and there is masses of manure everywhere, which rejoices my heart because it usually goes on William's cabbages.[11]

The flower-carpeted paving of the Lime Walk was so carefully guarded by Vita on Harold's behalf, but perhaps she just longed to get at it herself, for it figures in her dreams? She had seen in Yorkshire the paved court of an old house sprouting snapdragons and thought it delightful; it led her to dreaming of what she would like to do: 'How much I long sometimes for a courtyard flagged with huge grey paving stones. I dream of it at night, and I think of it in the daytime, and I make pictures in my mind, and I know with the reasonable part of myself that never in this life shall I achieve such a thing.' She suggests 'lakes of aubretia, bumps of thrift, mattresses of yellow stone-crops, hassocks of pinks, rivulets of violets: you see the idea?'[12] She goes into more details:

> There was once a play called *Boots and Doormats* ... in modern jargon I suppose they would be called tramplers and tramplees; I prefer boots and doormats ... Many big boots will walk down a paved path and there are some meek doormats prepared to put up with such gruff treatment. The creeping thymes really enjoy being walked on ...Pennyroyal does not mind what you do with it, and will give out its minty scent all the better for being bruised underfoot ... all the Acaenas are useful ...[13]

Round the edges where there is no danger of things being walked upon she would plant *Bellis* 'Dresden China', 'as pink and pretty as its name suggests'; 'and sun-roses foaming in all the delicate colours of terra-cotta, buff, yellow and rose; and the little trailing *Gypsophila fratensis* ... the tiny iris-like *Sisyrinchium angustifolium*, sometimes called Blue Eyed Grass ... and I should also have some tufts of the small *Iris pumila* ...'[14]

As even Sissinghurst had not room for everything she never did get her planted pavements, but her dreams came out in her *Observer* 'sticklebacks' as she used to call them. The above passage seems to illustrate well just why those Sunday breakfast-time conversations over the years seemed to captivate so many readers, even those who did not imagine themselves gardeners (for they also could indulge in dreams);

she gave good gardening advice, but unlike so many gardening columnists she was not afraid to admit her mistakes and that she didn't always know the answers; she told of the doings of her famous garden, though she never mentioned it by name, and she clearly put herself out to find the answers to readers' queries even if they were about something that did not apply to her garden. But, perhaps more than all these reasons for her appeal, it was just the feeling that one was having a Sunday morning conversation with an old and amusing friend, who was full of bright anecdotes and constant surprises; Vita's column enjoyed the accolade of being turned to first, even before the sports page!

It is through the columns of the *Observer* that Vita's Sissinghurst, in its prime, can be most clearly seen; she began her pieces in the autumn of 1946 and continued them for fourteen years. The first notes of endearing character to be caught by the observant visitor were the sink gardens on their brick supports in the courtyard, against the walls of the 'barracks' and the Big Room. In December 1953 she wrote:

> I find, unless I am much mistaken, that I have not written about sink or trough gardens since June 1949. Yet this is one of the handiest and most intimate forms of gardening, adapted to the large garden or the small, the town garden or the country; and especially, as I see I remarked then, to the rheumatic or the sufferers from lumbago, or the merely rather stiff-jointed elderly.[15]

Good practical advice (a big hole for drainage, a covering of crocks, some rough fibrous leaf-mould and then the soil) was followed by the possibilities – for growing lime-haters, scree-lovers or peat-loving plants – the choice is open. The Sissinghurst sinks were of the middle variety, tumbling out

> *Thymus serpyllum* for carpeting; saxifrages of the Kabschia or the encrusted kinds, tiny Alpine forget-me-nots, alpine poppy; *Bellis* Dresden China daisy [again], *Erinus alpinus*, pink variety; *Veronica allionii* with violet spikes, *Allium cyaneum*, a 5-inch high blue garlic, midget roses and bulbs of crocus, scillas, grape hyacinths ... the list would be endless...[16]

The idea was extended, or rather concentrated, into pan gardens (in an old saucepan or an outsize alpine pan), which Vita used to make for house-bound friends such as Katharine Drummond, and which Jack Vass would patiently spend hours making for Vita. She wrote about them in April and August, and they probably came as a boon of an idea for the inevitable wet days of the Easter and summer holidays. Small plants were grubbed from the garden; moss lawns and looking-glass lakes were recommended but 'not miniature gnomes or toadstools'. For Christmas, plates were filled with berried twigs and coloured leaves and precious freak primroses or rosebuds and Christmas roses. The windowsills of Sissinghurst in winter and early spring were aglow with bowls of bulbs – hyacinths, which she felt could not qualify for grace or beauty but were indispensable for their scent, and the narcissi 'King Alfred', 'Winter Gold', 'Carlton', 'Fortune' and 'Soleil d'Or'.

Though the very first tastes of Sissinghurst, the avenue of Lombardy poplars emphasizing the entrance and the arrangement of the front entrance court, were

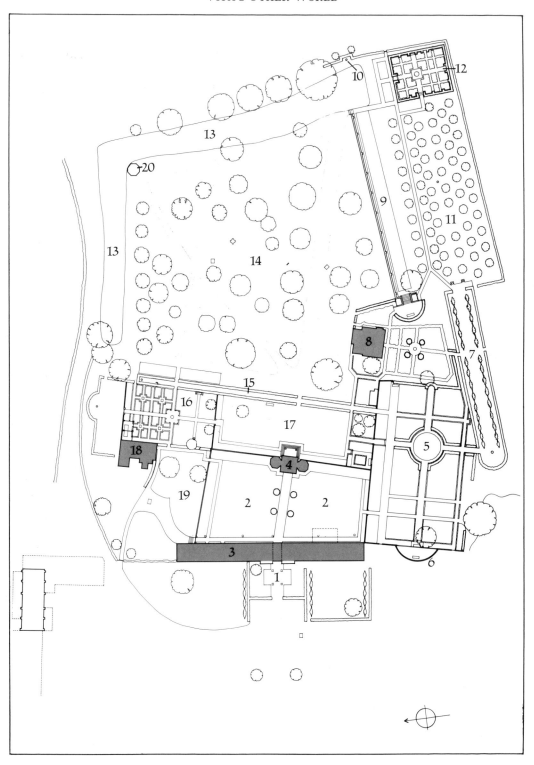

Harold's, once the courtyard was entered Vita took over as the dominant personality for a while. This courtyard that caught the shadows of the Tower, as in the Green Court at Knole, with shrubs and flowers bringing the dusky pinks, wines, clarets and purples of Florentine brocades, the ripening fruits of the warm south turned to flowers against the russet and pink old English walls, this courtyard is a brief introduction to the châtelaine of Sissinghurst. And beyond the south wall the Rondel Rose Garden [87] is her spiritual home, a room as expressive of her personality as her writing room, a room furnished with lilies, peonies, pinks, irises among masses of old roses, all in those warm, rich, *ancien régime* colours that are part of herself. Vita did perhaps really believe that she could qualify as an expert (but not with a capital E) on old roses. Her collection was at its peak during the fifties and she must take much of the credit for showing off the roses that first her old friend Edward Bunyard and later Graham Stuart Thomas wrote about. From where we stand now, the success of the revival of old roses owes a lot to her. She was quite fierce on the subject:

> May 28 1950. The roses are coming out, and I hope everybody will take the opportunity of seeing as many of the *old* roses as possible. They may be roughly described as roses which should be grown as shrubs; that is, allowed to ramp away into big bushes, and allowed also to travel about underground if they are on their own roots and come up in fine carelessness some yards from the parent plant.[17]

She was, she admitted, drunk on roses – and another reason must lie in the following romance, always irresistible: 'Take this phrase alone,' she wrote in one of her many pieces on the subject. 'In the 12th century the dark red Gallic rose was cultivated by the Arabs in Spain with the tradition that it was brought from Persia in the 7th century.'[18] Whether accurate or disputatious it does not matter, the romance was all, and she found in roses all the dusky pedigree that she was so proud of in herself. She collected them passionately. In May 1948 she listed them for new metallic embossed labels that would adorn them; her list includes the *gallicas* 'Alain Blanchard', spotted crimson, maroon and purple, 'Anaïs Segales', mauvy crimson which fades to lilac, the remarkable ('one of the most remarkable' says Graham Stuart Thomas)[19] striped 'Camaieux', the practically thornless old rose pink 'Du

89. *(opposite)* Sissinghurst Castle and its garden: a new plan surveyed and drawn by Stuart and Christine Page. The 'obtuseness' with which Harold Nicolson had to contend is all too evident; his achievement can be appreciated better than ever.

KEY
1. The entrance
2. The courtyard
3. The Big Room
4. Vita's Tower
5. The Rondel with its surrounding rose beds
6. Powys's wall
7. The Lime Walk
8. The South Cottage and its garden
9. The Moat Walk
10. The statue of Dionysius
11. The Nuttery
12. The herb garden
13. The moat
14. The orchard
15. The Yew Walk
16. The White Garden
17. The Tower lawn
18. The Priest's House
19. Delos
20. The gazebo erected in 1969 and dedicated to the memory of Harold Nicolson

Maître d'École', and the splendid 'Cardinal de Richelieu'. Besides her Pemberton hybrid musks 'Danae', 'Pax', 'Cornelia', 'Felicia' and 'Pink Prosperity' (of which she had three each) and the hybrid perpetual 'Roger Lambelin', whose lovely scented blooms with serrated edges hung from a weakly plant which was a candidate for training over hazel hoops (an idea which Vass claims he brought to Sissinghurst having seen it done at Cliveden), she wrote of her Bourbons. 18 August 1957:

> If you were born with a romantic nature, all roses must be crammed with romance, and if a particular rose originated on an island the romance must be doubled, for an island is romantic in itself. The island I refer to lies off the south-east coast of Africa, near Mauritius. It used to be called the Ile Bourbon, now called Reunion. The inhabitants of this small island had the pleasing habit of using roses for their hedges: only two kinds, the Damask rose and the China rose. These two married in secret; and one day, in 1817, the curator of the botanic garden noticed a seedling he transplanted and grew on, a solitary little bastard which has fathered and mothered the whole race we now call the Bourbon roses.[20]

Her Bourbons included the wonderfully scented 'Mme Isaac Perière' with shaggy purple flowers, and 'Mme Pierre Oger', a pale silvery pink lady with flowers like small waterlilies; 'Souvenir de la Malmaison', blushing powder pink, of course the thornless cerise-pink 'Zéphirine Drouhin', and the splashed and striped rose-madder 'Commandant Beaurepaire' which she (along with many others) thought might be a *gallica*. The Bourbons, because of their mixed parentage, caused further confusions; she grew the 'most swagger boastful bush' of reddish purple flowers 'Zigeuner Knabe' (which we now rather provincially call 'Gipsy Boy'), and the large and proud 'Mme Lauriol de Barny':

> I wish I could find out who Mme Lauriol was in real life, to have so sumptuous a flower called after her. I suspect that she may have belonged to the *haute cocotterie* of Paris at that date, or possibly I misjudge her and she may have been the perfectly respectable wife of some Mr de Barny, perhaps a rose-grower of Lyon. Someone ought to write the biographies of persons who have had roses named in their honour. Who was Madame Hardy? Who was Charles de Mills? I don't know, and I long for a Who's Who to correct my ignorance.[21]

Though forever loyal to her old roses she did venture to consider others; she was actually prepared to admit that others had merits – as long as they smelt as roses should. Her visit to Mrs Reiss's Tintinhull inspired another grudging admission – that even some floribundas had some merits – she liked the sumptuous red 'Frensham' and the fine yellows 'Sandringham' and 'Sunny Maid', but on the whole felt that they would be a fleeting fashion. Hybrid teas were a more secret vice. She

90. Sissinghurst: the South Cottage garden in June. The verdigris copper has been filled with *Mimulus glutinosus* and surrounded with a carefully haphazard array of thymes, iris, aquilegias and helianthemums. The climbing rose 'Madame Alfred Carrière' has now taken over South Cottage just as she did Long Barn.

had admired the yellow tea 'Mrs Van Rossem', the deep apricot 'Duchess of Atholl', cherry pink 'Mrs Edward Laxton' and fragrant yellow 'Lady Forteviot' on a visit to Queen Mary's Rose Garden in Regent's Park; at Sissinghurst they were confined to the vegetable garden, thus never to be seen by the visitors, but she liked to have them for the house. Her dozen bushes for cutting were mostly old favourites – 'Emma Wright', a pure orange, and another McGredy rose, coppery orange 'Mrs Sam McGredy' (which only suffered in Vita's eyes from its name), the crimson scarlet 'Ena Harkness', 'Charles Mallerin', darkest crimson with an almost black glow, the velvety crimson 'Christopher Stone', 'Crimson Glory' and 'Etoile de Hollande', and the silvery pink, verbena-scented 'The Doctor'.

The Rondel roses were the yardstick of the Sissinghurst year: 'The garden has really been lovely this summer,' Vita wrote to one of her hundreds of American admirers, Andrew Reiber, on 31 July 1955, 'the roses have flowered as never before, and now they have been succeeded by masses of white lilies. It won't last much longer for August is always a bad month here – it gets nicer again in September and October.'[22] There was a very prosaic reason for the massed underplanting of the roses – to deter the massings of ground elder to which Sissinghurst is so susceptible. But there were other reasons as well; they had already tried tall white eremurus spikes waving against the dark Rondel hedges, and Harold's first thought was that white peonies would be just as delicious, but then, at a Chelsea Show, 'a great temptation came to me with the shape, size and speed of a cockchafer – it is still with me – it is to fill the bays corresponding to the eremurus bays with lilies of all sorts'. *L. regale* was to be massed at the back with other sorts – 'we should not have to get more than some 24 other lilies to form a frontage ... I do not want very rare ones.' He realized that *L. auratum* was difficult but it would be a triumph if it came off, and he wanted *L. tigrinum*, which he thought lovely.[23] Lilies were a shared passion, though Vita had difficulties with them, and many failures, but, at last, a blazing success (which is still there to be seen) which made her triumphant. She ended by making the white *regale*, the Tiger lily, yellow and purple Turk's Caps and Madonna lilies the most glorious of Sissinghurst impressions; she had a particularly determined assault on Madonna lilies, for their 'inverted snobbishness' in persisting to grow well only in cottage gardens! The 'towering heroism' of the Himalayan lily, *L. giganteum (Cardiocrinum giganteum)* which belonged aptly to the 'appallingly majestic' scenery of her mountain home, was an honoured guest in Sissinghurst's birch woods.[24]

If lilies were a shared passion, so were peonies, but they were not quite so sacred: 'I have been looking at lists of peonies', wrote Harold in July 1951 – 'some of the descriptions made me laugh by their appropriateness – is it possible that Mr Kelway has a sense of humour? The Duke of Wellington, soft white, yellowish in the centre,

91. Sissinghurst Crescent in spring, with South Cottage and the entrance beyond, and the wave-backed seat, originally designed by Edwin Lutyens, placed to look directly down the Moat Walk.

bomb shaped, fine; Her Majesty, full and large; His Majesty, very distinct and handsome; Lord Kitchener, intense maroon red, the Duke of Devonshire, deep rosy mauve, large and fine, not tall.'[25] Vita loved her 'gross Edwardian swagger ladies' who shed their vast petticoats 'with a bump' on the polished table and she grew the pink 'Sarah Bernhardt', the dark red 'Martin Cahuzac', and the white 'Duchesse de Nemours'. In the late forties and early fifties peonies were quite difficult to find and expensive (she got most of hers from Kelways at Langport, and bemoaned the fact that the splendid yellow *Paeonia mlokosewitschii* cost 30s. a plant – she reared hers in the South Cottage garden from seed – when the other varieties were about 6s. each). Tree peonies were little known and even more rare for English gardeners then (she planted two on 21 December 1949 – 'now I must get on with Christmas') and quite a lot of gardeners must have learned of the beauties of *Paeonia suffruticosa* from Vita and seen its enormous white flowers veined with purple for the first time in her White Garden.

Alliums, another plant lavishly used in the Rondel rose beds but also elsewhere, must also owe much of their present popularity to Vita. Alliums recommended themselves to her on several counts – they were of Persian origin, at least her favourite *Allium albo-pilosum* was, they came in all sizes, and in many wonderful shades of mauve, purple and blue. She used *Allium cyaneum*, a blue mite, in her sink gardens, she recommended the big round lilac heads of *Allium rosenbachianum*, and treasured *Allium giganteum* in the White Garden.

And lastly, the Rondel rose beds would have been sadly bereft without their pinks. Vita's beloved 'Mrs Sinkins' swept everywhere (she was proud of the rarer 'Miss Sinkins', who was tidier and more prim in her habits), and so did the Cheddar pinks (*Dianthus caesius*). Soon old clove carnations and Linda Bruce carnations, 'Bookham Beauty', 'Harmony' and 'Lavender Clove', were added.

Although visitors never saw the vegetable garden, which lies behind Powys's great wall at the west end of the Rondel Garden, it did not mean Vita did not write about vegetables. In spite of what she had said about only being interested in them when they were cooked, she did enjoy growing them first. Eleanor Sinclair Rohde's book *Uncommon Vegetables and Fruits*, which was published by Country Life in 1943, took over from Edward Ashdown Bunyard as her guide on the subject, and she later bought plants and seeds from Miss Rohde's successor, Kathleen Hunter's nursery at Callestick near Truro, and recommended her to her readers. Along with mangetout, peppers, calabrese, apple cucumbers and red cabbage, which we take for granted now (forty years on), she also grew figs 'Brown Turkey' and 'Brunswick', the grapes 'Royal Muscadine', 'Muscatel', 'Golden Drop' and 'Dutch Sweetwater', peaches, nectarines, quince, medlar, bullace, greengages and her favourite the cherry-plum, the myrobalan. And on one famous occasion sacks and sacks of letters poured into the *Observer* office requesting more advice on growing the strawberry grape, which really does taste of alpine strawberries and which was growing productively at Sissinghurst. The plants could be bought for 10s. 6d. from Clarence Elliott's Six Hills Nursery; by way of thanks – 'what Hadji would call a rake-off',[26] she wrote – an enormous box of rock plants arrived as a gift for Sissinghurst the following year.

Eleanor Sinclair Rohde's book *Herbs and Herb Gardening* (published in 1936), and perhaps the herb garden she planted at Lullingstone Castle for Lady Hart-Dyke, must also have influenced Vita. She had tried a herb garden at Long Barn, but perhaps a real interest in herbs comes only to those who cook them and use them in other time-worn ways. Vita had served her apprenticeship at pot-pourris and lavender bags but she was no cook – she was interested in the finished dish but not the culinary arts. When she had first planted Sissinghurst's herb garden before the war she had timidly used but twelve small plants. Jack Vass remembers that when he returned there were no herbs, just ground elder. He used potatoes to clear the ground, and then they discussed how the four beds that existed could be further divided with grass paths. It is odd that, as at Long Barn, the herb garden should be the farthest from the house. During the war Vita had understood that a tablecloth-sized patch of chives, lovage, mint, tarragon, garlic and thymes should be kept outside the kitchen door (she liked lovage to transform a dull lettuce into a worthy salad and tarragon with her eggs) – but after the war Vita the non-cook sent the herbs far away again. Her collection was more for foliage and colour contrasts and bees, but she was, typically, lavish. According to her Acme labels list, she acquired over sixty varieties – all the expected ones and the more unusual – melilot, clary, elecampane, costmary, woad, herba barona, vervain, horehound, Old Lady and Old Man and comfrey and Good King Henry. Thymes were something special – she tracked down twenty-four varieties and grew about six. 'To smell the thyme', she noted, was a phrase used by the Greeks to express a literary elegance of style.

Sissinghurst, the herb garden: list of herbs in the garden in May 1948.

Caraway	Yellow allium	Calamint
Melilot	Silver thyme	Tansy
Burnet	Camphor	*Iris fiorentina* (Orris root)
Clary	Hyssop	Catmint
Elecampane	Pink hyssop	Fennel
Costmary	Vervain	Angelica
Marjoram	Balm	*Artemisia maritima* (Old Lady)
Woad	Mullein	*Artemisia abrotanum* (Old Man)
Borage	Bronze fennel	Santolina
Anchusa 'Dropmore Opal'	Dill	Coriander
Lemon mint	Horehound	Lemon thyme
Apple mint	Bush basil	Balkan sage
Eau de Cologne mint	Purslane	Winter savory
Black peppermint	Coriander	Sorrel
White peppermint	Pennyroyal	Good King Henry
Herba barona	Wormwood	Comfrey
Lovage	Bergamot 'Cambridge Scarlet'	Germander
Giant chive	Bergamot 'Rose Queen'	Marigold
Garlic	Bergamot 'Rare Pink'	Musk mallow

92. Sissinghurst: the Moat Walk in spring with Dionysius at the end. The wall, part of the walls of the original Sissinghurst Castle which Vita had been so overjoyed to unearth over forty years before this was taken in 1975, is decorated with the dainty urns she bought one at a time from Bert Crowther with the proceeds from articles. A list of her azaleas appears on page 195.

93. *(opposite)* Sissinghurst: Dionysius admiring himself in the moat. Harold bought this statue from Crowther in February 1946, and Vita voted him 'a real triumph'.

Outside the herb garden hedge, at the side of the moat, were two beds which she wanted to use to good effect. She tried hollyhocks, which reflected grandly in the water but were immediately smashed by the wind, so she turned the beds into a Persian carpet of creeping purple, white and red thymes with a few crocus, miniature narcissus, and cyclamen. Of course, the thymes did not confine themselves to their lawn, but crept along all the pavings of Sissinghurst – their scents and softness contributing much to the luxuriance and comfort of Vita's garden.

The orchard and the Moat Walk were homes for some of the rarest planting ideas, highly individual ideas which were of their nature transitory, except, that is, for the billowing white crinolines of 'Madame Plantier' trained up the apple trees, the stems

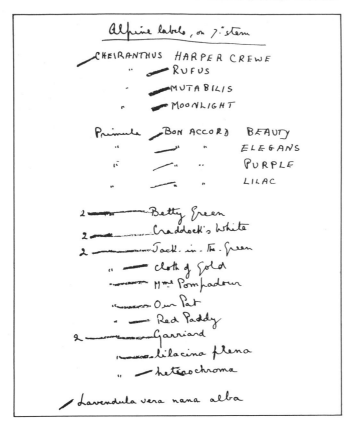

94. In May 1948 Vita made long lists of the plants in her garden for the purpose of buying Acme labels; these lists give a good inventory of parts of her garden.

List of irises, shrubs and trees (probably mostly in the Rondel Rose Garden) grown at Sissinghurst in May 1948. Most of these shrubs are tender and difficult to grow, and most of them were very rare in garden cultivation in England in the 1940s.

Iris 'Shah Jehan'
Iris 'Cleo'
Iris 'Lagos'
Iris 'Natal'
Iris 'Oliver'
Iris 'Quaker Lady'
Iris 'Blue Boy'
Iris 'Ambassador'
Iris 'Melchior'
Iris 'St Crispin'
Iris 'Lilias'
Iris 'Warwick'
Syringa 'Marechal Foch', carmine rose (cultivar of *Syringa vulgaris*)
Syringa 'Massena', reddish-purple (cultivar of *Syringa vulgaris*)

Syringa 'Mrs Edward Harding', double, claret red, shaded pink (cultivar of *Syringa vulgaris*)
Philadelphus virginiana
Hibiscus 'Hamato' (actually 'Hamabo', pale blush, crimson eye)
Hydrangea sargentiana
Populus candicans ('Balm of Gilead poplar')
Davidia involucrata
Crataegus prunifolia crus-galli
Lonicera tellmanniana
Lonicera tragophylla
Vaccinium corymbosum (swamp blueberry, pale pink/white flowers in May)

Prunus subhirtella autumnalis rosea ('Autumn cherry', semi-double flowers, blush pink)
Prunus subhirtella ascendens ('Spring cherry', pale pink)
Chionanthus virginica
Rhus cotinoides (now *Cotinus americanus*, rare, brilliant autumn colour)
Pittospermum tobira
Cotoneaster dielsiana
Cotoneaster bullata floribunda
Eucryphia pinnatifolia
Magnolia delavayi
Clematis orientalis
Ceanothus 'Indigo'

curving under the weight of her white flowers. Vita grew beds of gentians over the old castle foundations (which pepper the orchard but are thickest just beyond the Yew Walk):

> I spent much of yesterday picking apples, with regret because they looked so pretty on the trees, I filled two barrows, I was very happy ... The gentians were like the Mediterranean at my feet, my thoughts wandered vaguely round and round my new book and Masefield – not a poet I greatly love or admire but one line of his comes constantly into my head, 'The days that make us happy make us wise' ...[27]

Her gentians were *Gentiana sino-ornata*, only four inches high but brilliant in colour 'like the very best bits of blue sky landing by parachute on earth'. She planted *Cyclamen europaeum* beside them, as they both like semi-shade and the spongy mixture of peat and leaf mould she gave them, and they were one of her happiest associations of flowers. The gentians finally failed because they disliked the then newly acquired mains water.

Vita did her spring gardening in the orchard, spreading sheets of colour in contrast to Harold's intricately patterned rug of the Lime Walk. She was content to be an amateur about narcissi, preferring to call the trumpet flowers daffodils and mixing them in drifts with the flat-faced narcissi. She planted out her favourites which were used for the bowls indoors ('Fortune', 'Carlton', 'Golden Harvest', 'King Alfred' and 'Winter Gold'), added 'Mrs R. O. Backhouse' when Harold could spare that lovely pinky lady from his Lime Walk, and the white trumpets of 'Tunis', 'Beersheba' and the yellow/white mixture 'John Evelyn' – the latter increased so rapidly she could scarcely keep pace with digging them up and replanting. Narcissi

---

Azaleas in the Moat Walk at Sissinghurst as listed in May 1948. The Nicolsons' azaleas, all deciduous, in shades of flame, red and orange with a touch of purple and violet, have another thing in common – they are all 'old', i.e. to an expert eye they conform to a patina'd taste, but possible shortfall in quality, that dates them all before 1900. This would have appealed to Vita very much. The key to the source of many of these plants is probably 'Rouge Brique''s connection with Sunningdale, where Vita was of course friends with the young owner, James Russell.

'Cardinal'[1] (Ghent), vivid salmon red with top petal edged in deeper red

'Josephine Klinger' (Ghent), salmon pink with a lemon blotch

Coccinea speciosa (Ghent), 'one of the best of all', brilliant orange/red

'Rouge Brique' (Ghent), rich red, in cultivation at Sunningdale since 1898

'Guelder Rose' (Ghent), white with orange blotch

'Prince Henri des Pays Bas' (Ghent), marvellous light crimson with orange eye

'Sang de Ghentbrugge' (Ghent), rich crimson scarlet with deep orange flare

'Dr Charles Baumann' (Ghent), carmine red with frilled petals, gold blotched

'Louis Hellebuyck' (Ghent), dark pink with white stripe and yellow flare

'Ignea Nova' (Ghent), carmine red with golden eye

'Julius Caesar' (Ghent), dark crimson, blotched saffron yellow

'Saturne' (Ghent), cerise shading to pink, white inside

'Grandeur Triomphante' (Ghent), dark violet rose (a very old variety)

Calendulacea, the most brilliantly coloured of all wild azaleas – red, orange and yellows, growing to 10 feet high

'T. J. Seidel' (*mollis* hybrid), salmony orange

'Nicolaas Beets' (*mollis*), bronze yellow

'Franz van der Bon' (*mollis*) light apricot orange

'Cheerfulness', 'Abundance', 'Medusa', 'Soleil d'Or' ('now so charmingly turned into the vernacular Sally Door by our English gardeners ...') joined them.[28] Fritillaries grew here too, the native *Fritillaria meleagris*, which she discovered from Christabel Beck's monograph (which she recommended to her readers) coming up white as well as 'the familiar dusky gridelin', and that strange flower, still met at Sissinghurst, *F. pyrenaica*, greeny black and yellow inside its bell. Harold had romantic ambitions that the orchard should become banks of eglantine and sweeps of more of his beloved lilies; but the castle foundations had their say and defeated, and still do, any intensive cultivation. Vita was happy with the spring glories, the bees among the wild flowers and waving grasses of high summer and her pensive apple gathering.

In Sissinghurst's creating Vita had indelibly stamped her romantic personality, leavened with her fine good taste, on the courtyard, dominated by her Tower, in the Rondel Rose Garden and in the orchard. Harold's classicism, tinged with the sentimentality which he was only too aware overcame him at times, rules the Lombardy poplared entrance, his Lime Walk, the Nuttery and the Yew Walk. That these elements combine with such harmony is the measure of their complementary souls; it was indeed a joint effort, '*our* lovely garden', as they never ceased to remind each other and everybody else. It is perhaps fitting, therefore, that the last great Sissinghurst effort should be a joint one – the White Garden belongs to both of them.

Nothing more nor less than Vita's being a 'night owl' seems to have been responsible for her first idea about masses of white flowers. Her days were not only too well occupied to spare much time, she actually preferred to walk abroad in the dusk and darkness. She loved 'that stolen hour' between tea and supper, when she could settle to nothing, and so could wander freely off, with Rollo her alsatian lapping at her heels, out through the garden to the lake and woods in the dusk of spring and autumn. In summer a fine warm night was almost guaranteed to entice her out after supper, neither could she resist Sissinghurst under frost or snow and a full moon. It was in *Some Flowers*, written before the war, that she had first mentioned the white lilies 'seen by twilight or moonlight gleaming under the shadow of a thick wood', and she was enchanted by the white field daisies that turned luminescent in the summer dusk. Vita's very first suggestion was for a scheme of white flowers for the Lion Pond, in the south-west corner of the Tower lawn, which was being drained and filled in in December 1939: 'I have got what I hope will be a really lovely scheme for it: all white flowers, with some clumps of very pale pink. White clematis, white lavender, white agapanthus, white double primroses, white anemones, white camellias, white lilies including *giganteum* in one corner, and the pale peach-coloured *Primula pulverentula*'.[29]

It must also be remembered that the occupants of Sissinghurst Castle saw far more of their garden at night than most garden owners do ... they had to walk through it to reach their beds and any meal. The South Cottage garden, planted by Vita for Harold and so a joint effort of another kind, was bright with the optimism of morning (a first view for both of them out of their bedroom windows) and the comforts of the sunset ... 'a muddle of flowers, but all of them in the range of colours you might find in a sunset. I used to call it the sunset garden in my own mind before I even started to plant it up.'[30] The little walled garden of the Priest's House, though, where they dined and entertained, was suitable for more sophistication – even a touch of that old Sackville melancholy? 'I cannot help hoping that the great ghostly barn owl will sweep silently across a pale garden, next summer, in the twilight, the pale garden that I am now planting, under the first flakes of snow.'[31] They had discussed the idea fitfully through 1949, Harold sticking perhaps more firmly to it than Vita, so that at times she referred to it as 'his' idea. On 8 June 1949 she had made the decision to work out the planting; a week later Harold, while being drawn by Felix Topolski, contemplated the matter further: 'I think of it as cineraria in masses, rabbit's ears in masses, lad's love, santolina and the whole background being predominantly as grey as the rabbit's ears, then out of this jungle of growth I wish *regale* to rise . . .'[32] He was especially conscious that the garden got rather dull in July and August and he wanted the white planting to ride this period.

> I am not happy about the Erectheum garden, I think it is such a lovely shape and we see so much of it that it ought to be turned into a July garden. When the rest have declined – I believe that when we scrap the delphiniums we shall find the grey and white garden very beautiful and then we shall regret the scraggy, unhappy 'Night' roses. I want the garden as a whole to be superb in 1951 for the British Fair or Festival, with heaps of overseas visitors, and many will come down by car . . . I should like to concentrate on having at least the Erectheum lovely for July – with *regale* and silver we shall do that . . .'[33]

The 'unhappy' roses, I think, must have been the wonderful *Rosa centifolia muscosa* 'Nuits de Young', with flowers like camellias of black velvet, which the family nicknamed 'Lady Sackville' in affectionate memory of a very black velvet lady, with thorns but much beauty. She was grandly underplanted with purple pansies and pinks, and beyond the rose beds were Harold's delphinium beds, massed spikes to keep company the tower spires which overtopped the wall, complementing the pinky bricks with their shades of mauves and blues. All these eventually gave way to the box- and lavender-edged beds of what Vita wanted to call her White *Garth*. It was Harold who wanted a little colour – pink of China roses – but he deferred to Vita's better taste for a touch of yellow; it was Harold who went scouring for treasures and brought back a white gladiolus, an English iris, 'White Pearl', pompom dahlias, 'small eremurus' (a Shelford hybrid?) and the wonderful *Verbascum broussa* (*V. bombyciferum*).

> There is an underplanting of various artemisias, including the old aromatic Southern-wood; the silvery *Cineraria maritima*; the grey santolina or Cotton Lavender; and the creeping *Achillea ageratifolia*. Dozens of the white *Regale* lily (grown from seed) come up through these. There are white delphiniums of the Pacific strain; white eremurus; white foxgloves in a shady place on the north side of a wall; the foam of gypsophila; the white shrubby *Hydrangea grandiflora*; white cistus, white tree peonies, *Buddleia nivea*; white campanulas and the white form of *Platycodon mariesii*, the Chinese bell flower. There is a group of the giant Arabian thistle, pure silver, 8 ft high. Two little sea buckthorns, the

grey willow-leaved *Pyrus salicifolia* sheltered the grey leaden statue of a Vestal Virgin. Down the central path goes an avenue of white climbing roses, trailing up old almond trees. Later on there will be white Japanese anemones and some white dahlias . . .[34]

The *Pyrus* had been a Christmas present from Katharine Drummond in 1939 and had first been planted in the Rondel garden; it was moved to robe the frail Virgin, a lead cast that Vita had made in 1934 from the walnut original carved by the Yugoslav Tomas Rosandic. The Virgin, an object of great mystery and affection for the sensual Vita, had started her life at the end of the Moat Walk, but had now found her real home. Sending the Virgin to be cast and anticipating and then enjoying her return, doing these things for her garden, were the highlights of Vita's acquisitive instincts – she never, never, got excited about clothes or furniture in the same way. (She did about cars!)

And so, among her flowers, as the war decade of the forties slipped hopefully into the fifties, the châtelaine of that castle somewhere in Kent reached the crest of her life. She was now so famous that dealing with her post took a major part of her mornings. Her Companion of Honour, awarded in the New Years Honours of 1949, had given her dignity (if she needed it) and her *Observer* column was bringing her popularity (if she desired it). A letter addressed to 'The Hon Mrs Nicolson, A Castle Somewhere in Kent' would find her, and so would one marked simply 'Miss V. Sackville-West, The Novelist'. That delighted her. Sometimes she was rather overawed about the sackfuls of letters that resulted from her *Observer* pieces – whether it was about the strawberry vine or snails. She tried to reply to them all with her innate politeness, which made her readers feel special; some, however, in the way of the world, made impositions and demands for plants and advice, or even turned up without asking at strange hours of the day and night. But most of her correspondents and visitors were a pure pleasure; her readers answered her questions, they gave *her* the benefit of their experience, they deluged her with postcards and photographs of their efforts made out of her advice. She appreciated the kind of gentleman who swopped two magnificent lobsters and some prawns for rose cuttings, and happily exchanged the 'friendly little parcels' in what Anne Scott-James has called the 'freemasonry' of gardening . . . 'Lily regale seeds to Mrs Kelly. Myrtle cutting for Mrs Carey. A root of comfrey for Mrs Youle, Grand Drive, Raynes Park, SW20.'[35] 1950 was the year that Sissinghurst really noticed its visitors, who paid 1s. a time into the honesty box in the porch. A good Sunday brought something like £5 (always with the odd mystifying 9d or 3d), but their garden was hardly in the big league – in the same year Bodnant had had 10,000 visitors by mid June. Some of Vita's visitors offered to work – dead-heading the roses – and she made many friends among them. Especially welcome were those she felt were genuine

95. The famous castle somewhere in Kent: Sissinghurst on a summer's afternoon in the 1950s, with Vita's 'darling clock' at twenty-five past three and the flag fluttering from the Tower. The flag is made up of quarters for Sackville and West: '1st and 4th argent with fesse-dancettee sable' (West) and '2nd and 3rd or and gules a bend vair' (Sackville). The only sign of life is Harold's terrier.

and wrote really valuable thank-you letters – '… some people just moving from Horsmonden to Devon who felt they could not go without saying what constant happiness they had found in our garden', others 'who came in quietly and were Cecils'.[36] They both got very indignant when accused of not working; Harold said how he enjoyed his weeding week-ends .. possibly partly because he was seen to be making his contribution! On 21 April 1957 Vita was spurred to add a postscript to her *Observer* column: 'May I assure the gentleman who writes to me (quite often) from a Priory in Sussex that I am not the armchair, library fireside gardener he evidently suspects … and that for the last forty years of my life I have broken my back, my finger nails and sometimes my heart, in the practical pursuit of my favourite occupation.' And she did devote pieces to grit, propagating, fertilizers, weed killers and even vermiculite when she felt it necessary … 'Interest is being increasingly taken in vermiculite, so although I do not know very much about it I think I should at least be fulfilling a duty in mentioning it.'[37] Oh, wonderful Vita … it seems hardly surprising that after two years more of her observations she noticed that *Punch* was parodying her![38]

The master of Sissinghurst's quiet and not so quiet days was the clock in her Tower. They had debated for some time over the taste, the cost and the wisdom of having a clock, and in the end it seems that Vita, who was most pro-clock, won. It was eventually installed during the July and August of 1949 after considerable works to strengthen the Tower to carry the bell cradle. Every part of the process alternately terrified and delighted Vita … 'Today [18 August] they have got the dial out. It looks superb. Not only does it not clash with what you call the quiet sleepiness of the tower, but it adds enormously to its dignity.'[39] Harold liked the idea of the bell echoing over the fields, but wondered about the effect on Vita in her Tower. September 6, Vita again: 'Oh, there's our darling clock gathering itself together to strike twelve.'[40] She assured him that it did not keep her awake at night, and only a delicious quiver went through her Tower when it struck. It was a comfort. The clock, like so much of Sissinghurst's routine, was cared for by the faithful Copper.

> … Oh, what mistakes one makes in life. I met Copper descending the tower staircase with the grandfather of all screwdrivers in his hand – a patriarch of a screwdriver it was – and incautiously I said something about a pause or stammer of the clock (it reminds me of Arnold Bennett) – this brought a flood of tappets, fulcrums, spledgits, spigots, puchens, ratchets, pommels, angers … anyhow I gather it does not matter and will not harm our beloved clock … but I think I shocked Copper to the depths of his soul. 'Had I not noticed' he asked, 'that at midday it had not struck at all' (I had not noticed) … he looked at me as a doctor might look at a mother who had not noticed that her child had a temperature of 105 – 'These electricity cuts', he said sorrowfully, 'they take all the guts out of him,' and went on down the stairs.[41]

The clock, like the statues, and the lead urns she was collecting one by one from Bert Crowther at Syon Lodge to go along the top of the Moat Wall – these acquisitions were the excitements of Vita's days.

23. Sissinghurst: the iron gates (once in the entrance court at Long Barn) leading from the courtyard to the Rondel Garden are flanked by a glorious company of iris with long-spurred aquilegia hybrids.

24. Sissinghurst's country garden character is in evidence in the Rondel Rose Garden, with lavish masses of flowers just a step away from . . .

25. *(opposite above)* . . . the extreme formality of the main vista through the Rondel Rose Garden, closed by a Lutyens seat set in the curve of Powys's wall.

26. *(opposite below)* Sissinghurst: the White Garden viewed from the Tower. It is one of the great pleasures of Sissinghurst that the design can be appreciated from on high.

27. *(above)* Sissinghurst: the White Garden at ground level, with Rosandic's Virgin beneath her weeping pear, *Pyrus salicifolia*.

28. *(right)* Sissinghurst: the White Garden. Textural contrasts in planting at even closer inspection. The roses in the background are 'Iceberg'.

29. *(overleaf)* Sissinghurst: the orchard in springtime.

The clock paced her life, whether it was to keep an appointment in the village to open the Festival of Britain bus shelter, to go to Maidstone for a Committee for the Preservation of Rural Kent meeting, or to Cranbrook where she sat on the Magistrate's Bench (she was a very conscientious magistrate, but a little too soft-hearted and inconsistent, in the opinion of her fellows); whether it was to meet the timber merchant to walk the woods and mark the trees for felling (once she recorded a blue/black rage because the Forestry Commission had dared to refuse her a licence to fell the trees she wanted and had the temerity to suggest it would be better to fell others that would expose her to the buses along the Sissinghurst to Biddenden road), or, on rare and enjoyable occasions, to go over to the Beales at Castle Farm.

> The Beales had a party of Kent and Sussex farmers yesterday which I had to attend – I do like these sort of people – there were Scottish farmers who had settled in Kent and they talked about the worrld and the worrk – and there were all our Kentish farmers, the big fruit growers of apples and cherries, the Days, seven brothers all superb fruit growers, and there was Sir Edward Hardy, ex Chairman of Kent County Council, who loved my father and said some lovely things about him.[42]

Perhaps finest of all, on Wednesday 4 June 1952, came that long-awaited and frantically readied-for day when the Queen Mother came for lunch and to walk around the garden. Vita adored and admired Queen Elizabeth and had longed for her to come (much of her adoration stemmed from the Queen's commiseration with Harold during the war on his homesickness, which she called a personal kind of patriotism), but they must have made an unusual couple, wandering among the roses, the diminutive bandbox Queen in her silks and organza and Vita, as pictured by James Lees-Milne at about this time:

> She was totally indifferent to her clothes and appearance in a way that few women and most men are. Yet she always looked immensely distinguished. She could never be overlooked in a crowd, this tall, upright woman, with the oval face, straight nose, melancholy mouth and deep, sad brown eyes. Her usual dress was a plain blouse with open V neck, adorned by a single string of pearls. She wore drop earrings. Seldom to be seen in a skirt, she preferred in winter breeches laced below the knees, and long, laced boots, into the left one of which a pair of secateurs was stuck. In the summer she favoured loose linen trousers.[43]

She would have put on a skirt for the Queen.

Her more usual afternoon occupations were her gardening, and her gardening visitors: Jim Russell, frequently ('if we had a daughter I should like Jim Russell for a son in law'[44]), with gifts of old roses and cuttings of all kinds and much talk; Laura James with clumps of omphalodes and Mrs Tennant from Great Maytham with silver plants. Mrs Nathaniel Lloyd from Great Dixter with her sons; Colonel Frederick Stern from Highdown, his chalk garden at Worthing; Edward Hyams with 'something strong to kill the wasps'; Constance Spry, eager to buy flowers. 'Cherry' Collingwood Ingram, Freya Stark ... Jackmans, Hillings ... all the gardening world.

She happily allotted afternoons to planting her roses, received with much excitement from Hilda Murrell at Shrewsbury or from Nancy Lindsay; she loved her parcels from Hillier's, Wallace and Barr's, the receiving of treasures from Harold's hunting at the shows ... Peter Coats took photographs that 'made Sissinghurst look like Stowe', and there was, all the time, the growing fame of the garden to be fed. She allowed herself a kind of amused pride in prestigious commissions like 1,000 words for the *Observer* 'covering Chelsea' and an article on her own garden for the *R.H.S. Journal*; there were lectures and talks to be given and, increasingly, fan letters to be answered and interviews to be endured ...

> There hangs about the personality of the Hon. Victoria Sackville-West, C.H., F.R.S.L., J.P. much of the same ancient quality of calm and truth that illumines the works by which she has set the standard for feminine literary prowess of the 20th century ... Nothing from her hand is far removed from the poetry which first claimed the gentle, aristocratic scholar who married the vivacious Hon. Harold Nicolson, and whose mastery of gardens and gardening has made her name the authority in every home which cares for its flowers.

Thankfully unidentified! but taken from a cutting stowed away in an envelope in Vita's writing room.

There was life to be carried on as well, and they were not getting any younger. When Harold finished *George V* and saw it published triumphantly in the early autumn of 1952, he was shorn of an all-absorbing project; he kept writing, lecturing, travelling and book reviewing, and, that year, he moved thankfully from South Kensington into an apartment in Albany, where he was happy. 1952 held the Queen Mother's visit but also the death of his brother Freddy, for whom he felt a great pity, the feeling that he was growing old, fat and liverish (he was sixty-six), and worry that Vita's arthritic back was bending her proud shoulders. But it was generally a good year – Nigel was in the House of Commons and Ben was editor of the *Burlington Magazine*. In the New Year's Honours of 1953 Harold was awarded a K.C.V.O., and the remainder of the year was taken over by Nigel's wedding to Philippa Tennyson d'Eyncourt, from Burley in the New Forest (his constituency was Bournemouth East); the Nicolsons became enthusiastic in-laws and soon, to their utter delight, prospective grandparents. But Vita was still largely dreaming of her garden – on 23 September 1953 she wrote:

> ... how I wish I had another 50 years to look forward to and 10 gardeners and 10 thousand pounds bequeathed to me by a grateful shilling to be expended on nothing but the garden – then we would restore the lakes and make a water garden down there and a lovely approach to it via the calf orchard, plant the calf orchard with avenues of peaches and nectarines, very straight and simple with mown grass walks and bulbs for spring – darling, I must stop dreaming impossible dreams and get on with practical life.[45]

But at the end of the year she could write:

> My own darling Hadji, so ends 1953. My darling, happy new year to you as you read this, and oh, my God, you ought to know how much I mean it. May M.L.W. exceed all your

expectations, may ducky ducks lay many fertile eggs, may we have a broody hen just at the right time, may you write your books and keep your health and your now lissom figure and may there be no more wars. Amen.[46]

Her letters of the spring of 1954 were, as usual, full of news about the flowers that were coming out. The summer brought Juliet Nicolson, their first grandchild, with whom they were delighted, and who was always to hold an especially enchanted place in the heart of her paternal grandfather. In August Vita and Harold had the last of their truly carefree, happy holidays together, motoring in the Dordogne. It meant a great deal to them both; on their return she wrote to him:

> ... And we can think back on that lovely country with the poplars and the green grass and the hanging woods and the quiet river and the strange caves and the patient pious oxen and the castles and the *manoirs*. But I can't tell you how happy it makes me to think that you liked and understood the Dordogne in exactly the same way as I do. It is horrid having to communicate with you by letter instead of just shouting 'Hadji'! whenever I want you. But as a result we have stored up a great cellar full of vintage happiness and love as we always do when we get away together alone.[47]

On Tuesday morning, 15 November, Vita's post included a letter from the Royal Horticultural Society, which she opened casually thinking it was a circular. It announced the award to her of their Veitch Memorial Medal for 'services to horticulture'. She immediately wrote to Harold:

> Now, Hadji doesn't know about this any more than I knew about the C.H. I never was more surprised in my life, but *you must not say anything about it* until it is published early in December. I must say I was rather pleased but even more astonished, it is all due to those beastly little Observer articles I suppose – haven't I always said that one got rewarded for the things one least esteemed ... to get a gold medal for a bit of journalism is really a bit odd, perhaps [they] won't cut my articles so mercilessly in the future. I might put my price up. Your Mar VMM. I say, I hope Vass will be impressed.[48]

At the end of the year Harold was 'sorry to say goodbye to 1954 which has been a sweet year to me, Juliet and that lovely holiday in the Dordogne'. There is no doubt that Vita would have agreed with him. Fame, though not perhaps quite as she had expected it, had settled lightly and serenely on her world.

10

ANOTHER WORLD THAN THIS
1954-62

How fair the flowers unaware
That do not know what beauty is!
Fair, without knowing they are fair,
With poets and gazelles they share
Another world than this.
V. Sackville-West, *The Garden: Spring*[1]

I N RETROSPECT, that 'sweet year' of 1954 was the year that the world Vita had
constructed around herself was in its prime. From then onwards the door seems
gently to close on her life, a halting closing, with occasional bright rays coming
through, but nonetheless a calm and dignified decline, as befitted her nature.

They planned a rare party to celebrate the New Year of 1955 at Sissinghurst, and
when Harold returned to his London home in Albany armed with his 'scoop', his
special basket full of Sissinghurst's offerings, his mood – so beautifully caught by
James Lees-Milne – was 'suffused with happiness':

> While the weather was bitter outside he felt warm and cosy in his comfortable rooms
> with picked branches of balsam poplar . . . a vase of myrtle, fresh bay, and witch hazel,
> and another of jasmine and arums, all arranged for a party he was giving for a few
> friends. 'I love you very much,' he wrote to Vita, 'My health is good. I have many friends.
> I have two sons and a granddaughter. I am going to the ballet tonight. I am interested in
> politics, love books and enjoy architecture. So why should I worry?'[2]

As the year made its way, though, things did not turn out so well. There came the
beginning of their obsession that they would be parted by death or by a severe
illness that the other could not cope with; Harold had two mild strokes in the spring,
and his deafness began seriously to worry him. He was the first to have to give up
his gardening. Vita's arthritis spread from her back to her hands; it became a slow
and painful process for her to write, and then almost impossible for her to do
anything in the garden. She fell down her Tower stairs – a thing she had dreaded
doing – which further sapped her confidence. The garden, untouched as yet by
human frailties, was more glorious than ever; 1,000 people came for the Sunday

96. Summer 1959: the Nicolsons at home – Harold Nicolson and Vita Sackville-West outside the door
of South Cottage.

97. Vita in the Cottage Garden at Sissinghurst with a garden visitor – she was always around to talk to the visitors and answer questions.

opening for the Nurses' charity, and a gentle torrent of visitors, paying and invited, all summer. Vita and Harold loved and deserved to rest on their laurels a little and stroll round or sit beneath the Tower, passing the time of day directing or answering questions in a patriarchal manner. They enjoyed the thought of Sissinghurst being dynastic, and the hope that it would now pass to their grandchildren.

Harold had a premonition that he would die in 1956, but he was wrong. Of their old clan it was Dorothy Wellesley who died that year. Harold celebrated his seventieth birthday on 21 November, and though he and Vita most appreciated his telegram from Winston Churchill, they were to enjoy most the cheque for £1,370 which some 200 of his friends gave him. They discussed spending it on a greenhouse, or a cruise. The cruise won. In early January of 1957 they set out for the first of their five winter cruises, in the *Willem Ruys* to South America. That first cruise, in the

206

most luxurious and fashionable cruise liner of her day, was, with some irony since Harold called it a second honeymoon, perhaps the sharpest push to the closing of the door on the Vita that this book has sought to know. Simply because they were now to be annually together for weeks on end, for the longest periods of their whole married life, there are not only not so many letters to be read, but not such a need for them to be written. They became very close during this last period of Vita's life, and the urgency of their relationship by correspondence consequently lessened. On the cruises their letters home to Nigel and others were of politics, books and shipboard gossip – Vita especially seemed to let go, to succumb to a shipboard ennui. Her own unusual life, absorbed in poetry, books, flowers and being in love, had left her with a streak of voyeurism towards the ordinary, the mundane. What fascinated her in horse racing and football on television and going to popular films in the local cinemas at home also absorbed her in shipboard society, souvenirs and those irritating domestic eccentricities of the English abroad.

But the first cruise was also significant for what was happening at home, for at the end of January they received a telegram to say that Captain Beale had died. Vita sat down to write to Dorothy Beale of the 'very dear and trusted friend' that she had lost – 'never was there a man I have honoured more, and as you know, I loved him too'.[3] Perhaps it has never been acknowledged just how strongly Oz Beale supported Vita's Sissinghurst world for her; the Nicolsons were really very isolated in their local community, or would have been so but for the Beales. Apart from her Sissinghurst intimates, Bunny Drummond, Vi Pym, Edie Lamont,[4] Vita had no close friends around her, and Harold was never there for long enough to make any close friends at home. Oz Beale was always there – after all, it had been his brother (who was land agent to the Wellesleys) who had found Sissinghurst in the beginning; Oz had been farming at Bettenham ever since he had resigned his commission in 1920, and when he added the tenancy of Castle Farm to his own land he had become a substantial farmer, ruling 500 acres of Kent. He was a pillar of county society, a fellow magistrate with Vita on the Cranbrook bench, a kind, gentle and upright gentleman who calmly surrounded the castle and its garden with the well-ordered ploughings and harvestings of twenty-five years; he housed the house cows that supplied the Nicolsons, supplied hay and straw and any other garden needs, rose to all the crises, and shared commiserations (with perhaps a twinkle in his eye) when the worst calamity of all took place, and the cows got into the garden. Oz Beale was, by luck or grand design, the perfect farmer for Sissinghurst. Harold wrote, in his appreciation of him in the *Kentish Express*,[5] of 'his deep devotion for the fields and orchards', love of the old traditions that was modified by his intelligent approach to new techniques, to adapting to new methods without betraying his beloved land. Sissinghurst, and Vita knew it, would never be quite the same again.

Perhaps, for somewhat different reasons, Jack Vass knew that too, for he left just after Vita and Harold returned in January 1957. There had been a long-running and unexplained disagreement the previous year between Vita and Vass over the local flower show, but it was also that Mrs Vass did not fit into the tight Sissinghurst community. It was an amicable parting, Vass going with Vita's recommendation to Otto Lucas at Husheath Manor at Goudhurst.[6]

Their second cruise, in the winter of 1957/8, was in the *Reina del Mar* to the West Indies and South America. Vita was ill for part of the trip but recovered to enjoy Peru; in Lima they had tea with the Ambassador, William Pollock, in a garden filled with humming-birds, blossoms, lovely trees and arum lilies – Harold was overjoyed to see Vita so excited about a beautiful place. When they got home this time there were no major dramas, though the garden now seemed to lose its place as a prime concern – it was just a settled background. The family took over: Nigel and Philippa now had two children, Juliet and Adam, and Ben and his wife Luisa had a daughter, Vanessa. Harold went faithfully to his flower shows but hardly ever found anything that was better than what they already had – was it Sissinghurst's glory or his older eyes? He grumbled about the vulgarities of modern tastes – 'crocus as fat as tulips and what is the point of that?'[7] Vita recorded a sample of her morning post – the price of fame – a request for fritillary bulbs from California 'from someone who obviously thinks I am a nurseryman', an invitation to open a flower show in Chicago and be entertained by Mrs Richard Nixon, a request for advice on a flower border in Rome and for a lecture on some literary subject in Canterbury.[8]

The letters home from their third cruise to Japan were disappointing, and confirm just how Vita, once the traveller *extraordinaire* and so *sympathétique*, was losing touch. Nothing seemed to kindle her, even a visit to that mecca of garden mysticism, Kyoto; Harold's ingrained dislike of the Japanese and their country seems to have been catching. They had an uncomfortable ride on a crowded train through a land of mudflats, shacks, chimneys and enormous advertisement hoardings, jostled by Japanese women with babies on their backs and men with sleeked black hair. Quentin Crewe met them at Kyoto and took them to a Zen temple garden and Maryana Park, which she dismissed as 'a garden surrounding other temple buildings painted a hideous Pompeian red' ... 'Our dislike of Japan increases every moment,' she wrote, 'the garden must be quite colourful in its way when the pyrus, azaleas, cherries are out but there is nothing except a few miserable camellias, ponds, bridges and stepping stones.'[9] After lunch with Quentin Crewe he drove them to the station past the old Shogun palace – 'the only pretty building in this hideous place'. They returned to the boat in a slightly less crowded train, across a countryside of wet paddy fields, shacks and rows of lettuces in the rain.

This time when they got home Vita had to face Sissinghurst without her beloved alsatian Rollo (immortalized as Svend in her novel *The Easter Party*), who had died. There was a not new but very sad crisis in Ben and Luisa's marriage, and a new worry for Harold because Guy Burgess was claiming him as his only true and loyal friend in an attempt to get home from Moscow. Ronald Platt, Vass's successor, gave in his notice. Vita was very ill through the summer of 1959 with bouts of fever which were the undiagnosed beginnings of her fatal cancer. But the magnetism that made other women adore her was undimmed, as Victoria Glendinning has revealed.[10] It was also inconvenient. There were times when Sissinghurst became a nest of squabbling women, as Bunny Drummond, Vi Pym, Edie Lamont and Alvilde Lees-Milne all quite genuinely tried to protect Vita from disturbance and worry; poor Harold, in paroxysms of fear when Vita was ill anyway, and conscious that he could be of no practical use, was kept at bay. During these last years his weekends were longer – he usually came home Thursday evenings and went back Tuesday mornings; now it was he who saw the visitors and gathered bunches of Vita's favourite flowers to offer at the sick room door – otherwise he just worked in his writing room and kept up the routines.

Vita was determined that they should have another winter cruise, so to pay for it she sent two pairs of the Bagatelle vases to Sotheby's, plus some of the silver from the Rue Lafitte apartment. In early January 1960 they set out for South Africa, leaving Sissinghurst in the capable hands of the new head gardeners Pamela Schwerdt and Sybille Kreutzberger, who had started work the previous October.[11] The South African cruise was 'a dream of happiness' for them – alone and together and reasonably well, and Cape Town and the sights were unimportant.

For the summer of 1960 the garden's beauty droned on, now safe in the care of the *Mädchen*, as Pam and Sybille were called. Vita was ill a lot again and took to going back to bed in the afternoons. The following winter's cruise was to South America, but again the scenery was unimportant. When Vita returned she gave up doing her *Observer* column, and suddenly her own garden re-asserted its position of highest priority. There were some very good moments in 1961: the garden's visitors included Princess Margaret, Cecil Beaton, Cyril Connolly, Clive Bell and Elizabeth Bowen, Vita gave a lecture on roses to the R.H.S. in Vincent Square, using her own slides of Sissinghurst as well as some illustrations of Redouté prints – according to Harold she was wonderful – and her gardening life assumed normality again. 'I am trying to decide what to do today,' she wrote to him on 20 June, '(1) write letters (2) write an article on Sir Thomas Sackville which I ought to write (3) order plants and seeds which means systematically going round with my garden notebook (4) attack a pile of Christopher's literary remains or (5) write a story for which I have been offered £100. I think on the whole (3) will win.'[12] She even recaptured some of the moments of her youth with an escapade to the west country – she had always still managed these occasional outings, lately with the lovely and elegant Alvilde Lees-Milne, in the cause of recapturing romance, and she had visited for the last time Bramshill, Avebury, Owlpen and Berkeley Castle. She thought of the past more and more, especially of Virginia and Violet. Violet came to lunch at Sissinghurst and they gazed at each other nostalgically – it was all so very long ago and far away. By the autumn she and Harold were thinking about another voyage to the sun. On 1 November she wrote to him:

> Rabbits – a radiant day and the woods looking like the best verdure tapestry, brown and green and gold. If we were 18th century landowners and very rich we would construct a little romantic ruin something like Scotney on the edge of what was once the upper lake – Horace Walpole would have liked that; meanwhile we have done our best and have made a garden where none was. Your whizz kid Mar.[13]

It would be nice to leave her there, but a little more has to be said. They had their winter sun – it did not really matter where – and were home in February to enjoy the early spring garden briefly before she went into the Royal Free Hospital in Hampstead for a hysterectomy, which revealed the cancer that was inoperable. She was at home in April and May writing shakily to Harold about his taking care amidst the 'perils of Piccadilly'. Clinging to his routine, he went to the Chelsea Show as usual. He wrote to her sadly how they took his ticket away from him, saying it was 'NOT TRANSFERABLE'; it had always been in her name, she was the Royal Horticultural Society member, ever since the early Long Barn days, and on this occasion, of all, officialdom caught up with him.[14] Vita regretted missing Chelsea, and also a trip to Hilda Murrell's that she knew she would not make; her last triumphal journey was made across the White Garden, through the Bishopsgate, across the Tower lawn to M.L.W. in its glory, down through the Nuttery and back up the Moat Walk, in a wheelchair pushed by Copper feeling 'like Queen Victoria'. On 24 May Harold wrote his last note to her from Albany and came home the next day. She died, in the Priest's House, on 2 June 1962.

After her funeral service in Sissinghurst church her mortal remains, in a small pink marble sarcophagus, were taken to the Sackville crypt at Withyam. In James Lees-Milne's two-volume biography of Harold there is only the short Epilogue to come after Vita's death; just under six quiet years later the same funeral service was held for him in Sissinghurst church, and he was buried in the nearby churchyard. On 16 May 1968 St James's, Piccadilly was filled for a joint memorial service to them both.

Now, twenty-two years after Vita's death, time has given her life perspective. It is perhaps possible to judge just how well she coped with the discrepancies between the circumstances of her life and the world of poets, gazelles and flowers that she so longed to inhabit. For me, the fascination of her has always been that her longing was not enough, she managed to make her 'other world' real. The question that remains is, was she justified in her way of life, or was she extremely selfish? There are also questions I have to ask of myself. I said at the outset that this book would be a pursuit, a pursuit of a guiding thread – but does it lead to treasure? Does it lead anywhere? These are daunting questions, having come this far, but sometimes the gods that preside over the garrets of writers are kind. The candle in my gloom has been lit by picking up, by chance, Mark Girouard's *Return to Camelot*.[15] In this delightful book he traces the revival of chivalry through nineteenth-century upper-crust England to the Great War. Like many a good dramatist he begins on the brink of doom, at the high point that puts his story into focus, before the final dénouement. His high point is 1912, and particularly an Elizabethan joust that took place in the Empress Hall of Earl's Court on 11 July, when, as part of the great festival of Shakespeare's England, the flower of English society played their second to last act. Vita was there, with Violet Keppel, and on rose-wreathed palfreys they rode into the arena as 'wayting ladyes' to the Queen of Beauty. Violet was perfect for her part,

98. The photographer Edwin Smith was due to visit Sissinghurst on 2 June 1962 – they did not tell him not to come, but it was the day Vita died.

she was always to be the doomed lady, calling from her tower, never quite to be rescued. Vita would probably have chosen another part for herself – as poet-courtier in disguise, mounted on a faithful Arab, white of course. And that is just it – the point of my book. If Vita had been less Vita, less intelligent, less talented, less aware of the injustice of being female, she would have been doomed too. She would have married one of her contemporary knights, who were to be the lost generation, and then would never have recovered from his loss and frittered and flounced away a purposeless existence. But she was set apart; and so was Harold Nicolson. He was of that same generation, just as chivalrous as the best of them, and those that were to be lost – the Grenfells, Edward Horner, Patrick Shaw-Stewart, Charles Lister, John Manners, Percy Wyndham – were his friends. He had wanted to go with them, but he was too useful where he was and, over his head, it was determined that his war effort should be in the Foreign Office; in turn he came to realize that to work hard, long hours at the endless negotiations that are the background to war, and peace, was *his* best method of fighting.

So neither of them were doomed. The strengths or weaknesses of character, the vagaries of sexuality, the companionship of souls, or what you will that had drawn them together, made them survivors, sailing almost alone, but together, into a new world. They came to terms with each other – and that is the story of their marriage; how Vita came to terms with her new world, which she didn't instinctively like very much, is what I have to assess.

It took her almost all her life to come to terms with losing Knole, but she did it. For over twenty years she fretted over the day, 9 October 1928, when she had driven home to Long Barn in tears after seeing her house as the home of her Uncle Charles Sackville-West and *his* daughter Diana. She kept a key to the garden gate in a green leather box, and used it once, but it was lost, and perhaps momentarily forgotten, in the move from Long Barn. Then came the echo of the bomb-shattered glass around the courtyards, reported to her immediately, which maimed her heart. In wartime she could defend Sissinghurst with all her might and will, but she could not protect Knole. She tried to take her feelings in hand, and in the New Year of 1945 she wrote to Harold about the things she cared for most. It didn't take her long to eliminate everything but Harold, Knole and her writing:

> ... then I went on sifting. Knole would have to go in the last resort. But Hadji and my writing? Suppose God appeared (and I thanked God that he wasn't given to playing such tricks) and said to me, 'You shall write such poetry as Shakespeare and Dante put together never wrote, but your poor Hadji shall go blind. Choose!' Well, yes, you will be flattered to know that my whole being, my subliminal self, screamed NO, no, no, and I never wrote another line.[16]

After the war it was agreed that Knole should eventually pass to the National Trust, with the usual proviso that Lord Sackville and his heirs should continue to live in the house. James Lees-Milne had kept Vita informed about the negotiations (she would have been the first to admit that tax problems and financial agreements were hardly her forte) and then asked her to write a guide book for the Trust. She set about the task with a will, wrote it 'quite coldly and unmovedly', corrected the proofs 'quite efficiently' . . .

> . . . and then suddenly it will bite like rodent teeth closing and I awake to the truth – my Knole, which I love more than anything in the world except Hadji and then it bites and I can't bear to go on with this little book about Knole which has been given to someone else and not to us. Oh, Hadji, it is silly to mind, but I do mind, I can't quite understand why I should care so dreadfully but I cannot get it out of my system, why should stones and roofs and shapes of courtyards matter so poignantly, they ought not to, but they do . . .[17]

To comfort her, Harold returned her own explanation of her feelings of earlier years. Knole was so wrapped up in her life, her father, Violet, Virginia, himself, that it was 'far more a person than a house'. It was heartless of Eddy not to sympathize; Eddy, the successful rival who had won Knole, was unappreciative of its beauties, and Vita, the only one who really cared, was excluded – he understood, he wrote, 'the aching feeling that you alone know and really understand, that you alone are kept apart from it'.[18]

After that Vita kept Knole to herself and her private thoughts in her Tower, except for one occasion, when – like all loves – it surfaced at a very good moment. It was 22 November 1949 when she wrote to Harold: 'Oh what a happy day I have spent – except that you weren't here . . . Today was so especially happy because I did a lot of odd jobs, things I have been meaning to do, but chiefly because the sky was so peculiarly lovely . . .' She describes how the shapes of the trees in Roundshill Wood found cloudy reflections in the sky and how such things moved her so much:

> I know it is all out of proportion, like the way that one mentions Knole upsets me – I wish I didn't feel so violently about Knole; it is a nuisance to me and it must be a worry to you, and I apologize for having cried in your room the other night, but Knole seems to touch me on an exposed raw nerve and gets me all hysterical, which I'm not normally; something about Knole touches me right down to the roots of myself – I can't help it and I shall never be able to help it – Knole is mine and I am Knole's and that is that. I know every bit of stone in it and I love it, and I think and hope and believe that it loves me as I love it – a sort of mystical feeling about this which you may or may not understand. I know you haven't much sympathy with my feelings but you may be wrong and there may be more things in heaven and earth, Horatio, than is dreamed of in thy philosophy. Oh, how often I quote that to myself and think how wise a man Shakespeare was . . .[19]

This seemed to be Vita's catharsis, and Knole bit no more. In 1957 when Eddy Sackville-West decided to go and live in Ireland, he felt he was doing the right thing by suggesting that Vita could go and live at Knole if she so wished. She didn't. She did not go back until the spring of 1961, after the death of her Uncle Charlie's American wife Anne, whom she did not like. She was pleasantly surprised; she seemed to forget how she had hated things being sold (particularly the Hoppner painting of the Dorset children), and how the furniture had been changed around to her distaste (the chairs in the Brown Gallery that sit in line like a dentist's waiting-room) by both her uncle and the National Trust. She had learned after all that sometimes things had to be sold, and she seemed to understand and accept that at least something of Knole would now survive far beyond her ability to make it do so, and she enjoyed several visits to a Knole 'looking lovelier than ever' in that last summer of her life. Or had her allegiance finally changed? Once, a few years previously, Nigel had asked her whether she would ever consider making Sissinghurst over to the Trust.

> I said Never never never. Au grand jamais, jamais. Never, never never . . . Nigel can do what he likes when I am dead, but so long as I live no Nat Trust or any other foreign body shall have my darling. No, no. Over my corpse or my ashes; not otherwise. It is bad enough to have lost my Knole, but they shan't take S/hurst from me. That, at least, is my own. Il y a des choses qu'on ne peut pas supporter. They shan't; they shan't; I won't; they can't make me. I *won't*, they can't make me, I never would.[20]

And how did she fare in the world of poets? As I said in my introduction, her poetry was both popular and highly praised in the twenties and thirties. Her poems were frequently printed in both prestigious and popular papers – *Time and Tide*, the *Poetry Review*, the London *Mercury, New Statesman and Nation* and the *Daily Express*. She gave regular critical talks on the radio, which rather made her the voice of living poetry to thousands of listeners, and she was elevated to the reigning aristocracy of English poetry, into the company of Walter de la Mare, Edmund Blunden and Edith Sitwell. Vita was not given to self-delusion, but among the poets she knew she occupied a position that made her believe she would succeed John Masefield as Poet Laureate. Fortunately Masefield outlived her. Of course, the establishment that rules any art is a laggard show, and she was an astute enough critic to know that the Eliot/Auden/Spender school were unstoppable. Despite this knowledge she carried on writing her kind of poetry for the two best reasons of all – because it was the one thing that made her 'truly and completely' happy and because she felt she was writing about more lasting things than politics. But she knew, when she was finishing *The Garden*, that her poetry meant nothing to her son Ben's generation. She asked Harold sadly: '. . . will it ever mean anything to anyone's generation? I doubt it.'[21]

Now, in the burgeoning business of totting up the twentieth century's offerings, Vita's doubts seem sadly fulfilled. In a dozen modern critical anthologies, filled with Auden, Eliot and Dylan Thomas, there is no mention of her; C. H. Sisson's assessment of the 'best English verse' from 1900 to 1950 omits hers;[22] Michael Schmidt manages to find fifty Modern British Poets to guide his readers towards, without her;[23] Allen Tate does not mention her in his collected reviews (though he does include two of her poems in *Modern Verse in English*),[24] and Robert Ross's classic assessment of the Georgians makes only a brief single mention of the 'bloodless verse' of the volume that includes her work.[25]

If on the strengths of *The Land* and *The Garden* this seems, at the least, unfair, what are the reasons? I think there are three. Firstly, Georgian poetry has suffered a vast and complete critical assassination. The champions of D. H. Lawrence, Edward Thomas, Siegfried Sassoon, Isaac Rosenberg, Wilfred Owen and even Blunden and Masefield have been hastily dragging them out of the wreckage of the Georgian fold and declaring them innocent of any part in it at all. The reasoning goes: '... whether or not they appeared in *Georgian Poetry* is, according to such critics, totally irrelevant. What matters is the quality of their work: if it is good it cannot be Georgian; if it is Georgian it must, *ipso facto*, be feeble.'[26] Perhaps, as the Georgian era is deemed to have ceased in 1919, or at the latest 1922 (according to whom one reads) Vita and her epic poems should be dragged out too?

The other two reasons are, though, more serious than the vagaries of poetic fashion. When, in 1914, Richard Church included Vita in his *Eight for Immortality*,[27] he lighted upon them both. Church found her 'a poet in a tradition' – who could be antique, timid and aloof. In this 'ivory tower' guise she is not worthy of attention, let alone immortality (he quotes *Absence* as one of her 'most repressive moments'[28]) but, and it is the biggest of buts, he *knew* her and he knew she did not inhabit an ivory tower but a tower of brick ... 'a richly coloured house set in a richly coloured land, and furnished with a collection of treasures gathered by her as she has ranged over time, scholarship and life'.[29] *Knowing* Vita, and her true personality, the aloofness in her poetry becomes (as with Thomas Gray) 'reserve and dignity' that forbids and therefore invites approach; *knowing* Vita, her poetry assumes her own quality of grace (as does that of Cowper). How she must have enjoyed those comparisons. But the important thing is that Church found the best in her poetry through knowing her. Is this a failing in her work? I think not. I think it is rather that critics who did not find her within their ken dismissed her image as 'the Kidlet' of the tabloids, a Bloomsbury hanger-on with an unsuitably aristocratic aura. This 'image' was, after all, a common one at the end of the twenties, despite *The Land*, when she immersed herself in Sissinghurst, and from then on her anti-socialness became a way of life. Vita would have intensely disliked our even more media-image conscious times – she did not like the self she was forced to display at social gatherings, at lectures and committee meetings she was reserved and shy unless she knew her subject or her company extremely well, and then the shyness became a calm and attractive detachment.[30]

The paradox to this, her public detachment, was her private magnetism. To have supper with her, or talk with her in her Tower for an evening, was to be overwhelmed by her patina of dignity, kindness and grace of personality; this Vita, in a one-to-one relationship, was as enchanting as a gazelle, or one of the skipping deer in Knole's park, and one felt privileged to win the company of such a creature. This was the secret of her lifelong attraction for a series of lovers and intimates. But, whether blinded by her magnetism, as her lovers were, or by her anti-socialness, as her critics are, the end result is the same sad one – the barrier into the secret worlds of *The Land* and *The Garden* remains unbreached.[31]

And then, of course, the secret world went out of fashion. After *The Waste Land* the only voice of poetry that was listened to was the urban voice. Poets sat in cities and remembered the countryside only in nightmare or fantasy; as Professor William Keith has written, in *The Poetry of Nature*[32] (which also does not mention Vita), the poetic landscape of the twentieth century 'is made up of Auden's derelict industries, abandoned branch-lines, and harvests rotting in the valleys, or Philip Larkin's diminished England of raw estates and acres of dismantled cars'. Have we not had enough of this mourning for a lost paradise, which need not be lost if we are prepared to love a living and changing view of paradise rather than one mummified in the eighteenth century.[33] *The Land*, after all, does not mourn, it celebrates the eternal values of a landscape that we still search for – and it is *so* valuable for today:

> The power of being alone with earth and skies,
> Of going about a task with quietude,
> Aware at once of earth's surrounding mood
> And of an insect crawling on a stone.[34]

This, as Richard Church acknowledged, 'is a concise summing up of the poet's function; his universality, his particularity'; this is the permanent worth of *The Land*, of much more value than the shifting values and scenes of cities.

It might also be said that another need of the twentieth century has been for war poetry. And is not *The Garden*, in one of its guises, of rare value as poetry from the home front?

> Strange little tragedies would strike the land;
> We sadly smiled, when wrath and strength were spent
> Wasted upon the innocent.
> Upon the young green wheat that grew for bread;
> Upon the gardens where with pretty head
> The flowers made their usual summer play;
> Upon the lane and gaped it to a rent
> So that the hay-cart could not pass that way.
> So disproportionate, so violent,
> So great a force a little thing to slay.
> – Those craters in the simple fields of Kent![35]

A similar fate has befallen Vita's prose writing. In the literature of the English country house *Knole and the Sackvilles* and *The Edwardians* have secured her a safe place, though it is a place of privilege as well as of merit.[36] Without her obvious label of Knole, posterity has found her elusive – though parody should have pointed the way: '. . . and oh, I've such a darling description of a cornfield. I make you *feel* England!' said Ronald Firbank's Vita-character in *Flower Beneath the Foot*.[37] Is it only the nostalgic voyeurism of the vanished world of *The Edwardians* and Chevron (the fictional Knole) that is worth remembering? What about the superbly sinister *Dragon in Shallow Waters* (which Lord Curzon admired), the mystical *Grey Wethers* and the *Country Notes*, all dominated by writing that defines the spirit of a place as ably as Thomas Hardy or Edward Thomas? The veil of Knole, the Sackville inheritance and *The Edwardians* can safely be lifted and Vita's deep understanding of the English landscape, and her ability to project it, will be found. In *The Edwardians* she posed her own quandary – whether to sit and mourn for a lost world or go out and learn the value of a new one – and in her own life she made her choice. It was not easy, nor an instant success – there was much of the

> Advance, relapse, advance, relapse, advance,
> Regular as the measure of a dance[38]

that is the gardener's lot – but she persisted all the same.

At this point I have to express my wish that Vita had written more essays or *Country Notes*, for in these her belief in her new world (our new world) could be clearly seen, and she was at her best in bringing her literary past to bear upon our present. It is August 1939, and she has gone out into the orchard alone in the evening, as was her wont, to carry on cutting the hay:

> The scythe slid regularly through the long grass, laying the swathe quite neatly for so inexpert a mower, like fesses across a heraldic field; and, mixing poetry, war, and blazon in my mind, I thought of Marvell:
>
> > Thus, ye Meadows, which have been
> > Companions of my thoughts more green,
> > Shall now the Heraldry become
> > With which I shall adorn my Tomb.
>
> I had no wish to adorn my Tomb; only to supply free bedding for my cows; still the conceit pleased me. The spirit of Marvell came very near: not only did ripe apples drop about my head with big thuds into the grass, falling from sheer maturity although not the frailest breeze arrived to stir the moonlight – but the scythe occasionally sliced through one of them with a juicy sound which would certainly have touched the fancy of my most delectable poet.[39]

There, alone, in the darkening orchard, tiring from the swinging of the scythe, gleaning satisfaction from the physical effort, she is closer to Marvell, and brings us closer, than a thousand words of minute examination of his 'sacramental experiences' in the meadows of Appleton House made by modern critics could possibly do. She has that wonderful literary ability, both in poetry and prose, to whisk us back into her past, our pasts . . . and then share with us her present:

> Everything . . . seemed smooth and useful until the wedge dropped out of the scythe and I couldn't find it anywhere to knock it in again. This is a thing which does easily happen with scythes, when the blade swivels round and points impertinently at the sky.[40]

What Vita said and wrote in the matter of conservation was an extension of her literary belief. As early as 1928 she spoke to a meeting of the National Trust and told them, 'it was all very well for the Trust to preserve the old beauties of England but what about the new beauties? . . . since it was no good trying to resist change, see whether beauty couldn't be made out of [new] things too.' That was quite a breath of fresh air in 1928, and she was made aware that it shocked the audience – 'their minds being entirely focused on the shrikes and corncrakes of Wicken Fen' – but she was this, the best kind of conservationist, all her life.[41] Her years of work with the Committee for the Preservation of Rural Kent (the Kent branch of the Council for the Preservation of Rural England) were those of the calm, persistent stemming of the tide of bad taste in the countryside, rather than the flagrant confrontation that is 'Conservation' now. In her chapter on 'Outdoor Life' from a book called *The Character of England*,[42] published in 1947, she pleaded for the retention of the craft virtues and patience of the country lifestyle – 'it would be merely foolish to oppose anything in the nature of true progress towards the relief of a harsh existence or the increased fertility of the land' but please, don't let the distinction, the spirit of the English landscape be destroyed in the process. She was speaking seriously, with the most liberal voice of conservation, and *now* we know that she was right. Vita possessed an almost unique blend of the virtues of the caring aristocrat and the ability to express this care in words – what she did not possess were the acres in which to demonstrate the best English landowning characteristics and the political will to force her enlightened opinions on others. Her poetry and prose, therefore, has to do it for her; not only can she resurrect the fascinating particularity of Marvell and make us turn again in curiosity to the prosaic Rector of Aston, William Mason, and his eighteenth-century version of *The English Garden*, but she can show that their virtues and delights still decorate our world if we will but enjoy them. I feel that the same can be said about her writing, or much of it, as Edward Thomas said of Richard Jefferies: 'Lighter than gossamer, words can entangle and hold fast all that is loveliest, and strongest, and fleetest, and most enduring, in heaven and earth.'[43]

Which leaves me with the world of flowers. Vita's place as a romantic gardener is secure, high in the annals of gardening legend; the twentieth century has been enchanted to find that someone possessed of the single-minded devotion to her art that was the mark of Henry Hoare of Stourhead, Charles Hamilton of Painshill and even William Beckford of Fonthill has wandered into our own time and worked a miracle with considerably less resources than they had. But, of course, it is now not enough to be a legend, one has to be a *good gardener* too, so the question repeatedly occurs – how *good* a gardener was she? She was not a plantsman, in terms of a collector or breeder who spends hours chasing rare characteristics, patiently bringing his children to glorious life in the garden. She did not spend hours in her greenhouse, though from the very first small house at Long Barn to the much larger ones at Sissinghurst she delighted in the greenhouses and their products; she enjoyed a string of gardeners who had been brought up to such things – one cannot see her patiently pricking out the primrose seedlings or the lilies, and growing these things was for economy and quality first and the pride of achievement at second move. She did, as I have told in the Long Barn chapters, work hard, digging, planting, weeding – all the basic grinds of gardening – but her energies were always towards producing the flowers rather than cutting the lawns or trimming hedges. She *always* did a lot of the pruning at Sissinghurst, for as every good gardener knows, that is where the fine touch comes in evidence, the single most effective stamp of personality on a garden once the plants are there. I think she must have physically gardened, 'hard, involved gardening' – the sort that communicates with the plant as one breaks it up, weeds round it – at some time almost every spring, summer and autumn day of her life until her health gave out, and then, in her last summer, she found the strength to garden again. Often, this was in the early evening, alone, for I think she was supremely conscious that the professional gardener *never* concedes that an amateur can do anything right; Jack Vass gives her unending credit for her taste in colours, plant varieties and planting ideas, but says that he usually had to replant anything she had planted while she wasn't looking! I think that is a situation that will never be changed!

But Vita did know her plants. She had (what many professional gardeners lack) an ability and patience to look into flowers and divine their characteristics; much of the quality of Sissinghurst came from her taste for flowers 'which require to be looked at very intimately, if their queerness of beauty is to be closely appreciated. They are flowers which painters have delighted, or should delight, to paint.' Her flowers had to 'gain from being intimately observed', whether in the garden or in a pot on the table, when she had moments with nothing else to do;[44] her daily tour of the garden was made with her eyes open, constantly judging the effects made by neighbouring colours and textures. If she had a planting idea she tested it out by carrying a picked flower and leaf spray around until she found its rightful new place. These entry tests to Sissinghurst for flowers and shrubs were stiff, and she was ruthless in keeping only the plants which earned their places. Nothing remained on sufferance just to fill a space. Harold admired this in her (he being more timid about throwing things out) but he could exact a firm judgement on what was, or was not, allowed into their garden; he would not have rhododendrons at any price – 'fat stockbrokers whom we do not want to have to dinner' – and he rejected many of the marvels of the shows, such as blue primroses, for their harsh colours and being too far removed from their originals. However, there were few overall rules, and both had their moments of what the other would call bad taste: Harold developed a passion for auriculas, with all their purple splashings and green frillings, and Vita nurtured red-hot pokers, kniphofias, in the South Cottage garden (perhaps she remembered them from the Victorian borders at Knole), though he could never understand why.

If these things make a good gardener – hard work, involvement, evening hours scouring catalogues, patient mornings filling out order forms, excited afternoons checking deliveries, meticulous ordering of where everything is planted, planting much herself (but, most importantly, inspiring her gardeners with her own enthusiasm and devotion to the garden) – all overlaid with the energy to write and earn money for her garden and her exquisite Florentine taste, then she was a good gardener. If a good garden imparts a sense of well-being then a knowledge of soil structures and pH values can be taken as read; if it has an abundance of flowers of a peculiar quality then the presence of weeds is not of importance; if there is some special delight – a white wand of *Prunus subhirtella autumnalis* blossom against the pale blue of a winter sky, or the flowers of *Magnolia grandiflora* 'like great white pigeons settling among dark leaves', or even a rosemary bush shrouded in dewed gossamer – for every day of the year, is that not enough to ask from paradise on earth? One final thing is certain, when someone feels like sitting down and listing the fifty best twentieth-century gardeners, Vita will be in the top ten. I think she should easily be in the top ten of all time.

Would she be bitterly disappointed to find that her status as a gardener has perhaps outrun her status as a poet? I think she answered this question herself:

> Gardening is a luxury occupation; an ornament, not a necessity, of life. The farmer is not at all concerned with the eventual beauty of his corn as a feature in the landscape, though, indeed, he gets a certain satisfaction out of it, as he leans against his gate on a summer evening, and sees his acres gently curving to the breeze. Still, beauty is not his primary aim; the gardener's is. Fortunate gardener, who may preoccupy himself solely with beauty in these difficult and ugly days! He is one of the few people left in this distressful world to carry on the tradition of elegance and charm. A useless member of society, considered in terms of economics, he must not be denied his rightful place. He deserves to share it, however humbly, with the painter and the poet.[45]

And was she selfish, thus to pursue her secret world of beauty? She is still, by too many people who should know better, branded for ruining Harold Nicolson's brilliant career by refusing to be a diplomatic wife, live where she was bidden and be the shadow of her spouse. Yet one of the truths of love is that it must stand its ground, retain its strength; if Vita had surrendered to convention (which was quite impossible) she would have destroyed both Harold and his love for her. As it was he died 'one of the happiest men who had ever lived'[46] – better known, more beloved, probably more influential than he would ever have been as an ambassador, after an 'alpine meadow' of a life, which for nearly forty years was secure against the backdrop of a place that even he with his high standards could love more than anywhere else in the world.[47]

T HE thread has run out. I have arrived back where I started when I began work on this book by reading through Harold and Vita's letters at Sissinghurst. It is the last morning of April; it was raining early and the castle has been wreathed in greyness. Now, just before noon, the garden is open, and while I work I hear beneath my window the gentle rise and fall of quiet English voices discussing horticultural niceties. I have done a fair morning's work and the sun and the birdsong beckon me outside. In the courtyard the rosiness has been drained from the bricks in the cold light but the grass is vividly green, with an impeccably mown pattern; the deep cerulean blue of the violas in the terracotta pots is echoed in the diminutive blue violets around the Irish yews and the blue flowers of the rosemary clumps at the Tower door. The Rose Garden is quiet, expectant, hopeful. There are wonderfully bright bunches of polyanthus of deepest crimson, but little else to detract my eyes from the careful needlework of the roses arched on their hazel hoops, the figs trained on Powys's wall. Everything – roses, delphiniums, lilies, geraniums, foxgloves, rain-spattered alchemillas – is bursting with young life … and waiting. But in the Lime Walk the show has started: the grey paving is flooded with muscari, anemones, primroses, fritillaries and powderpuff-pinky tulips, with scillas and jonquils, whose white winged trumpets look as though they are about to fly away. It is a sight, and smell, that takes my breath away. Through in the South Cottage garden, russet wallflowers and salmony 'Orange Emperor' tulips warm themselves in the sun beside Harold's empty chair by the door. From the seat in Sissinghurst Crescent – the seat with the breaking wave along its back made to the design that Lutyens had first sketched out twenty years before he first met Vita or her mother – the moat wall is seen to be busy with blackbirds and bumblebees attending to the perennial purple wallflower, 'Mr Bowles's Variety', on its top. In the distance Dionysius, freed from his winter coat of canvas and straw, seems to stretch in the sun as he admires himself in the moat. The orchard is a sea of white and yellow narcissi, which upon closer inspection is sprinkled with fritillaries, anemones and wild flowers. My last port of call, the White Garden, is especially beautiful with hope – the hopeful creamy edges of the young *Hosta crispula* leaves, with white tulips and more bees busy with white pulmonaria; the *Rosa longiscuspis* on the centre arbour is in good leaf, the flowers of the camellia 'Janet Waterhouse' gleam brightly among her dark leaves, and there are drifts of delicate epimediums, pads of silver salvia and *Stachys olympicus*, and uncurling young fronds of Solomon's Seal. Back in the courtyard my last glimpse is of the purple border, awash with wallflowers, honesty and pale mauve tulips. A jolly coach party has arrived; it is time for me to go in.

SISSINGHURST is no longer the Nicolsons' garden, but it is their memorial. It is lavishly and skilfully maintained with loving care by the National Trust as a national work of art: this is a difficult and demanding task, but then Sissinghurst Castle's garden is a rare and particular treasure. Here, more than anywhere else, the pretty days must go on for the spirit of this place to survive. The flowers unaware are Vita's gift to us, gardeners or non-gardeners alike, an ever-renewable hope and belief in what we do.

> Still there are moments when the shadows fall
> And the low sea of flowers, wave on wave,
> Spreads to the pathway from the rosy wall
> Saying in coloured silence, 'Take our all;
> You gave to us, and back to you we gave.
> You dreamed us, and we made your dream come true.
> We are your vision, here made manifest.
> You sowed us, and obediently we grew,
> But, sowing us, you sowed more than you knew
> And something, not ourselves, has done the rest.[48]

NOTES

INTRODUCTION

1. V. Sackville-West, 'Sonnet', Long Barn, 1917, *Orchard and Vineyard*, John Lane, 1921.
2. V. Sackville-West to Harold Nicolson, 22 October 1945.
3. Peter Quennell, *Customs and Characters: Contemporary Portraits*, Weidenfeld & Nicolson, 1982, p. 45.
4. Harold Nicolson to V. Sackville-West, 16 March 1954.
5. Anne Scott-James, *Sissinghurst: The Making of a Garden*, Michael Joseph, 1975.
6. V. Sackville-West, *In Your Garden*, Michael Joseph, 1951; *In Your Garden Again*, Michael Joseph, 1953; *More for Your Garden*, Michael Joseph, 1955 and *Even More for Your Garden*, Michael Joseph, 1958.
7. *V. Sackville-West's Garden Book*, ed. Philippa Nicolson, Michael Joseph, 1968 and subsequent editions. At the time of writing, Robin Lane Fox is editing a new version of the *Observer* garden notes, to be published by Michael Joseph in 1986.
8. V. Sackville-West to Harold Nicolson, October 1957.
9. V. Sackville-West to Harold Nicolson, 5 November 1954.
10. Harold Nicolson to V. Sackville-West, 2 October 1957.
11. Michael Stevens, *V. Sackville-West – A Critical Biography*, Michael Joseph, 1973 (quote from *The Times* on the dust jacket).
12. Victoria Glendinning, *Vita*, Weidenfeld & Nicolson, 1983; Penguin edn, 1984.
13. Nigel Nicolson, *Portrait of a Marriage*, Weidenfeld & Nicolson, 1973.
14. Harold Nicolson, *The Development of English Biography*, Hogarth Press, 1927, pp. 9/10.
15. V. Sackville-West, letter to Mrs Howard, 7 July 1944, Sissinghurst Papers.

PROLOGUE

1. T. S. Eliot, *Little Gidding*, stanza 5, quoted from *Collected Poems 1909–1962*, Faber & Faber, 1963, by kind permission.
2. Virginia Woolf, *Orlando*, Hogarth Press, 1928; Granada edn, 1982, p. 9.

3. V. Sackville-West, *Knole and the Sackvilles*, Heinemann, 1922, p. 17.
4. Virginia Woolf, *Orlando*, Granada edn, p. 12.
5. ibid.

1. KNOLE: THE MIGHTY SHADOW IN THE GARDEN'S DIP

1. V. Sackville-West, 'To Knole Oct. 1 1913', in *Poems of West and East*, John Lane, 1917, and *Collected Poems*, Hogarth Press, 1933.
2. The story of Pepita Duran and Lionel Sackville-West is told in V. Sackville-West, *Pepita*, Hogarth Press, 1937.
3. Lionel Sackville-West, as British Minister in Washington, was indiscreet enough to express in 'the Murchison letter' his hope that President Cleveland would be returned for a second term. His brother died a month after the letter was made public and, now the 2nd Lord Sackville, he was able to return home to tend his estate, thus masking the end of his diplomatic career. See Nigel Nicolson, *Portrait of a Marriage*, Weidenfeld & Nicolson, 1973, Part 2 (paperback edn, Macdonald Futura, 1974).
4. Vita always preferred plain V. Sackville-West as her pen name, partly from her belief that art dispenses with sex barriers but also, it must be said, as a small revenge on her cousin Edward Sackville-West, who also wrote, but whose chief crime in Vita's eyes was to be a boy and thus able to inherit Knole. Once Eardley Knollys introduced Eddy as 'the writer Sackville-West', at which their companion replied, 'Oh, I thought the writer Sackville-West was a woman!' Vita related Eddy's mortification joyfully to Harold, adding that she suspected he had a complete vis-à-vis over this, much as she did over Knole.
5. Nigel Nicolson, *Portrait of a Marriage*, Part 2. In February 1910 in the High Court Vita's uncle, Henry Duran, claimed that Lord Sackville had married Pepita Duran and that he, Henry, was the legitimate heir to the title and estate. He was unsuccessful. Three years later Sir John Murray Scott's family contested his will and his lavish legacy to Lady Sackville. They too were unsuccessful.

6. V. Sackville-West, 'To Knole Oct. 1 1913'.

7. Knole had passed through the male line for eight generations until the 4th Duke of Dorset was killed hunting in 1815 when he was only twenty-one. He had no brothers, so Knole was left to his sisters Mary and Elizabeth in turn. Elizabeth's sons became the 1st and 2nd Lord Sackville in their turn; the 2nd Lord Sackville was Vita's grandfather. As her mother refused to have any more children, the only threat to Vita's inheritance came if her uncle Charles Sackville-West married and produced a son. This he did – Edward Sackville-West was born in 1901.

8. These woods are included in a survey of Knole's adjacent woodlands carried out in the year that Vita was born – 1892. Kent County Archives, ref. E118, Report on the Woods, dated 23 September 1892.

9. V. Sackville-West, 'Leopards at Knole', in *Poems of West and East*

10. V. Sackville-West, *Knole and the Sackvilles*, Heinemann, 1922.

11. The Hoppner painting of the 4th Duke of Dorset and his sisters was one of Vita's most loved treasures of the house; it hung in the private sitting room when she was a child. It was also one of the first things to be sold by her Uncle Charles when he inherited the house in 1928.

12. The Knole Visitors' Books are in Kent County Archives.

13. George Cornwallis-West, *A Little About a Lot of Things*, Putnam, 1930.

14. V. Sackville-West, *Knole and the Sackvilles*, p. 20.

15. ibid.

16. ibid.

17. Roy Strong, *The Renaissance Garden in England*, Thames & Hudson, 1979.

18. Comparisons and similarities can be drawn from illustrations in John Harris, *The Artist and the Country House: A history of house and garden view painting in Britain 1540–1870*, Sotheby Parke Bernet, 1979.

19. The following quotations come from documents in Kent County Archives, ref. U269 E21/2/3.

20. V. Sackville-West, 'Knole and Its Owners', printed in the National Trust Guide to Knole, 1980.

21. The first contract with Thomas Akres is dated 15 January 1710; the second is undated. Kent County Archives, ref. U269 E21/2/3.

22. Virginia Woolf, *Orlando*, Hogarth Press, 1928; Granada edn, 1982, p. 69. For a time Vita owned a pet bear called Ivan, a gift from Ivan Hay.

23. V. Sackville-West, 'Knole and Its Owners'.

24. John H. Brady, *The Visitor's Guide to Knole in the County of Kent with Catalogue of Pictures*, printed in Sevenoaks, 1839.

25. The Knole garden books are in Kent County Archive.

26. Virginia Woolf, *Orlando*, Granada edn, p. 12.

27. How and why the family split into two branches, de la Warrs and Sackville-Wests, and how the former could not inherit Knole, is told in George Cornwallis-West, *A Little About a Lot of Things*, pp. 28/9.

28. V. Sackville-West, 'Gardens and Gardeners'', *Country Notes*, M. Joseph, 1939, p. 96.

29. ibid.

30. ibid., p. 97.

31. ibid.

32. V. Sackville-West, 'To Knole Oct. 1 1913'.

33. V. Sackville-West, *Knole and the Sackvilles*, p. 20.

34. Violet Trefusis, *Don't Look Round*, Hutchinson, 1952, p. 42.

2. THE GRAND TOURISTS

1. V. Sackville-West, 'Song: Let us go back', dedicated to 'the unkindest of critics H.G.N.', in *Poems of West and East*, John Lane, 1917.

2. 'Mar' was Vita's childhood name, given to her by her parents, meaning *little* or *vulnerable* in Sackville family language. Harold adopted it as a term of endearment and Vita used it throughout her life in her letters to him.

3. V. Sackville-West to Harold Nicolson, letter, 29 March 1929.

4. Dorothy (Dottie) Wellesley was born Dorothy Ashton in 1889. In 1914 she married Harold Nicolson's friend Gerald Wellesley and they became a close foursome. Dottie was constantly at Long Barn, as Vita was at her home, Sherfield Court, at Sherfield-on-Loddon, near Basingstoke, during the twenties; they had absent husbands, young children, poetry and gardening in common. Dottie was Vita's physical opposite – slight, fragile and fair with dazzling blue eyes. She was proud to claim Vita as 'one of the great literary friendships of my life'.

Geoffrey Scott was nine years older than Vita; they first met on one of her Italian trips just before her marriage, probably in 1911 or 1912 when Scott was working for Bernard Berenson at Villa I Tatti and writing his classic *The Architecture of Humanism*, first published by Constable in 1914. The story of Vita's affair with Scott is told by Victoria Glendinning in *Vita*, Weidenfeld & Nicolson, 1983 (Penguin edn, 1984), Chs 12 and 13; there is no doubt that Scott's attraction was his brilliant conversation on art, architecture and Florence and that he in turn felt that he had found in Vita someone who met both his physical and intellectual needs. The affair was doomed, as were all Scott's emotional relationships, and makes sad reading. I feel, however, that Vita had a deeper intellectual relationship with Scott than with any other person in her life.

Virginia Woolf came to Long Barn for the first time in June 1924, and later that year the Hogarth Press published one of Vita's books for the first time – *Seducers in Equador*, which is dedicated to Virginia. At this early stage in their relationship Virginia was dazzled by Vita's aristocratic glow, by her confidence, experience and popularity. Vita, in turn, had begun to worship, as she always would, Virginia's vulnerability, her sparkle and her mystical genius.

5. Robin Lane Fox's review of Victoria Glendinning's *Vita* in the *Financial Times* ended with this sentence:

'Hard, involved gardening, and a rare love of nature, and the lonely silence of a garden at dusk: these tastes connect with her mythomania, her Orientalism, her Georgian poetry, the barriers beyond which not even lovers could pass.' For these words I thank him.

6. V. Sackville-West to Violet Trefusis, 13 October 1948 (quoted in Philippe Julian and John Phillips, *Violet Trefusis: Life and Letters*, Hamish Hamilton, 1976, pp. 227/8. Violet's castle, St Loup de Naud, is outside Provins about 80 km from Paris – a romantic and mysterious tower perched on a hill 'like an illumination in some fifteenth-century missal'. See Violet Trefusis, *Don't Look Round*, Hutchinson, 1952, pp. 97/8.

7. Violet Trefusis, *Don't Look Round*, p. 42.

8. The period of *The Land* (dedicated to Dorothy Wellesley) and the buying of Sissinghurst marked Vita's closest friendship with Dottie; after that Dottie became absorbed in her passionate literary friendship with W. B. Yeats, and after his death in 1939 she became more and more isolated at Penn's Rocks. Vita only visited Penn's out of duty. Dorothy Wellesley published a disappointing autobiography, *Far Have I Travelled* (James Barrie, 1952), and she died in 1956.

9. Philippe Julian and John Phillips published *Violet Trefusis: Life and Letters* in 1976 to set the record straight after what they felt was a misleading representation of Violet in Nigel Nicolson's *Portrait of a Marriage*.

10. This totally delightful side of Vita's mother is revealed in Susan Mary Alsop's *Lady Sackville*, Weidenfeld & Nicolson, 1978, pp. 152/3.

11. This was Nether Swell Manor, built in Renaissance style by E. Guy Dawber and decorated by Marcel Boulanger of Paris to provide a setting for Sir John's French furniture. See Clive Aslet, *The Last Country Houses*, Yale University Press, 1982. The house was chiefly inhabited by his sisters, the Misses Alicia and Mary Scott, very formidable ladies, who may not have welcomed Lady Sackville and her daughter. Untypical though it was of the Arts and Crafts mood of most of the Gloucestershire houses of this period, Nether Swell may have been Vita's introduction to a countryside she came to love second only to Kent.

12. Sir John Murray Scott had been secretary and virtually the adopted son of Sir Richard and Lady Wallace – Sir Richard was the illegitimate son of the Marquess of Hertford. Sir Richard left him the contents of his Paris apartment and of La Bagatelle and the use of both for life. Vita's mother benefited most of all because Sir John, her 'Seery', could refuse her nothing and left her a fabulous treasure when he died on 17 January 1912. Though the Misses Scott contested the will, Lady Sackville won; the rest of her life became a constant drama of possession or dispossession of these valuables. See Nigel Nicolson, *Portrait of a Marriage* and Susan Mary Alsop, *Lady Sackville*.

13. The Wallace treasures that Vita valued most were the magnificent bronze vases attributed to Claude Balin, which adorned the garden at La Bagatelle when she went there as a child. They had been copied in the 1860s by the Marquess of Hertford from the originals at Versailles, by special permission from Napoleon III. Sir John appears to have given Lady Sackville several pairs soon after their meeting in 1897, and she took them to Knole. Eventually at least four pairs (possibly six pairs) ended up at Sissinghurst; two pairs were sold at Sotheby's on 20 March 1959 for £1,850 (to pay for the Nicolsons' winter cruise), and these were bought by the National Art Collection Fund and returned to the Wallace Collection. Nothing about the vases is absolutely certain, as there were so many original designs and they have been copied again and again. The statue of a Bacchante playing the cymbals, now in the Lime Walk at Sissinghurst, was also one of the Wallace treasures from La Bagatelle.

14. Nigel Nicolson, *Portrait of a Marriage*, part 2.

15. Victoria Glendinning, *Vita*, p. 36.

16. ibid., p. 40.

17. André Barret, *Florence Observed*, translated from the French by Stephen Hardman, Kaye & Ward/O.U.P., 1973.

18. Victoria Glendinning, *Vita*, p. 34.

19. Harold Acton, *Florence*, Thames & Hudson, 1961, p. 6.

20. ibid., p. 5.

21. *Violet Trefusis: Life and Letters*, pp. 27/8.

22. Harold Acton, *Florence*, p. 5.

23. J. C. Shepherd and G. A. Jellicoe, *Italian Gardens of the Renaissance*, Alec Tiranti, 1953 edn (1st edn Ernest Benn, 1925).

24. See ibid., and Iris Origo, *Images and Shadows: Part of a Life*, John Murray, 1970. Iris Origo remembers that her mother (Sybil Cutting, who married Geoffrey Scott in 1917) bought Villa Medici in 1911. The villa was approached 'down a long drive overshadowed by ilex trees to a terrace with two tall trees – paulownias – which had scattered on the lawn mauve flowers I had never seen before. At the end of the terrace stood a square house with a deep loggia, looking due west towards the sunset over the whole valley of the Arno' (p. 116).

25. Geoffrey Scott, *The Architecture of Humanism*, Constable, 1st edn 1914; 2nd edn 1924, p. 66.

26. ibid., p. 150. Vita's copy in her Tower room has a conversation piece: it has Harold's name inside, then, '*Not at all* – V. Nicolson from G. Wellesley – 'Quite Right, G.W.' 'Very gratifying G.S.'

27. V. Sackville-West to Harold Nicolson, October 1937.

28. V. Sackville-West to Harold Nicolson, 17 September 1928.

29. V. Sackville-West to Harold Nicolson, 18 July 1929.

30. Vita tossed this phrase off lightly whenever Spain was mentioned!

31. V. Sackville-West to Harold Nicolson, 5 March 1949.

32. Nigel Nicolson, *Portrait of a Marriage*, p. 40.

33. ibid., p. 41.

34. V. Sackville-West to Harold Nicolson, from a group of letters Vita wrote on a trip to the west country in September 1913, the month before her marriage.

NOTES

35. 'St Fagan's Castle', *Country Life*, 20 September 1902.
36. 'The Manor House Sutton Courtenay', *Country Life*, 6 February 1904 and 16 May 1931.
37. Jack Vass (Head Gardener at Sissinghurst, 1938–57) remembers forty gardeners at Cliveden when he was one of them between 1929 and 1933, and he learned to do flowers for the house there. Nancy Astor visited Sissinghurst after the war and said how much she liked it; on 19 February 1953 Vita wrote that Nancy had telephoned asking her to design the garden for 'the old Abbey' she had bought near Plymouth. However, I have not been able to find further mention of anything that Vita did.
38. 'Mells Manor', *Country Life*, 10 November 1917.
39. Francis Bacon, 'Of Gardens'.
40. V. Sackville-West, 'MCMXIII', in *Poems of West and East*.
41. Coker Court was lent to them by Dorothy Heneage, a friend of Violet's, of whom there is a marvellous description on p. 102 of *Violet Trefusis: Life and Letters*. To go there today is an experience which pulls together threads of Vita's life – its dreamlike atmosphere is perfectly retained and it is to the church beside the drive that pilgrims flock to pay tribute to T. S. Eliot – the lines from *Little Gidding* quoted in my Prologue (p. 16) come to life here.
42. During Harold Nicolson's childhood his father actually lived in St Petersburg, Budapest, Teheran, Constantinople, Sofia and Tangier; Harold was particularly happy in Tangier. His first real holiday 'abroad' on his own was to Lac Champex in Switzerland, and he came to adore the mountains; while he was at Balliol that affection was endorsed for him by visits to the chalet of his mentor, F. F. 'Sligger' Urquhart, at St Gervais-les-Bains in the Haute Savoie. See James Lees-Milne, *Harold Nicolson: A Biography*, Chatto & Windus, 1980, Vol. 1, Ch. 2.
43. Harold Nicolson, *The Desire to Please*, Constable, 1943.
44. James Lees-Milne, *Harold Nicolson: A Biography*, Vol. 1, p. 53.
45. Harold Nicolson, *Helen's Tower*, Constable, 1937, p. 40.
46. Harold Nicolson, *Lord Carnock (Sir Arthur Nicolson Bt): A Study in the Old Diplomacy*, Constable, 1930, pp. 43/4.
47. James Lees-Milne, *Harold Nicolson: A Biography*, Vol. 1, p. 1.
48. Harold Nicolson, *Helen's Tower*, Ch. 1.
49. Clandeboye, in County Down, is described at great length and with great wit in Harold Nicolson's *Helen's Tower*. See also Edward Malins and Patrick Bowe, *Irish Gardens and Demesnes from 1830*, Barrie & Jenkins, 1980, pp. 31/2.
50. Harold Nicolson, *Helen's Tower*, p. 73.
51. ibid., pp. 73/4.
52. ibid., pp. 85/6.
53. Edward Malins and Patrick Bowe, *Irish Gardens and Demesnes from 1830*, p. 31.
54. Harold Nicolson, *Helen's Tower*, p. 97.
55. ibid.
56. ibid., p. 41.
57. V. Sackville-West, 'Dhji-han-Ghir', dedicated 'for HN', in *Orchard and Vineyard*, John Lane, 1921.
58. James Lees-Milne, *Harold Nicolson: A Biography*, Vol. I, p. 67.
59. Harold Nicolson, *Sweet Waters*, Constable, 1921, p. 202.

3. AN ELK-HOUND AND A ROSE BUSH: LONG BARN 1915–25

1. V. Sackville-West, 'Night', dedicated to H.G.N., in *Orchard and Vineyard*, John Lane, 1921.
2. Harold Nicolson to V. Sackville-West, undated letter.
3. V. Sackville-West, 'Gardens and Gardeners', *Country Notes*, M. Joseph, 1939, p. 96.
4. V. Sackville-West, *The Garden*, dated Long Barn, Summer 1915, in *Orchard and Vineyard*.
5. 'Aunt Bumps' was Lutyens's name for the portly Miss Jekyll and it symbolized the affectionate relationship he had had with her since their first meeting in 1889, when she was 45 and he was just 20. She was very influential on his early career; he built her home, Munstead Wood, near Godalming, for her in the 1890s and she helped him to design gardens for his other houses from that time. Lutyens had met Lady Sackville at the opera in June 1916, and their relationship developed as she employed him to make lavish alterations to 34 Hill Street, W1 (left to her by Sir John Murray Scott) and subsequent houses that she owned. See *Edwin Lutyens: A Memoir*, by his daughter Mary Lutyens, John Murray, 1980.
6. Victoria Glendinning, *Vita*, Weidenfeld & Nicolson, 1983, p. 85.
7. Susan Mary Alsop, *Lady Sackville*, Weidenfeld & Nicolson, 1978.
8. Gertrude Jekyll, *Wood and Garden*, Longmans, 1899, p. 156.
9. Barrington Court, Ilminster, Somerset – Miss Jekyll did the complex planting plans for the architects Forbes and Tait and the owners Colonel and Mrs Lyle in 1917, when she was 74. The original plans are in the Reef Point Gardens Collection at the College of Environmental Design, University of California, Berkeley.
10. All these roses listed by Vita in her earliest Long Barn notebook (except the miniature 'Juliette') were then in current use by Miss Jekyll in garden schemes. Most of them are in her list of 'choicest varieties' in the back of *Roses for English Gardens*, Country Life, 1901. It is also interesting to note that Vita went to visit the Princess Dolgorouki at Nashdom near Taplow in July 1919, and here she would have seen a round pergola'd rose garden designed by Lutyens and planted to Miss Jekyll's taste.
11. V. Sackville-West to Harold Nicolson, 19 July 1919.
12. James Lees-Milne, *Harold Nicolson: A Biography*, Chatto & Windus, 1980, Vol. 1, pp. 87/8.

13. *Catalogue of the Lutyens Exhibition*, ed. Colin Amery and Margaret Richardson, Arts Council, 1980, note by Gavin Stamp, p. 174.

14. Lutyens's philosophy on garden design is expressed in notes for a lecture to the Architectural Association in April 1908, from the Lutyens Family Papers, R.I.B.A. Ridley MSS, letter to Lady Emily Lutyens dated 8 April 1908. See also my book *Gardens of a Golden Afternoon*, Allen Lane, 1982 (reissued Viking, 1985), pp. 96–131, on the Lutyens/Jekyll design philosophy.

15. Warlincourt Halte British Cemetery at Saulty, dated October 1917, Lutyens's office layout plan with Miss Jekyll's planting added in her own handwriting – a holly hedge all round the cemetery, regular planting of four fastigiate oaks, and a carpet of *Berberis aquifolium* (to be kept cut at two inches high) around the Great War Stone. The Trouville Hospital Area plan (now called Tourgeville Military Cemetery) has borders of pansies, London pride, myositis, geranium, dicentra, centranthus, aquilegia, iberis, erigerons and stachys between the headstones. All these plans are in the Reef Point Gardens Collection, University of California, Berkeley. Are they what Harold saw?

16. Lutyens's original note makes an interesting comparison: 'The man whose range of conception is small will constantly repeat himself, but the man who has a larger and better grasp will perceive a more diversified capability of the problem for which he has to find a solution.' Lutyens Family Papers, letter to Lady Emily Lutyens, 8 April 1908.

17. Peter Coats, *Great Gardens of the World*, Weidenfeld & Nicolson, 1953, Introduction by Harold Nicolson.

18. V. Sackville-West to Harold Nicolson, 24 July 1919.

19. Victoria Glendinning, *Vita*, p. 84; and there are Lutyens 'sketches' in the first Long Barn garden notebook.

20. Letter to the author from Nigel Nicolson, 8 March 1981.

21. V. Sackville-West to Harold Nicolson, June 1919.

22. V. Sackville-West to Harold Nicolson, 11 July 1919.

23. Reply from Harold Nicolson to V. Sackville-West, no date but July 1919.

24. V. Sackville-West to Harold Nicolson, no date but July 1919.

25. V. Sackville-West to Harold Nicolson, 29 October 1919.

26. Nigel Nicolson, *Portrait of a Marriage*, Part 1.

27. ibid.

28. Virginia Woolf, *Orlando*, Granada edn., p. 90.

29. *The Heir* (Heinemann, 1922) is the story of the ineffectual Peregrine Chase, who finds his identity and resolution by having to fight for his inheritance, an Elizabethan manor house. The descriptions are of Knole – upholstered depths of velvets and damasks, like ripe fruits, the fairy-tale backgrounds of the tapestries, the reflections in the cloudy mirrors, bowls of coral-coloured tulips bright against the sober panelling, and the vistas of the garden and the peacocks. These are what Chase realizes he really loves ... his familiar background and former life recede: '... *this* was reality; *this* was home.' Vita named the heroine of the story, the house, after Blackboys Manor at Possingworth in Sussex, which Violet had rented as a trysting place: *The Heir* was a farewell to Knole and to Violet.

30. 'Notes on a Late Spring', *Evening Standard*, quoted in Victoria Glendinning, *Vita*, p. 137.

4. PARADISE: PERSIA 1926 AND 1927

1. 'Nostalgia', in *Collected Poems*, Hogarth Press, 1933, p. 176.

2. James Lees-Milne, *Harold Nicolson: A Biography*, Chatto & Windus, 1980, Vol. 1, p 241.

3. Harold Nicolson to V. Sackville-West, 13 November 1925.

4. Harold Nicolson to V. Sackville-West, 27 November 1925.

5. Harold Nicolson to V. Sackville-West, 5 December 1925.

6. ibid.

7. V. Sackville-West, *Passenger to Teheran*, Hogarth Press, 1926, p. 8.

8. ibid., p. 10.

9. ibid., p. 25.

10. ibid., p. 26.

11. ibid., p. 30.

12. ibid., pp. 31, 32.

13. ibid., p. 50.

14. V. Sackville-West, diary, 16 February 1926, Shrove Tuesday.

15. V. Sackville-West, *Passenger to Teheran*, pp. 57, 58.

16. H. V. F. Winstone, *Gertrude Bell*, Cape, 1978, pp. 257, 258.

17. ibid., pp. 32, 33. Gertrude Bell died from an overdose of barbiturates early in the morning of the following 12 July (1926). She poisoned herself because she knew that she was ill and she could not bear the thought of having to leave Baghdad and go home to a useless existence. She was two days away from her fifty-eighth birthday.

18. V. Sackville-West, *Passenger to Teheran*, p. 69.

19. ibid., p. 89.

20. ibid., p. 111.

21. ibid., p. 112.

22. ibid., p. 145.

23. ibid., p. 90.

24. ibid., pp. 91, 92.

25. Sylvia Crowe, 'The Persian Background', in *The Gardens of Mughul India*, Thames & Hudson, 1972, p. 20.

26. V. Sackville-West, *Passenger to Teheran*, p. 132.

27. ibid., p. 134.

28. ibid., pp. 93, 94.

29. ibid., p. 106.

30. ibid., p. 136.

31. V. Sackville-West to Harold Nicolson, letter, 26 September 1926.

32. V. Sackville-West, *Passenger to Teheran*, p. 10.

NOTES

5. THE CONSTANT LURE: 'THE LAND' AND LONG BARN 1927–30

1. V. Sackville-West, *The Land: Winter*, Heinemann, 1926.
2. Victoria Glendinning, *Vita*, Weidenfeld & Nicolson, 1983, p. 166.
3. Richard Church, 'V. Sackville-West: A Poet in a Tradition', in *Eight for Immortality*, Dent, 1941. (The other seven were W. H. Davies, Walter de la Mare, Robert Frost, 'the later Yeats', Edmund Blunden, T. S. Eliot and Robert Graves.) Church knew Vita after she moved to Sissinghurst.
4. V. Sackville-West, *The Land: Winter*.
5. Professor A. N. Duckham to V. Sackville-West, 20 August 1957, Sissinghurst Papers.
6. Harold Nicolson to V. Sackville-West, 26 July 1919. 39 Sussex Square was the Brighton house that Lutyens was converting for Lady Sackville.
7. Both *The Land* and *The Garden*, as well as other poems, demonstrate what I feel is Vita's special affection for autumn; it produces her best writing. In his anthology *And So To Bed*, Phoenix House, 1947, p. 84, Edward Sackville-West wrote: 'I have discovered that others beside myself consider that each new year starts on October 1st.' He felt himself to be a child of autumn though he admits that Henry Vaughan and Thomas Traherne would not have agreed – for them 'the enchantment of spring held no overtones of disillusion, of *déjà vu* – none of that latterday sadness which caused Mallarmé to stigmatize Spring with the epithet *maladif* – morbid.' It is an interesting proposition – Vita was extremely close to her cousin in some things. Was she on the side of Traherne and Vaughan or of Eliot and her cousin? Being Vita she was probably on both!
8. Vita wrote the *Dictionary of National Biography* entry on Dorothy Wellesley, remarking on what W. B. Yeats had called her 'passionate precision' – 'an almost myopic observation of Nature that was Tennysonian in detail' – and wishing that she had nurtured this talent for the greater benefit of her poetry. See notes 4 and 8, Ch. 2.
9. Lord Gerald Wellesley (1885–1971), later 7th Duke of Wellington, was a diplomat, architect and journalist. As a contributor to *The Spectator* from 1924 to 1926 he wrote a witty and waspish piece (22 November 1924), 'The Week-End Cottage', about rich, luxurious, complicated people who are prepared to put up with the dangerous little stairs and low doors of their (otherwise modernized) habitations of long dead rustics 'to imagine with smug satisfaction that they are leading a wild and primitive life'. Down to the new door latches of medieval design and the red tennis court, 'his' cottage bears a very strong resemblance to Long Barn.
10. V. Sackville-West to Harold Nicolson, 7 July 1929. 'Penn's Rocks', *Country Life*, 23 and 30 March 1961, by Christopher Hussey. Penn's became famous for Dorothy Wellesley's poetical gatherings and also for its interior decorations by Roger Fry and Rex Whistler.
11. Victoria Glendinning, *Vita*, pp. 179–87.

12. ibid., p. 187.
13. V. Sackville-West to Harold Nicolson, 1 November 1927.
14. V. Sackville-West to Harold Nicolson, 9 January 1928.
15. V. Sackville-West to Harold Nicolson, 4 May 1928.
16. V. Sackville-West to Harold Nicolson, 16 May 1928. B.M. (Bonne Maman) was the family name for Lady Sackville.
17. V. Sackville-West, *The Land: Autumn*.
18. Vita carefully planned her first sink garden, filling it with a mixture of *Campanula* 'Will Paine', *Saxifraga Coryphylla, S. irvingii, S. griesebachi, Erodium chaemaedryoides roseum, Thymus coccineum, Soldanella alpina, Wahlenbergia* 'Maltby's White', *Iris gracilipes, Dianthus frequii* and *D. alpinus*.
19. Colonel Charles Hoare Grey of Hocker Edge, Cranbrook (on the Cranbrook to Goudhurst road), was a Hoare of the banking family and descended from Henry Hoare who made Stourhead gardens – he apparently inherited a considerably grandiose taste in garden design. He had added Grey to his name under the terms of his father-in-law, the 7th Earl of Stamford's, will in 1927. He was an alpine expert and collector, and in return for some Persian bulbs Vita brought him he had given her primulas from Sikkim and Andean saxifrages. He also cultivated lilies, dwarf rhododendrons and azaleas and water plants at his nursery at Hocker Edge and in his garden at nearby Hartridge Manor. He was known to be very haughty and ride roughshod over people, but *not* Vita; they became good friends. His three-volume classic on *Hardy Bulbs* was published in 1937 with illustrations by Cecily Hoare Grey. After the Second World War they moved from Kent to Yorkshire, where Colonel Grey was instrumental in the making of Harlow Car, the Northern Horticultural Society's garden at Harrogate.
20. V. Sackville-West to Harold Nicolson, 21 June 1928.
21. V. Sackville-West to Harold Nicolson, 22 June 1928.
22. V. Sackville-West to Harold Nicolson, 3 May 1928.
23. This and the other quotations in the preceding paragraph are from letters between V. Sackville-West and Harold Nicolson in the period 22 May to 19 June 1929.
24. V. Sackville-West to Harold Nicolson, 10 July 1929.
25. Bodiam Castle in Sussex, a romantic ancient castle islanded in a large moat, was another of the beautiful places which Vita dreamed of as a home. This time Harold shared her dreams, in part because of his affection and respect for his boss, the Foreign Secretary, Lord Curzon. Curzon's passion for ancient houses, for renting and restoring them as he did with Montacute, Hackwood and Bodiam among others, was something both Nicolsons completely understood – if *they* had been rich enough it was a pastime that would have suited them both. After Lord Curzon's death in 1925 Harold edited his book on Bodiam (it was published in 1926), and he eventually wrote a biography of the great man, *Curzon: The Last Phase*, Constable, 1933.

6. THE CASTLE AND THE ROSE 1930–39

1. V. Sackville-West, *Sissinghurst*, Hogarth Press, 1931.
2. Harold Nicolson, diary, 4 and 5 April 1930.
3. V. Sackville-West, *Family History*, Hogarth Press, 1932, p. 117. The description seems to fit approaching Sissinghurst from the northern side of the 'circular' drive – in fact the old entrance did come past Horserace Cottage but apparently Vita did not discover this until 1942 – so she may have just thought it more poetic to come in this way.
4. ibid., pp. 117–222.
5. Harold Nicolson, diary, 6 April 1930.
6. Harold Nicolson to V. Sackville-West, 24 April 1930.
7. The Surveyor's report from E. Glasier, Grafton House, Grafton Street W1, for Meynell and Pemberton Solicitors, 30 Old Queen Street, Storey's Gate, Westminster, dated 29 May 1930, is in the Sissinghurst Papers (Purchase File).
8. Anne Scott-James, *Sissinghurst: The Making of a Garden*, Michael Joseph, 1975, pp. 36/7.
9. The news of the Castle being for sale had actually come to Dorothy Wellesley from her land agent, whose brother Captain Oswald Beale had farmed Bettenham Farm since resigning his army commission in 1920. Captain Beale took over Castle Farm when the Nicolsons bought it, and eventually came to live in Castle Farm house in 1936. Another brother ran the family building firm which did most of the work at Sissinghurst Castle.
10. Anne Scott-James, *Sissinghurst: The Making of a Garden*, pp. 57–60.
11. Harold Nicolson to V. Sackville-West, 24 October 1934.
12. The Hayters, Sidney and George, came with Sissinghurst, i.e. they were living in one of the farm cottages when the Nicolsons bought the property. They were the chief labour force for clearing and making the garden, though it is not clear whether they were employed by Hollamby's Nurseries, the contractor, or by Vita herself.
13. V. Sackville-West to Harold Nicolson, 16 and 17 October 1930.
14. William Robinson's letter to Vita is dated 12 December but there is no year; she records her visit in reply to this invitation in 'Gardens and Gardeners', printed in *Country Notes* – she says he was 'nearing eighty if, indeed, he had not passed it' when she met him, but she must have been wrong as he was eighty in 1918. *The Land* was published in 1926 – did she mean ninety?
15. This 'official' letter dated 8 October 1931 was from the editor of *Action*, 5 Gordon Square, WC1, and signed 'yours sincerely, Harold Nicolson'.
16. Long Barn remained empty until 1934; Vita visited it on 30 October 1934 when it was let to Sidney Bernstein, who was 'making every room as hideous as possible'. It was subsequently let to Charles and Anne Lindbergh and Desmond MacCarthy, and finally sold in 1943.

17. Harold Nicolson, diary, 6 March 1932.
18. ibid., 20 March 1932.
19. ibid., 27 September 1933.
20. See Note 14 above. Vita's visit to Robinson inspired her to place him into the context of English gardening history in 'Gardens and Gardeners', *Country Notes*, pp. 96–108.
21. *The Times*, 4 October 1930, quoted by Clive Aslet in *The Last Country Houses*, Yale University Press, 1982, p. 209.
22. Albert Reginald Powys, born 16 July 1881, was the middle one of the eleven children of the Rev. C. F. Powys and was brought up at Montacute House in Somerset, where he was imbued with the spirit of old English craftsmanship. He went to Sherborne, was articled to C. B. Benson for three years from August 1899, and worked for William Weir and Walter Cave, concentrating on the rebuilding of churches in the William Morris tradition. He was married in 1905, and was appointed Secretary of the Society for the Protection of Ancient Buildings in 1911. He ran the S.P.A.B. and his partnership with John MacGregor from 20 Buckingham Street in the Strand.
23. A. R. Powys, *From the Ground Up*, Dent, 1937, Foreword by John Cowper Powys.
24. A. R. Powys to Harold Nicolson, 3 November 1932.
25. ibid.
26. ibid.
27. ibid.
28. The Hammann busts were of Eddy Sackville-West, Raymond Mortimer, Paul Hislop, David Herbert, Dorothy Wellesley, Edward Knoblock, two of Harold Nicolson and possibly one of Cecil Beaton. Paul Hislop now has the first three, one of Harold is at Sissinghurst in South Cottage, another of Harold with Nigel Nicolson, and the whereabouts of the others is unknown to me. They are only plaster busts, so was Harold going to have them cast or was it all a joke?
29. Harold Nicolson to V. Sackville-West, 14 January 1935.
30. V. Sackville-West to Harold Nicolson, report on Powys's visit, 13 February 1935.
31. A. R. Powys to Harold Nicolson, 22 March 1935.
32. V. Sackville-West to Harold Nicolson, 13 February 1935.
33. The wave-backed seats designed by Lutyens became a feature of most of his gardens. The original design was made in the late 1890s or very early 1900s – the first picture of such a seat is at Little Thakeham, finished in 1902. The first seat for Sissinghurst came from Lady Sackville, from either 34 Hill Street or Sussex Square, Brighton, and has been copied for those at present in the garden.
34. Nigel Nicolson has recorded that William Copper was engaged as the Nicolsons' chauffeur (Harold never learned to drive a car) on 16 August 1931 'until the Income tax goes up'. He was still there to push Vita's wheelchair on her last trip round the garden before she died in 1962.

35. V. Sackville-West, 'Sissinghurst Castle', *Country Life*, 3 September 1942.

36. *Family History* was dedicated to Evelyn Irons (see Victoria Glendinning, *Vita*, Weidenfeld & Nicolson, 1983, Ch. 22, for the story of her relationship with Vita). It may be Evelyn Irons with Vita standing next to the Priest's House in the aerial photograph of 1932 [pl. 66].

37. Harold Nicolson, diary, 31 December 1932.

38. Harold Nicolson to V. Sackville-West, 23 February 1935, from Cuernavica.

39. Harold Nicolson to V. Sackville-West, 3 September 1936.

40. James Lees-Milne's chapters in *Harold Nicolson: A Biography*, Chatto & Windus, 1980, Vol. 2, 'The Thread of Peace 1935–37' and 'The Brink of Catastrophe 1938–39', are an evocative commentary on 'the landslide into war', with a clear insight into Harold's lonely opposition to Appeasement and his reasons and reactions to events.

41. The Sackville flag was Vita's atavistic gift to Sissinghurst. The first flag arrived amid great excitement on 5 March 1939, but its colours were wrong and it had to go back – a week later the correct one was hoisted on to the flagstaff between the towers, where Harold had decided it looked best. On 24 March Vita wrote: '. . . the flag streamed out 5 minutes after I had passed under the porch and made me feel awfully grand.'

42. V. Sackville-West, 'On Buying a Motor Mower', *Country Notes*, p. 61, is amusing on her feelings about grass-cutting methods.

43. V. Sackville-West, 'The Garden at Sissinghurst Castle', *Country Life*, 11 September 1942, has a picture of Delos, the path to the Priest's House (see pl. 78). The stones in the distance are mainly parts of Harold's atavistic gift to Sissinghurst, stones forming a column festooned with garlands and rams' heads which one of his ancestors had brought from Greece to Ireland, to Shanganagh Castle, and set up to commemorate the Reform Bill of 1832. Harold bought the column at a sale and it arrived at Sissinghurst in October 1936.

44. Edward Ashdown Bunyard (1878–1939) was the son of George Bunyard, whose nursery near Maidstone reared the famous 'Allington Pippin' apple and other notable varieties; Edward Ashdown was an epicure as well as a nurseryman. He published *The Anatomy of a Dessert* in 1933, *The Epicure's Companion* in 1937, and *Old Garden Roses*, his classic monograph on his favourite flowers, in 1936.

45. V. Sackville-West to Harold Nicolson, 20 January 1937.

46. Gordon Farley came as a gardener to Sissinghurst on 13 May 1936.

47. Harold Nicolson to V. Sackville-West, 8 June 1937.

48. Harold Nicolson, diary, 1 October 1938.

7. THE WAR AND 'THE GARDEN' 1939–45

1. V. Sackville-West, *The Garden*, Michael Joseph, 3rd imp., 1947, p. 14 (first published 1946).

2. Henry Reed, 'The Naming of Parts', from *A Map of Verona*, Cape, 1946.

3. James Lees-Milne, *Harold Nicolson: A Biography*, Chatto & Windus, 1980, Vol. 2, pp. 97–122, 'The Brink of Catastrophe 1938–39'.

4. Victoria Glendinning, *Vita*, Weidenfeld & Nicolson, 1983, p. 283.

5. V. Sackville-West, 'A Country Life', *Country Notes*, Michael Joseph, 1939, p. 11.

6. V. Sackville-West to Harold Nicolson, 13 February 1939.

7. V. Sackville-West, 'A Country Life', *Country Notes*, p. 11.

8. V. Sackville-West, 'Winter Colour', *Country Notes*.

9. V. Sackville-West, 'Snow', *Country Notes in Wartime*, Hogarth Press, 1940.

10. V. Sackville-West, 'February Frost', *Country Notes*.

11. V. Sackville-West, 'Colour in the Snow', *Country Notes in Wartime*.

12. *Faces: Profiles of Dogs* was Vita's last published book (1961). It is made up of one-page essays on forty-four different breeds, many of which she had known as the pets of her friends or herself. She mentioned the saluki Gertrude Bell gave her in Baghdad, Pippin her cocker spaniel, killed on the railway near Long Barn, Rollo her alsatian, Canute the elk-hound of Long Barn days (immortalized in Virginia Woolf's *Orlando*), and Dan her collie puppy, who was her companion in her last summer of 1961 before he had to be destroyed. See Victoria Glendinning, *Vita*, p. 401.

13. V. Sackville-West, 'The Urchin Wakes', *Country Notes*.

14. V. Sackville-West, 'Small but Vigorous', *Country Notes*.

15. V. Sackville-West, 'Controversial Topics', *Country Notes*.

16. V. Sackville-West, 'More Fishing', *Country Notes*.

17. V. Sackville-West, 'Fishing', *Country Notes*.

18. V. Sackville-West, 'Lilies and Lakes', *Country Notes in Wartime*.

19. V. Sackville-West, 'September 1938', *Country Notes in Wartime*.

20. V. Sackville-West to Harold Nicolson, 6 February 1939.

21. All these quotes are from letters between V. Sackville-West and Harold Nicolson during February/March 1939. 'Belated Haysel' is from *Country Notes in Wartime*. 'It has begun', James Lees-Milne, *Harold Nicolson: A Biography*, Vol. 2, p. 122.

22. V. Sackville-West, 'Blackout', *Country Notes in Wartime*.

23. V. Sackville-West, 'July 1940', *Country Notes in Wartime*.

24. ibid.

25. V. Sackville-West, 'War in the Country', *Country Notes in Wartime*.

26. V. Sackville-West, 'Dig for Beauty'.

27. *Country Notes in Wartime*, 'Lilies and Lakes'.

28. V. Sackville-West, *The Garden*, p. 14.

29. Edward Thomas, *Richard Jefferies*, Faber & Faber, paperback edn., 1978, pp. 120/21.

30. Compare this sentiment with a verse from Vita's 'To Knole Oct. 1 1913':

> So I have loved thee, as a lonely child
> Might love the kind and venerable sire
> With whom he lived, and whom at youthful fire
> Had ever sagely, tolerantly smiled:

31. 'Souvenir de Docteur Jamain is an old hybrid perpetual which I am rather proud of having rescued from extinction. I found him growing against the office wall of an old nursery. No one knew what he was; no one seemed to care; no one knew his name; no one had troubled to propagate him. Could I dig him up?' From *V. Sackville-West's Garden Book*, ed. Philippa Nicolson, Michael Joseph, 1968, pp. 143/4. She did take the rose home and 'he' flourished, so that she was able to give him back to several collectors, including Hilda Murrell.

32. The Rev. William Mason M.A., Precentor of York and Rector of Aston, filled his long poem *The English Garden* (or simply *The Garden*) with a review of the history of gardening and a complex examination of aspects of design. He gives endless advice on the setting out of vistas, alleys, arbours, groves and scenes of classical association. His poem is one of external examination, whereas Vita's poem explores herself. She did own a copy of *The English Garden*. See *The Works of William Mason*, Vol. 1, Cadell & Davies, London, 1811.

33. V. Sackville-West to Harold Nicolson, 19 December 1944.

34. Victoria Glendinning, *Vita*, pp. 341/2. Victoria Glendinning writes that in the March before *The Garden* was published, Vita had been to a meeting of the Poetry Committee of the Royal Society of Literature at Denys Kilham Roberts's rooms in King's Bench Walk, to discuss readings to be held at the Wigmore Hall in the presence of the Queen. It was *not* suggested that Vita should take part. In 1951, in a letter to Eddy Sackville-West, she said that something which hurt her so much that she never told anyone took place that day – 'they destroyed me forever'.

35. George Barker, quoted on p. 260 of C. H. Sisson, *English Poetry 1900–1950: An Assessment*, Hart-Davis, 1971.

8. VITA'S ENGLAND

1. V. Sackville-West, *The Garden: Winter*, Michael Joseph, 3rd imp., 1947, p. 32 (first published 1946).

2. V. Sackville-West to Harold Nicolson, 24 April 1941.

3. Clarence Elliott (1881–1969) was described by Vita as a large and shaggy gentleman who reminded her of Stephen Leacock when she met him on his first visit to Sissinghurst in April 1941. She liked him very much. Clarence Elliott had started his Six Hills Nursery at Stevenage in 1907; he collected plants with Reginald Farrer and from the Falkland Islands and South America, and propagated many rare and forgotten plants in his nursery. He was an expert on sink gardens, a special interest to share with Vita. They had something else in common too: he was gardening columnist for the *Illustrated London News* from 1949 to 1959.

4. Captain Collingwood Ingram, nicknamed 'Cherry' because he collected flowering cherries from the East and brought them home to English gardens, lived at The Grange, Benenden, a few miles away from Sissinghurst. He was a frequent visitor, and Vita obtained many of her plants from him, including the Japanese cherry, *Prunus* 'Tai-haku', for the orchard, and a Corsican rosemary, 'Benenden Blue'.

5. V. Sackville-West to Harold Nicolson, 27 February 1952.

6. Mrs Christopher Hussey of Scotney Castle, Lamberhurst, persuaded Vita to open Sissinghurst for the National Gardens Scheme. While Vita wanted to help – she felt that an organization that had worked so hard to open so many gardens for the public deserved success – she was a little loath to part with too much of the visitors' money. At 1s. a time this brought in an average of £5 on a good Sunday afternoon (though it could be nearer £50 for a busy charity Sunday), and she liked to use such money for the gardeners' wages.

7. *Observer*, 15 June 1947.

8. The National Trust Gardens Committee held its first meeting on 23 March 1948 at 42 Queen Anne's Gate, and it was constituted a month later. Its purpose was to approve gardens worthy of acceptance for the scheme, which would take over gardens for the nation and maintain them in a manner that conserved their original design intentions; the Committee also had to establish funds for their purpose, and Vita's first contribution to this was an appeal on the BBC on 31 October 1948. She also publicized the scheme in America and liaised with the National Gardens Scheme through Mrs Hussey. Otherwise her responsibilities were to give her opinions on the maintenance of the gardens that were acquired. I don't imagine she was ever paid a penny of expenses for her thirteen years' work, nor would she have expected to be.

9. Letter to the author from James Lees-Milne, 10 March 1984.

10. V. Sackville-West, *The Easter Party*, Michael Joseph, 1953; Mermaid edn 1955, pp. 20/21.

11. 'Littlecote Manor' in *Country Life*, 5 November 1927, shows the garden in Sir Ernest Wills's time as it would have earned Vita's wonderment. There were massive herbaceous borders flanking the lawn and running for 500 feet down both sides of the canal of River Kennet water which crosses the end of the garden. With the exception of one south-facing border beside the canal, these borders have now gone.

12. V. Sackville-West, *Grey Wethers: A Romantic Novel*, Heinemann, 1923, dedicated to Pat Dansey – 'Ces fantômes charmants que nous croyons à nous' (these charming ghosts which we believe are ourselves); the story of Clare Warrener, a spirit of the downs, not understood by the solemn Calladine who tries to capture

her in marriage, nor by her kind parson father. Clare eventually escapes into an undemanding, equal, soul-sharing partnership with Nicholas Lovel, who is half-gypsy and equally an outsider. But the Wiltshire landscape, the power of the ancient spirits of the downs, is the real substance of this book.

13. ibid., p. 19.

14. ibid., p. 21

15. Christopher Hussey, 'Cold Ashton Manor', *Country Life*, 21 February 1925.

16. ibid.

17. *Observer*, 10 October 1954.

18. Margaret Richardson, *Architects of the Arts and Crafts Movement*, Trefoil Books, 1983, p. 137.

19. ibid.

20. V. Sackville-West, *Royal Horticultural Society Journal*, Vol. LXXIV, part 11, November 1949; reprinted in *In Your Garden*, Michael Joseph, 1951, p. 222, and also in the National Trust Guide, 1976.

21. ibid.

22. Nancy Lindsay, Manor Cottage, Sutton Courtenay, to V. Sackville-West, undated, but in Sissinghurst Papers.

23. Cynthia Asquith on Stanway, from her autobiography *Remember and be Glad*, quoted in Jane Abdy and Charlotte Gere, *The Souls*, Sidgwick & Jackson, 1984.

24. Hilda Murrell (1906–84), 'a highly intelligent and charmingly eccentric woman of strong opinions', joined her father Edwin Murrell in the nursery business after reading English, French and History at Cambridge. She was an authority on roses – species, old roses and miniature roses – and she helped to make Murrell's one of the great nurseries of rose growing. 'A fierce but fundamentally gentle warrior, a Bunyan-like soul on a lonely and constant quest' (no wonder Vita loved her) is how she is described in an obituary note in *The Times*, contributed by Mr Charles Sinker after her tragic death on 21 March 1984.

25. V. Sackville-West to Harold Nicolson, n.d. but 1922.

26. Edward Malins and Patrick Bowe, *Irish Gardens and Demesnes from 1830*, Barrie & Jenkins, 1980, pp. 85 and 123.

27. ibid.

28. Ralph Cusack's nursery catalogue, 1951/2.

29. ibid., annotated by V. Sackville-West in the Sissinghurst Papers.

30. Lanning Roper, 'Exotic Plants in a Scottish Garden', *Gardening Illustrated*, January 1952.

31. ibid.

32. V. Sackville-West's introduction to *The Diary of Lady Anne Clifford*, Heinemann, 1923.

33. ibid.

34. The Hon. Robert 'Bobbie' James (1873–1960) was the younger son of the 2nd Lord Northbourne. He was managing director of a steel company in Barrow and made his garden at St Nicholas during the 1920s and 30s.

35. Lanning Roper, 'A Garden for Reflection', *Gardening Illustrated*, November 1953.

36. Edith Lamont (Mrs Newton Lamont), who lived at Chart Sutton near Maidstone, was one of Vita's last intimates; they apparently met in the garden at Sissinghurst and became close friends during the late fifties. Mrs Lamont was a painter and photographer and a very good gardener – she also shared Vita's passion for dogs, and I imagine she was always on hand with consideration and comfort when Vita was feeling ill and out of sorts. She went with the Nicolsons on their last cruise to look after Vita, and tended her until she died.

37. V. Sackville-West to Harold Nicolson, 9 October 1957.

38. ibid.

39. Between January 1949 and August 1951 Harold spent a great deal of time at Windsor Castle researching his most full-time book, his biography of George V, which was eventually published in August 1952. 'Harold felt like Byron when he woke up, famous,' says James Lees-Milne of this 'literary event'. See *Harold Nicolson: A Biography*, Vol. 2, Ch. 8.

40. Harold Nicolson to V. Sackville-West from Windsor Castle.

41. Some time after this, Harold had an idea to train clematis on to the trunks of the lime trees: '. . . would it not be fairyland with trees hung with purple and white? Or would it look like a Hollywood setting for a rumba? Or Maidenhead?' Vita despaired of clematis, which did not seem to like Sissinghurst, and she replied that they would ask George Jackman for advice as she felt he owed her a favour. Perhaps she was also trying to divert Harold from an idea that offended her impeccable taste! Harold Nicolson to V. Sackville-West, 12 April 1950.

42. Enid Bagnold to V. Sackville-West, 2 November 1952, in Sissinghurst Papers.

43. Edith Olivier, *Without Knowing Mr Walkley*, Faber & Faber, 1938, p. 255, and Cecil Beaton, *The Wandering Years: Diaries 1922/39*, Weidenfeld & Nicolson, 1961, p. 315.

44. Lanning Roper, 'Tintinhull Manor', *Gardening Illustrated*, January 1951.

45. See National Trust Guide to Montacute, 1977, p. 25, on the roses Vita planted and see V. Sackville-West to Violet Trefusis, 12 October 1948 (in Philippe Julian and John Phillips, *Violet Trefusis: Life and Letters*, Hamish Hamilton, 1976), saying how she was 'responsible for the garden' and had been down there. Also V. Sackville-West to Harold Nicolson, 13 October 1948, bemoaning the drought which had wrecked her planting – 'God's fault, not mine'. I suspect Vita tactfully withdrew from this long-distance commission (though she did love to be asked to advise on other people's gardens), and Mrs Reiss from Tintinhull took over.

46. V. Sackville-West, *Observer*, 26 April 1953 and *More for Your Garden*, Michael Joseph, 1955.

47. Michael Haworth-Booth to V. Sackville-West, undated letter, but 1948 and in Sissinghurst papers.

48. Laurence Fleming and Alan Gore, *The English Garden*, the book of the Thames Television series, Michael Joseph, 1979.

49. The surviving papers from Vita's correspondence course from the Horticultural Correspondence College are in the Sissinghurst Papers.

9. BLUNDERING INTO FAME 1945–54

1. Jack Vass was undoubtedly the gardener who had most effect on Sissinghurst. After being rejected by 'Lord Derby's and Maggie Greville's gardener', Vita wrote to Harold on 14 August 1939: 'I have heard from a younger man who has been with the Duke of Northumberland at Albury, the Astors at Cliveden and a gentleman called Sir Bernard Ekstein ... he is also recommended by the RHS ...' Vass started at Sissinghurst on 2 October 1939, and in January 1941 he went into the RAF for flying duties with No. 35 Pathfinder Squadron. He was in the crew of a Halifax shot down over the south of France and was posted missing, but eventually got home in April 1944 and finished his war with Transport Command, visiting places like Guatemala where he noticed the flowers growing wild that he had struggled with in greenhouses at home.
2. V. Sackville-West to Harold Nicolson, 8 October 1946.
3. V. Sackville-West to Harold Nicolson, 4 February 1947.
4. F. A. Mercer and Roy Hay, *Gardens and Gardening*, Studio Publications, 1950.
5. The carpet of crimson, tawny and gold polyanthus was restored to the Nuttery after the war and kept until at least the mid-fifties. There was, however, not enough time or labour to propagate new seedlings; they are gross feeders and the soil – completely renewed by Vass and the gardeners after the war – was played out after about twelve years. Massed polyanthus also set up a rejective reaction – for all these reasons the polyanthus had to be given up. (Miss Jekyll completely replanted and set new seedlings in new soil every year to maintain her polyanthus carpet!)
6. James Lees-Milne, *Harold Nicolson: A Biography*, Chatto & Windus, 1980, Vol. 2, p. 226.
7. Harold Nicolson to V. Sackville-West, 18 April 1945.
8. Harold Nicolson diary, on his 50th birthday 1936, quoted in his 80th birthday card, 21 November 1966; Sissinghurst Papers.
9. Harold Nicolson to V. Sackville-West, 28 April 1936.
10. Many of Sissinghurst's tulips and narcissi came from Barr & Son of Covent Garden and Surbiton, the firm founded by the great tulip- and daffodil-hunting Peter Barr in 1861. Vita bought from Barr & Son until the firm was amalgamated with Wallace's, landscape gardeners of Tunbridge Wells, in 1956. The bulb business is now de Jager's of Holland, based at Marden, Kent.
11. V. Sackville-West to Harold Nicolson, March 1952.
12. V. Sackville-West, *Observer*, 5 November 1950, and *In Your Garden*, Michael Joseph, 1951.
13. ibid.
14. ibid.

15. V. Sackville-West, *Observer*, 27 December 1953 and *More for Your Garden*, Michael Joseph, 1955, p. 169.
16. V. Sackville-West, *Observer*, 12 June 1949, and *In Your Garden*, p. 75.
17. V. Sackville-West, *Observer*, 28 May 1950, and *In Your Garden*, p. 70.
18. V. Sackville-West, *Observer*, 28 May 1950, and *In Your Garden*, p. 71.
19. Graham Stuart Thomas, *The Old Shrub Roses*, Phoenix House, 1956, p. 141.
20. *Observer*, 18 August 1957, and *Even More for Your Garden*, p. 128.
21. *Observer*, 25 August 1957, and *Even More for Your Garden*, p. 132.
22. V. Sackville-West to Andrew Reiber, 31 July 1955; *Dearest Andrew, Letters from V. Sackville-West to Andrew Reiber 1951–62*, ed. Nancy MacKnight, Michael Joseph, 1980.
23. Harold Nicolson to V. Sackville-West, 27 May 1948.
24. V. Sackville-West, 'Lilium giganteum' from *Some Flowers*, Cobden Sanderson, 1937.
25. Harold Nicolson to V. Sackville-West 28 July 1951.
26. V. Sackville-West to Harold Nicolson, 31 January 1948.
27. V. Sackville-West to Harold Nicolson, 8 October 1952.
28. *Observer*, 19 April 1953, and *More for Your Garden*, p. 68.
29. V. Sackville-West to Harold Nicolson, December 1939.
30. *Observer*, 5 July 1955, and *More for Your Garden*, p. 99.
31. *Observer*, 22 January 1950, and *In Your Garden*, p. 21.
32. Harold Nicolson to V. Sackville-West, 15 June 1949.
33. Harold Nicolson to V. Sackville-West, 4 July 1949.
34. *Observer*, 5 July 1955, and *More for Your Garden*, p. 99.
35. Anne Scott-James, *Sissinghurst: The Making of a Garden*, p. 107.
36. Both references from a letter of V. Sackville-West to Harold Nicolson, 3 July 1951.
37. *Observer*, 8 May 1955, and *Even More for Your Garden*, p. 70.
38. *Observer*, 5 May 1957, and *Even More for Your Garden*, p. 67.
39. V. Sackville-West to Harold Nicolson, 18 August 1949.
40. V. Sackville-West to Harold Nicolson, 6 September 1949.
41. V. Sackville-West to Harold Nicolson, 29 January 1951.
42. Harold Nicolson to V. Sackville-West, 1 August 1950.
43. James Lees-Milne, *Harold Nicolson: A Biography*, Vol. 2, p. 279.
44. V. Sackville-West to Harold Nicolson, 3 January 1950.

45. V. Sackville-West to Harold Nicolson, 23 September 1953.

46. V. Sackville-West to Harold Nicolson, 31 December 1953.

47. James Lees-Milne, *Harold Nicolson: A Biography*, Vol. 2, p. 278.

48. V. Sackville-West to Harold Nicolson, 15 November 1954.

10. ANOTHER WORLD THAN THIS 1954–62

1. V. Sackville-West, *The Garden: Spring*, p. 79.

2. James Lees-Milne, *Harold Nicolson: A Biography*, Chatto & Windus, 1980, Vol. 2, p. 283.

3. V. Sackville-West to Mrs Dorothy Beale, 30 January 1957, by kind permission of Dr John Beale.

4. Bunny Drummond was the daughter-in-law of Mrs Drummond (to whom *The Garden* was dedicated), and to some extent filled the void left by her mother's death; Edith Lamont, see Ch. 8, note 36; Violet Pym was the comforting, countrified wife of an ex-Irish Guards Major who farmed at Barnfield near Charing. 'She is like a cornfield, or a loaf of bread, or a brown egg, or bracken in autumn,' wrote Vita. Victoria Glendinning, *Vita*, Weidenfeld & Nicolson, 1983; Penguin, 1984.

5. *Kentish Express*, 1 February 1957, report of Captain Beale's death and an appreciation by Sir Harold Nicolson.

6. Jack Vass feels that Sissinghurst was at its peak about 1955. From Husheath Manor he went to Lady Eleanor Bennett at Matfield and is, at the time of writing, still working, winning prizes and arranging flowers for the house among the rhododendrons and azaleas at Borde Hill, Haywards Heath, Sussex.

7. Harold Nicolson to V. Sackville-West, 15 March 1956.

8. V. Sackville-West to Harold Nicolson, 20 June 1961.

9. V. Sackville-West to Nigel Nicolson, 6 February 1959.

10. The last three chapters of Victoria Glendinning's *Vita* reveal that Vita's magnetism for other women remained undimmed – perhaps it was something to do with her determination *not* to give up being a romantic to the last.

11. Pamela Schwerdt and Sybille Kreutzberger were Sissinghurst's first college-trained gardeners, both having diplomas from Waterperry Horticultural College. Vita took them as 'an experiment', but soon realized that their knowledge, energy and hard work was just what the garden needed.

12. V. Sackville-West to Harold Nicolson, 20 June 1961. 'Christopher's literary remains' refers to the papers of Christopher St John (a woman), of Smallhythe, whose literary executor Vita was.

13. V. Sackville-West to Harold Nicolson, 1 November 1961.

14. Harold Nicolson to V. Sackville-West, 23 May 1962.

15. Mark Girouard, *The Return to Camelot: Chivalry and the English Gentleman*, Yale University Press, 1981, p. 6.

16. James Lees-Milne, *Harold Nicolson: A Biography*, Vol. 2, p. 178.

17. V. Sackville-West to Harold Nicolson, 24 September 1947.

18. Harold Nicolson to V. Sackville-West in reply, 25 September 1947.

19. V. Sackville-West to Harold Nicolson, 22 November 1949.

20. Victoria Glendinning, *Vita*, Weidenfeld & Nicolson, 1983, p. 350.

21. V. Sackville-West to Harold Nicolson, 22 October 1945.

22. C. H. Sisson, *English Poetry 1900–1950, An Assessment*, Hart-Davis, 1971.

23. Michael Schmidt, *A Reader's Guide to 50 Modern British Poets*, Heinemann/Barnes & Noble, 1979.

24. David Cecil and Allen Tate (eds.) *Modern Verse in English*, London, 1958.

25. Robert Ross, *The Georgian Revolt 1910–1922: The Rise and Fall of a Poetic Ideal*, Faber & Faber, 1967.

26. Timothy Rogers (ed.), *Georgian Poetry 1911–1922: The Critical Heritage*, Routledge & Kegan Paul, 1977, p. 1.

27. Richard Church, *Eight for Immortality*, Dent, 1941, pp. 69–82.

28.

ABSENCE

No lights are burning in the ivory tower
Like a tall lily in the moonlight risen;
No light, to-night, within the ivory prison.
No golden glow behind the blackened panes
Like golden anthers in a pallid flower;
The gates are looped, to-night, with hasps and chains.
Only the little virgin coldly smiling
With carven finger raised to carven lip
In secrecy beneath the latticed moon
Preserves her secret, keeps her virgin watch
On silvered fields that to the silver heaven
Lie open as the restless summer sea
Crossed by one tall incautious sailing-ship,
Or love to lover generously given.

1931

(Collected Poems, Hogarth Press, 1933, p. 254.)

29. Richard Church, *Eight for Immortality*, p. 71.

30. Vita's shyness and lack of confidence were engendered in childhood by Lady Sackville's constant chiding of her for being unkempt and unsociable, rather than the pretty and pliable daughter she would have wished for. In consequence Vita was always determinedly unconcerned about her appearance (she always scowled for the three seconds a day she brushed her hair), and it was partly pride and partly genuine uncertainty that made her scorn social gatherings. The only time she felt herself to be either decorative or desirable was in the early years of her marriage – perhaps it was Harold's failing that he was unable to nurture this, her self-respect in social terms?

31. In 1938 Vita published *Solitude* (Hogarth Press), a long poem which expresses the gazelle-likeness of her personality – her darting, desperate searching for a refuge in a pure love, a certain God, that she knows she

is incapable of accepting even if she should find it. Think how the hunted deer flies ever onwards till it drops, think how the deer safe in Knole's park can be tempted to take a picnic bun but then shy out of reach, and you are approaching an understanding of Vita's attitude to her lovers. The 'picnic bun' being passionate physical love, which she is over and over again – because of something in herself – forced to reject as a cheap unworthy trick. Hilda Matheson, the most perceptive of her lovers, divined this in *Solitude*; see Victoria Glendinning, *Vita*, pp. 296/7.

32. W. J. Keith, *The Poetry of Nature: Rural Perspectives in Poetry from Wordsworth to the Present*, University of Toronto Press, 1981.

33. I firmly believe that Vita had this very enlightened view on a problem of perception of our surroundings – an obsession with the English landscape of the eighteenth century – that has bedevilled our thinking for the last fifty years. I have expressed my opinions, reasons and justifications for them in *The Everywhere Landscape*, Wildwood, 1982.

34. V. Sackville-West, *The Land: Winter*, Heinemann edn, 1934, p. 25.

35. V. Sackville-West, *The Garden*, p. 92.

36. In Richard Gill's *Happy Rural Seat: The English Country House and the Literary Imagination*, Yale University Press, 1972, Vita does get a respectable amount of space allotted to *Knole and the Sackvilles* and *The Edwardians*. Gill (p. 147) observes *The Edwardians* to be 'as inconclusive as *Heartbreak House*' and to survive mainly as 'satire rather than as sociology'.

37. Ronald Firbank, *Flower Beneath the Foot*, Duckworth, 1932, p. 91.

38. V. Sackville-West, *The Garden*, p. 14.

39. V. Sackville-West, 'Belated Haysel, August 1939', *Country Notes in Wartime*, Hogarth Press, 1940, p. 9.

40. ibid.

41. V. Sackville-West to Harold Nicolson, 6 November 1928.

42. V. Sackville-West, 'Outdoor Life', Ch. 20 from Ernest Barber (ed.), *The Character of England*, Oxford University Press, 1947, p. 408.

43. Edward Thomas, *Richard Jefferies*, Faber paperback, 1978, p. 298.

44. V. Sackville-West, foreword to *Some Flowers*, Cobden Sanderson, 1937.

45. V. Sackville-West, 'October', *Country Notes*, p. 173.

46. James Lees-Milne, *Harold Nicolson: A Biography*, Vol. 2, pp. 354/5.

47. Sissinghurst had quite a lot to live up to – the 'homes' for which Harold had the greatest affection were Balliol, the House of Commons, King's Bench Walk in the Temple and Albany, Piccadilly.

48. V. Sackville-West, *The Garden*, pp. 16/17.

❧ BIBLIOGRAPHY ❧

ALSOP, Susan Mary, *Lady Sackville*, Weidenfeld & Nicolson, 1978.

DESALVO, Louise, and LEASKA, Mitchell A. (eds.), *The Letters of Vita Sackville-West to Virginia Woolf*, New York, William Morrow, 1985.

GLENDINNING, Victoria, *Vita*, Weidenfeld & Nicolson, 1983; Penguin, 1984.

JULIAN, P., and PHILLIPS, J., *Violet Trefusis: Life and Letters*, Hamish Hamilton, 1976.

LEES-MILNE, James, *Harold Nicolson: A Biography*, Chatto & Windus, 1980.

LUTYENS, Mary, *Edwin Lutyens: A Memoir by his Daughter*, John Murray, 1980.

NICOLSON, Harold, *The Desire to Please*, Constable, 1943, and subs. paperback editions.

—— *Helen's Tower*, Constable, 1937.

—— *Sweet Waters*, Constable, 1921.

NICOLSON, Nigel, *Portrait of a Marriage*, Weidenfeld & Nicolson, 1973, and subs. paperback editions.

SACKVILLE-WEST, V., *The Garden*, Michael Joseph, 1946, and subs. editions.

—— *Knole and the Sackvilles*, Heinemann, 1922.

—— *The Land*, Heinemann, 1926, and subs. editions.

—— *Passenger to Teheran*, Hogarth Press, 1926.

—— *Pepita*, Hogarth Press, 1937.

—— *Sissinghurst*, Hogarth Press, 1931.

—— *Twelve Days*, Hogarth Press, 1928.

SCOTT-JAMES, Anne, *Sissinghurst: The Making of a Garden*, Michael Joseph, 1975.

STEVENS, Michael, *V. Sackville-West: A Critical Biography*, Michael Joseph, 1973.

TREFUSIS, Violet, *Don't Look Round*, Hutchinson, 1952.

WOOLF, Virginia, *Orlando*, Hogarth Press, 1928, and subs. paperback editions.

Note: A list of the works of V. Sackville-West appears in Victoria Glendinning's *Vita* and in Michael Stevens's *V. Sackville-West: A Critical Biography*.

INDEX

INDEX